MURDER IN ISTANBUL

JAMAL KHASHOGGI & THE CROWN PRINCE

by

Owen Wilson

This edition published for the first time by Gibson Square in 2019

UK Tel: +44 (0)20 7096 1100
US Tel: +1 646 216 9813

rights@gibsonsquare.com
www.gibsonsquare.com

ISBN 978-1-78334-069-9

Originally published with the title *Khashoggi and the the Crown Prince.*

Papers used by Gibson Square are natural, recyclable products made from wood grown in sustainable forests; inks used are vegetable based. Manufacturing conforms to ISO 14001, and is accredited to FSC and PEFC chain of custody schemes. Colour-printing is through a certified CarbonNeutral® company that offsets its CO2 emissions.

Printed by Clays.

Contents

Return from London

Having just spoken at a London conference, the courtier to the kings of Saudi Arabia says goodbye to a friend at Heathrow's steel-and-glass terminal 2, the Queen's Terminal, in the early evening one Monday in late September. Dressed in a light-yellow shirt and rolling a suitcase, the tall and bespectacled man walks through airport security to his 10pm Turkish Airlines flight to Istanbul. Just before take-off he sends one last text to his fiancée at home –

'*I'm on the plane right now, I'm coming home to you. In love, loving and passionate.*'

Landing at Atatürk Airport, he rolls his suitcase with his coat curled around the handle to the taxi stand and arrives at his new apartment in Istanbul around 4.30am. His fiancée joins him half an hour later at what will be their future home, carrying groceries for breakfast in a plastic bag.

At a quarter to 1pm, the tall man, now wearing a dark blazer, and the younger woman cross the busy streets of Istanbul. Hand-in-hand they hail a taxi.

Both are beaming and relaxed. He is about to collect the documents from his consulate that he needs to get married to her. On the previous Friday just before noon, four days earlier, they had also gone to the consulate together. But the administrative staff had not been able to process the paperwork in time before he had to catch his afternoon flight out to London, and they had asked him to come back. He had waited for as long as he could that Friday and had barely made the flight.

After the consulate visit, the couple intend to look for more furniture for their apartment near Istanbul's oldest district. They are planning to have dinner at around 5 or 6pm and to set the date for their marriage later that week. It will be a no-nonsense affair – just family and a few friends. He had been more interested in how they would celebrate it and what they would wear than she. Given the hardship in the world, she doesn't like spending much money on a wedding, or looking forever for dresses.

The man takes precautions just before going through the security road-block in front of the consulate. Top palace officials in his home country take a lively interest in him and have for five months been offering him high-level positions to entice him back home. They did so as well the year before when he moved to or, more accurately, escaped to the United States. As he enters the consulate's security zone to be patted down, he hands his mobile phones to his fiancée.

'See you, my dear, wait for me here'.

A few moments later he greets the smiling, nodding, elderly, light-blue blazered usher of the consulate and is gone.

The woman had taken the day off and had decided to wait outside anyway. How long could it take to pick up documents? On Friday she had waited for an hour and a quarter.

Three hours later, at 4pm, there is still no sign of him. She is getting anxious now that more than twice as much time has passed compared to the previous visit. She discovers that the consulate closed its doors at 3.30pm.

She goes up to the guard at the gate and then rings the consulate's number to see where he is...

1

Mysteries

On Saturday 6 October Turkish officials leaked to Reuters a blunt statement that a man had been murdered on the Tuesday in the Saudi consulate in Istanbul. The news about this untimely, violent death behind diplomatic doors ran as a thunder bolt through the world media. It is highly unusual for one government to accuse another government of criminal behaviour. It is even rarer for this to happen from a standing start and for state offices to be used as a killing ground.

Immediately, the international media was spell-bound by this real-life whodunnit. Over the next months the story would blow up to a running-news murder mystery akin to the hunt for Saddam Hussein and Muammar Gaddafi. The affair's tentacles would wrap around Turkey, Saudi Arabia, the US, Russia, Great Britain, Israel, Iran and Egypt.

Astonishingly, at the heart of it was a character who operated backstage and in the shadows rather than front-of-stage at the helm of important decisions. Both an affable conversationalist and someone used keeping cards close to his chest without friends realising it, this almost nineteenth-century character had slipped effortlessly backwards and forwards between roles as a spy and diplomat entrusted with explosive national secrets, war correspondent, newspaper editor, centrist pundit, as well as PLO champion and secret donor to subversive opposition movements. Straddling these contradictory roles, he had along the way established friendships with kings, princes, presidents, thinkers, and even super-villains such as the founder of al-Qaeda.

One person who got to know him in 2018 thought that this mercurial character 'did not appear to be guided by any particular ideology' but was 'sharp, quick-witted... always on the lookout for a good debate'. A long-standing friend concurred that 'he engaged people that disagreed with him' and could be wildly indiscreet. Another who had also known him for a long time called him the 'most intellectual person in Saudi Arabia'. A high-ranking prince said of him that he 'has always been honest'. Other words used to describe him were 'big and burly' and 'soft and humble' and also 'pushy but in a good way'. His sons said that their father was like a 'rock-'n' -roll star' in Saudi Arabia.

Turkey's media bombshell created the first big riddle in the Khashoggi affair with hindsight, and one of the reasons for this book. Why? What had prompted President Erdoğan of Turkey to go nuclear in a matter of days? And what was so special about this shadowy figure called Jamal Khashoggi few had ever heard of?

Furthermore, wrapped inside the Turkish allegation, was another great riddle – and another reason for wanting to write this book. Unlike nations such as Russia and North Korea, the desert kingdom had never before hunted down someone on foreign soil in order to assassinate them. It had never before murdered any Saudi nationals abroad in general, or Turkey in particular, full stop. At least, not openly. As a personal advisor to Erdoğan would say, 'It is an attack that destroys all traditions'. A UN report of 20 June 2019 would assess it as 'just unthinkable' before the killing.

Who was the main suspect? Saudi Arabia's *de-factor* ruler, Crown Prince Mohammed bin Salman, minister of defence, deputy prime minister, CEO of its single oil company, president of both its economic and security council, or more popularly 'MBS', looked like the man with his hand on the trigger. He was a relatively new entry on the world stage and had popped on the global-news radar only a few times since his appointment on 21 June 2017 – notably once for imprisoning senior royal relatives, officials and businessmen in a local five-star hotel for a shake-down relating to almost a trillion dollars to fill the royal coffers, and another time for kidnapping the Lebanese prime minister Saad al-Hariri on his visit to Riyadh and making him announce his resignation on television (as well as having him roughed up, it was rumoured). He seemed a colourful, feisty, unorthodox character who didn't hesitate to pick on people his own size. Unusual for a leading Saudi royal, age thirty three, he exuded youthful vigour.

Certainly, MBS, the new crown prince, was known to be cracking the whip inside Saudi Arabia to establish his authority. He had set up a hit team known to US intelligence as the Saudi Rapid Intervention Group or 'Tiger Team'. It was deployed to subdue dissidents inside and outside the kingdom. But the group was involved in Saudi Arabia's routine campaigns of forcibly repatriating and detaining nationals – including activist women – in royal palaces inside the kingdom. There were rumours of physical abuse and sometimes even torture. It wasn't pretty, but sadly nothing out of the ordinary for the authoritarian kingdom. And the group wasn't known to have a license to kill.

Why the dramatic break with the past on this occasion? What reason could be grave enough for Saudi Arabia's royal palace to disrupt long-standing tradition – if not Saudi (religious) laws – and assassinate a relative nobody? Why would the crown prince wager the house and his royal succession on a minion?

Saudi intrigue was consensus-based and non-violent compared to the desert-kingdom's neighbours (King Faisal's death in 1975 was tragic but not political). Indeed, Turkey's President Erdoğan had barely survived a precipitous coup against him on 16 July 2016, from which he was saved by Twitter by a fluke. Saudi royal succession was placid rather than violent, venomous and internecine, despite the unimaginable wealth involved. Yet here suddenly was one of Saudi Arabia's thirty-three million subjects slain outside the kingdom on palace orders in a consulate.

The overture to these two mysteries couldn't have been more mundane. On Tuesday 2 October, Jamal Khashoggi had flown into Istanbul from London. With a short greying beard, not in the greatest health but with an open, ready and inviting smile, he was a fifty-nine-year-old Saudi *bon vivant* who had recently become resident in the US.

The weekend before, he had spoken at a wonkish 25th-anniversary conference in London on the PLO Oslo Accords, the beginning of the Middle-East peace process, and stayed at the Ambassadors Bloomsbury, a short walk away. Although not a diplomat, he had in the past taken meetings with the PLO and Hamas on behalf of Saudi Arabia as a supernumerary emissary. Despite a severe cold, he had met up with friends from Saturday through Monday. On Tuesday he had arrived back in Istanbul and went to the Saudi-Arabian consulate in the Levent business district to obtain papers needed for a marriage license in Turkey.

His failure to re-emerge from his mission would have taken some time to percolate through to the media. Except for one thing. Since December 2017, Jamal Khashoggi had his own masthead on the website of the *Washington Post* in a new online section called Global Opinions. Every month the *Post* published one or two pieces of his in English but also translated them into Arabic – in which language his pages 'spiked in traffic'.

It was this media connection that had led to the first reports about the events on 2 October on the *Post*'s website, four days before the Turkish government's bombshell. Jamal Khashoggi's fiancée Hatice Cengiz had alerted *Washington Post* Istanbul-bureau chief Kareem Fahim that Jamal had mysteriously failed to re-emerge four hours after visiting the Saudi consulate in Istanbul.

Fahim duly posted the item on his own *Post* blog that day. The internet in the Middle East soon buzzed with rumours. The news that a former Saudi secret-service liaison to al-Qaeda had disappeared also instantly circulated among secret services around the world. Clearly, the CIA, MI6 – not to mention Russia's FSB and GRU, Mossad, France's Deuxième Bureau, Germany's BND, China's Ministry of State Security, and the intelligence services of other countries that sold arms to Saudi Arabia – took an interest in order to assess what the implications were for their country's leaders. Some of these agencies – the ones that had found out in advance of Saudi plans to strike against Jamal Khashoggi at the Istanbul consulate – were already secretly covering events for their paymasters.

From this point onwards the news machine gained a unique momentum. There was little chance that the *Washington Post* or other press would find out more on their own, however. In Britain, journalists had been able to do their own investigative work during the excruciating deaths of Alexander Litvinenko from Polonium 210 poisoning in London in 2006 or Dawn Sturgess's after the poisoning of Sergei Skripal and his daughter with a top-secret Soviet nerve agent in Salisbury in 2018. But both Turkey and, even more so, Saudi Arabia are hermetically shut to a free press – or indeed any type of researcher – trying to dig around sensitive subjects. The idea of a Freedom of Information request would be laughable. Both countries – like Russia, China, North Korea, or, for that matter, the world's other authoritarian regimes – had draconic ways of deterring infractions whether by a journalist or not. Even foreign-governmental intelligence agencies risked severe prison sentences or worse in the case of Saudi Arabia.

In the months that followed it would nonetheless appear as if the (Turkish) media had done its own investigative work on the Khashoggi affair. But any release of new information depended instead on a conscious decision by the government of Turkey or Saudi Arabia – or another country – and not on journalists hunting down independent sources like terriers. Starter releases were initially handed to a small number of global outlets, such as Reuters, the *Washington Post*, and the *New York Times*. But once the fire was lit, most were handled by *Sabah* (Morning) in Turkey. A one-time independent paper, *Sabah* had been seized on a technicality in 2007 and sold to media conglomerate Çalik Holding for a knock-down price with a government loan. Çalik's then CEO was President Erdoğan's son-in-law, who had since become his minister of finance. Occasionally a few other Turkish media with similar histories received leaks. The modest number of non-Turkish government leaks went to their home media, but not always as we will see.

When trying to establish the facts of the Khashoggi affair, the team of UN special rapporteur Agnes Callamard noted this lop-sided aspect of the case. She announced an international human-rights inquiry into his killing on 25 January 2019 and was joined by Helena Kennedy, QC, among others. Their report of 20 June 2019 addressed the issue of leaks and noted that 'there is rarely space for scrutiny from anyone outside the intelligence system. Outsiders may be readily manipulated'. As a result, the report set aside 'leaks reported by journalists' and only used them 'to corroborate information gathered independently by the inquiry'.

It is the third riddle the book aims to delve into, and the aim is the opposite of the pin-point aim of the UN inquiry – to nail down facts and apportion blame. Instead of ignoring media leaks on principle, as the UN inquiry team did, their time line is reconstructed here because they shaped the narrative of the Khashoggi affair. The power of these leaks created an evolving reality that had real consequences, rippling like a stone dropped in water. The UN report called this 'a worrying tendency to value Intelligence information and leaks of it, over facts and evidence.' While it should, perhaps, not have happened, it did.

Unlike in the Skripal case, these leaks were freely deployed by the leakers to 'manipulate' these consequences as there was no media counterweight to them in either Turkey or in Saudi Arabia, the places with facts on the ground. The press geographically located elsewhere had no access either. In fact, it only had leaks of its own. Instead of scrutinising the facts, as the UN report did, here it is the nebula that will be scrutinised. It is the riddle of government leaders' behaviour that is being tracked in this book.

By going back to the very first instance of a statement or release – rather than repeats elsewhere – as they were fed into the news-cycle questions 'who did it?' and 'will the culprits be punished?', a pattern emerged. This was particularly the case when considering the additional question what benefit such a press release sought to obtain and whether the release of leaks contained hard facts or merely suggestive facts.

Normally this isn't necessary, but it is when the suppliers are authoritarians or intelligence services.

From this not only a new story emerged in which Jamal Khashoggi's background took centre stage, but also one in which Ankara's role is as murky Riyadh's. And that theirs was not the only tenebrous one. Though the affair was mainly about hurt national pride inside Turkey, it is ironic that outside the country, due to opposition to Saudi Arabia as the villain of the piece, the authoritarian President Erdoğan came to be seen as a defender of honourable government.

Although on the face of it a stand-off between governments, the Khashoggi affair's tentacles would also brush and pinch some of the world's most visible billionaires. They included president of the US Donald Trump, his friend Tom Barrack, Vladimir Putin, owner of Amazon Jeff Bezos, King Salman of Saudi Arabia, his son Crown Prince Mohammed, while in the background hovered the world's richest man Sheikh Mohammed bin Zayed, the ruler of the UAE and bidder for Newcastle United Football Club. In addition there were the aspiring billionaires such as Jared Kushner, Donald Trump's son-in-law, and President Recep Erdoğan. In 2015 President Erdoğan already moved into the *Ak Saray* (white palace) in Ankara built at close to $1bn with taxpayers' money. Erdoğan's government had stopped publishing the palace's costs once they overran the budgeted $615 million. The Khashoggi affair was not just about geo-politics but also personal for this special class of the world's richest people in government. In the middle was the clubbable insider Jamal Khashoggi.

None of the governments involved in the affair come off as hugely principled. The temptation to tell tales (a flat denial – a tale one way or the other – of a previous statement was encountered in the process of this book, for example) is great because they can, they reckon the gravity of the situation demands it, and often perhaps because it is easier that way for all the officials, their promotions, and the institutions involved. But, while they may put up roadblocks in a pinch, Western officials know that they do not have sole control over the facts. Journalists, elected officials, and members of the public can check them over, decide whether what they are being told makes sense or not, and say so.

If there is one moral of the Khashoggi affair, it is that this individual freedom to establish the facts is still as potent as when it was accidentally reborn in the sixteenth-century Netherlands. If that freedom didn't (still) exist strongly in the leading country in the world, Jamal Khashoggi's rendition would be just another tool for the small population fraction in power to act increasingly as wizards of Oz over the others. Minute-maid facts – here today contradicted tomorrow – would be another. It is hard to see how the story in this book could be published in, say, Saudi Arabia, or Turkey.

By laying out all the media facts, the self-serving agendas and distortions created by all the governments involved reveal themselves. As a media phenomenon the Khashoggi affair is also significant because it shows what happens when official facts are always fudged and double, and echo-chambers are created. The media starts to look like a giant, national Truman Show and it becomes clear why Byzantine studies were the only non-political option in Soviet Russia.

The UN report of Agnes Callamard's team will feature in greater detail at the end of the book. But even this report didn't escape the manipulation problem. While having a determination to fight 'confirmation bias', more time, skills and money, better access than any 'outsider', the team was not given Saudi Arabia's raw data and Turkey provided highly screened access – as meticulously catalogued by the report. The Khashoggi affair was what daily life is like in these countries. 'Facts' are controlled by their stories – held until it becomes expedient to issue new ones.

In order to avoid depersonalising what happened to Jamal Khashoggi, he will be referred to as 'Jamal' in the story of this book as opposed to the affair that bears his surname. References are included where strictly necessary.

2

A Blip

On 2 October, Jamal Khashoggi's enigmatic disappearance was still but a spit on the radar. At some point, after the *Washington Post*'s blog and other coverage, it would have to be filed away as a loose end without further news rather than a red-hot developing story. All that could be said on the day was that Jamal Khashoggi might or might not have been arrested and repatriated to Saudi Arabia – fate unknown like repatriated Saudis before him. Ambiguous? Yes. Tragic? Without a doubt. A major global-news story? Less so in a world where people awkwardly vanish with regularity in authoritarian countries.

Yet four days after Jamal's unexplained disappearance, the story, instead of vanishing into a news haze, was saved from oblivion by precisely the country that had not time for its own independent journalists – Turkey.

After initially seeming as uninformed as anyone else, it was the Turkish government that lit the blue touch paper when two of its officials stated to Reuters that 'Mr Khashoggi has been killed at the consulate.' And, just to twist the knife further, the anonymous officials added 'We believe that the murder was premeditated and the body was subsequently moved out of the consulate.'

The officials leaked this information anonymously to the paper because they supposedly were not authorised to speak. It set the tone for the future and a variety of reasons would be given for this approach: protection of sources – intercepted communication or human informers – ongoing investigations, hampering of future prosecution, etc. It all also added to the fevered speculation and sense of mystery.

Yet no government makes such an accusation unless they have copper-bottomed evidence. They 'wouldn't announce this kind of thing, if they didn't have some other information which is leading them in that direction', a British pundit on al-Jazeera observed. That was the key.

Particularly, the Turkish government versus Saudi Arabia. With a tanking economy and over 100,000 of its citizens detained following a 2016 putsch – by a fraction of that number – Erdoğan's standing was fraying abroad and brittle at home.

Saudi Arabia, however, with its economy floating on oil and Mecca and Medina, the holiest places of Islam within its borders, could lay claim to Turkey's traditional leadership from Ottoman days over Sunnis in the Arab world – particularly under their new *de-facto* ruler, young and photogenic MBS.

Turkey's breath-taking accusation of premeditated murder immediately bracketed Jamal Khashoggi and the crown prince together before the world. This was because the day after the alleged killing, no less a person than MBS himself had officially and vocally protested Saudi innocence of Jamal's disappearance and current whereabouts.

'We have nothing to hide', he himself had said unequivocally on the record about Jamal in a Bloomberg website interview that covered a broad range of other topics and by chance was scheduled on the evening of 3 October.

From 6 October, when the Turkish government engaged the global news machine, its authorities began to leak a steady and grisly stream of detailed information about the murderous events in the Saudi consulate, destroying MBS's reputation in the process with a thousand cuts.

A new reputation would emerge. Gone was the image of young and dynamic new broom, carefully cultivated with the help of global advisors such as McKinsey, Booz Allen, lobbyists and top PR agencies, over the course of fifteen months – organisations which had been paid many hundreds of millions of dollars. He was now cast as a ghoulish potentate in the mould of Vladimir Putin, Saddam Hussain, and the Assads.

Fanning the flames further, President Erdoğan, MBS's fellow-authoritarian, signalled in a number of personal statements that he would not stop until he had achieved his objective – whatever that was exactly. Erdoğan – despite his own gloves-off vendetta against Turkish journalists – would write a column in billionaire Jeff Bezos's *Washington Post* on the matter, and called the murder 'savage' and 'planned'. He would give many press conferences.

Holding the line set by the crown prince in his Bloomberg interview, the kingdom pretended it had no idea what the fuss was about. But the Turkish drip-feed would prove irresistible and keep MBS and Jamal's assassination in the world's media-spotlight and would force Riyadh's hands again and again.

Yet that was but the tip of the iceberg. Other things were going on below the surface of the news pages.

3

Murder at the Consulate

A private Gulfstream jet with tail markings HZ-SK2 touched down at Istanbul's Atatürk Airport at 3.13am on 2 October 2018 and taxied to the private-jet terminal. It was owned by Sky Prime Aviation, a company whose shares had reportedly been transferred to the Saudi government after MBS's shakedown of his royal relatives in 2017 in the capital's Ritz Carlton. The jet had come from Riyadh with an elite force of nine Saudi soldiers and included two colonels, and a general. The jet idled on the tarmac awaiting further instruction after the nine men disembarked. Two hours earlier an advance team of three Saudi soldiers had flown in on a scheduled commercial flight, and the day before another forward trio of soldiers, including a general and a major, had arrived midday in Istanbul on a scheduled commercial flight from Riyadh.

All fifteen men checked in until at least Friday at two five-star hotels in Istanbul's Levent business district on the European side of the city – the nine-strong team at the Mövenpick Hotel and the two forward trios at the Wyndham Grand.

They were all caught on (subsequently leaked) CC-TV, passing through airport security and at their hotels' front desks. Both luxury tower-block hotels are close to one another and just a few minutes' drive away from the plain five-storey consulate, which is tucked away on a quiet street. At 7.20pm on 1 October, consular secret-service agent, Muflis al-Musleh made bookings at 7.20pm for the pack of the team, asking for 'seaviews'. From such rooms at the Mövenpick guests could eye-ball the nearby consulate.

Later that day a second Sky Prime Aviation Gulfstream IV jet, with tail marking HZ-SK1, would touch down at around 5.15pm at Atatürk Airport. It would immediately sweep up six of the fifteen-strong hit squad and their luggage, taking off again at 6.20pm. The idling Gulfstream jet HZ-SK2 would take off four hours later in the evening at 10.54pm with seven of the fifteen-strong hit-squad and whatever luggage they had with them. The remaining two members of the hit-squad would leave on a scheduled flight just after midnight. Meanwhile, there was another exodus. The Saudi secret-service chief-of-station of the consulate left for Riyadh on a commercial flight at 9.35pm with his family. Three of his Saudi secret-service officers stationed at the consulate would also disappear, *Sabah* would report.

The timing of the operation was so tight that the nine soldiers on the first Gulfstream could just about cross paths with Jamal Khashoggi in front of the main airport hall where, clad in a yellow dress shirt, he pulled a small suitcase to the taxi rank. He had taken Turkish airline flight TK1984 from Heathrow, the last flight out to Istanbul at 10.15pm, and had landed at Atatürk Airport at 4am, half an hour after the nine men.

It is a distinct possibility that Jamal Khashoggi had been tailed in London. The Gulfstream with the nine Saudi soldiers had departed from Riyadh at around 9.40pm (UK time), half an hour before take-off of the Turkish Airline flight from Heathrow. The Gulfstream's lift-off was likely exactly timed with passengers boarding the Turkish Airlines Airbus 321 and the flight closing to push off its standby 9.40pm. No one could get on or off while the plane taxied to its Heathrow runway for take-off at its scheduled 10.15pm time slot. The UN Inquiry established that the jet's flight plan and nine-strong passenger list were filed at 9:23pm under diplomatic clearance.

It seems equally possible that a couple of the nine Saudi soldiers went to the main Atatürk Airport arrivals hall to confirm that Jamal had gone through customs in Istanbul and that he was heading back to his apartment.

Although Saudi Arabia is immensely wealthy from oil money, its consulate in Istanbul is far from impressive. Over-shadowed by Levent's financial towers, it is a far cry from the modern Saudi Arabia dreamt of by its *de-facto* leader Crown Prince Mohammed bin Salman with his vision of skyscraper cities in the desert and luxury coastal-holiday resorts for sun-seekers around the world. Behind security barriers and razor wire, the plain, squat yellow-cream building with a huge specimen conifer, terracotta roof tiles crowned by a Saudi flag, and an air-conditioning unit flung against the masonry, is rather more Benidorm-utilitarian. It has the air of a worn, but well-maintained 1970s office, with light-blue painted metal window grills in elegant Islamic patterns and CC-TV cables slung over them, as well as a mysterious assortment of other types of electronic equipment dotted around the walls and windows. The ceilings of the harshly-lit public area facing the front are low, while the help-windows are sealed with bullet-proof glass. On the desks, stacks of papers wait to be rubber-stamped in a jumble of passport photos and visa applications. It is also an unlikely murder scene.

Jamal Khashoggi, the fifty-nine-year-old Saudi *bon vivant* and royal insider arrived at the consulate at 1.14pm. In self-imposed exile in Virginia, he needed Saudi documentation prior to his forthcoming marriage in Turkey. Unlike Saudi Arabia, Turkey did not recognise polygamy and in order for him to marry Turkish law required a certificate of celibacy stating whether he was single, divorced or widowed. He also needed an authorised copy of his birth certificate.

Jamal was wary of consular and embassy visits. As a former palace official, he was well acquainted with the furtive Saudi method of interrogations and forced repatriation. Apart from troublesome Saudi dissidents who needed to be placed under government control inside the kingdom, there were always a few privileged princes who misbehaved, or had become too Western and liberal in their opinions. It was a long-standing practice. He had worked for five years at two large Saudi embassies and he knew exactly what took place in them. It hadn't bothered him then, but now he was at the receiving end of those policies.

Diplomatic missions seemed safe in principle, though, in certain countries. He had visited the Saudi embassy in Washington, DC, in the late winter of 2017 and had been recognised by Saudi embassy staff. MBS's brother, Prince Khalid bin Salman, abbreviated as KBS, age thirty, was the US ambassador and he had called Jamal up for a visit of about half an hour in his spectacularly grand top-floor office. This was notwithstanding Jamal's strained relationship with MBS's government. KBS was charming to Jamal, with whom he had developed a friendly relationship – over time Jamal sent him several messages expressing his loyalty to the kingdom. 'We just had a nice chat, and he was quite nice', Jamal told a friend afterwards.

How safe was the Istanbul consulate though? Would the Saudi government dare cause trouble in defiance of the Turkish government, if not international treaties? Riyadh would never contemplate doing so in Washington, where it would be the equivalent of poking a hornet nest at the Capitol, or elsewhere in the US. But what about Turkey?

4

Caught

On Friday 28 September, Jamal had picked up the courage to go to the Istanbul consulate in the privileged Beşiktaş (stone cradle) district and walked in at 11.50am without an appointment.

Earlier in the month he had paid for a flat in a secure apartment complex in Istanbul's Zeytinburnu (cape olive) district. Located well south of Beşiktaş, it was a jumble of traditional nineteenth-century six-story textile and leather factories with modern apartment blocks built like cliffs among them. Though architecturally lawless, it faced the Marmara Sea at one end, adjoined historic Istanbul, and was only 15 minutes from Atatürk Airport. The apartment itself was a quick 30 minute drive from the consulate.

Jamal had been deeply apprehensive about the Friday visit. At the very least, he thought, they might refuse to help him with sorting out the documentation he needed. He had mooted to his fiancée Hatice Cengiz beforehand, 'maybe it's better if I don't go.'

Deep down he thought he would be safe in Turkey, but he reckoned that he might be questioned and this he feared most. 'Because he was a very emotional and delicate person, he was uncomfortable with tension', Hatice said about Jamal's hesitation.

But without the two certificates they could not get married in Turkey and Jamal had decided to risk it. As he did not announce his visit, Riyadh would have little time to get organised if they were so minded. On that day he had to catch a flight in the afternoon and, if he was being watched, taking a taxi with his luggage and fiancée was entirely logical.

It turned out, he told Hatice, that the consular staff had no prior warning that he might be coming in and that they were pleasantly surprised to see him. In fact, they were very warm in their response and people had come up to him. The person helping him had said 'they would do it for him'. He had worried for naught the consulate might refuse to supply the documents.

Jamal had waited for almost an hour. But then he had to apologise and said he had to leave for his flight in the afternoon. Perhaps it was one reason why he picked that Friday of all days. He had an excuse to leave quickly. Also, his London talk the next day was well-advertised and, perhaps that was another reason why it wasn't an obvious day to pick. If anyone was tracking his movements that is.

The consular staff said regretfully 'there is no time' to certify the paperwork against the civil registry in Saudi Arabia before he had to run off to the airport.

Hatice had been waiting outside the consulate roadblock for a little less than an hour. She was anxious because his flight was close to boarding. Another 15 minutes and he would have missed it, she reckoned. She took Jamal straight to the terminal, where he checked in with just his carry-on but without his large suitcase, which he asked her to drop off at their apartment. Later leaked CC-TV coverage showed her taxi turning into the apartment complex's security gate at 1.50pm and Hatice getting into the elevator up to the floor of their home at 2.04pm with the suitcase and talking to a worker at the complex.

Hatice felt relieved, too, despite all the tension of the day. She said Jamal was cheerful and thrilled with the 'nice treatment and hospitality' at the consulate. It had been an emotional experience and he felt less homesick after the visit among his country folk. It had made a weight fall off of his shoulders and at least some of the yearning for Saudi Arabia had abated. He had come out smiling and said, '*Inshallah* [God willing] I will get the papers after I return from London'. It had been 'unnecessary to worry' and 'everything was fine', he reassured her. He had told the consular staff that he would be back in Istanbul on Tuesday,

2 October, and they had said they would have all the papers ready by then.

TK197 is Turkish Airlines' last afternoon flight on Fridays to Heathrow, and scheduled for take-off at 2.40pm. Jamal flew to London to speak the next day at a conference at the Wellcome Collection on the Euston Road on Saturday 30 September. It was organised by the Middle East Monitor and other speakers included Tony Blair's former secretary of state for international development, Clare Short, and Sir Richard Dalton, consul-general in Jerusalem under John Major's government. Jamal stayed in London for the weekend, meeting up with London friends all day Sunday and Monday, such as the Arafat-family lawyer Saad Djebbar. Djebbar has been a friend since 1996 and Jamal helps fix 'matters regarding Saudi institutions'. They meet for an hour on Motcombe St at the Fine Cheese Company

Unlike Jamal himself, his London friends were deeply concerned about his safety in the city and worried about Saudi spies tracking him. They had offered to put him up at a low-key hotel rather than the four-star one arranged by the organisers.

But Jamal had waved the offer away. He felt 'relaxed and calm' after the visit to the consulate. A PLO friend at the conference even saw how Jamal left his mobile phone unattended on a table during the conference (the friend decided to keep an eye out until Jamal returned). When the director of the conference organisation, Daud Abdullah, asked whether the Saudi authorities might withdraw his passport, Khashoggi replied he didn't think 'they would go that far.'

On Monday, Jamal told his friend Azzam Tamimi – the British reformer of the Finsbury Mosque, post the one-eyed, hooked, militant-Islamist cleric Abu Hamza, and a broadcaster on an Arab channel – about the consulate. He had been received warmly, 'very warmly' in fact he said. The people working there were just 'ordinary people'. There would be no problem visiting again to pick up the certificates.

Despite his cold, Jamal had spoken with excitement about his future plans to his friend and was full of ideas. They had spoken about

Tamimi's interview of Jamal on his show on Thursday in Istanbul, and Jamal had talked about his forthcoming marriage and the apartment he had just purchased.

In actual fact, Jamal had triggered the Saudi trap laid for him. The diplomat who had first helped him at the consulate had passed Jamal and his query on to one of the Saudi secret-service officers stationed at the consulate. The officer had given him his name as 'Sultan' (or Saad, UN report detail 78) and his telephone number to call on Tuesday. It was later leaked that telephone records showed that calls had been made to Riyadh immediately after Jamal's visit. The return appointment to the consulate in Istanbul was the crucial bait for the trap to shut close.

The UN report (detail 78) gave greater insight into the beehive of activity inside the consulate from telephone wiretaps. At 2.22pm, while Jamal's plane was still waiting for clearance to take off for Heathrow, in Riyadh top intelligence agent brigadier-general Maher Mutreb confirmed over the phone to Istanbul consular attaché Saad al-Qarni (likely) that his 'videos and images' were being appraised. At 2.27pm, in a follow-up call, Mutreb asked al-Qarni whether Jamal would return on 2 October.

'Yes, we were all shocked. We just spoke. "I said how are you?" There isn't anything official but it's known that he is one of the people sought. However, we did not receive any letter from our service regarding whether there is any problem or not on him.' The surprise and warmth by the consular staff when Jamal walked in was genuine. At the same time – through the keen observance of watch-lists by its secret-service staff in the absence of a direct order to notify Riyadh – Jamal became a marked man when he could wait no longer for the paperwork to be processed in time before he had to leave for the airport.

Riyadh now knew when Jamal would be back inside the four walls of their diplomatic property. There were four days to plan how to disappear Jamal, who was well-known personally to MBS who called him by his first name. The level of involved parties in the affair would remain stratospheric. The Turkish authority who would reveal the most comprehensive official details of Riyadh's plot was none other than President Erdoğan himself.

On Friday evening, just before Jamal landed in London, Saudi attaché Abdulaziz al-Ghumuzi spoke to the consul-general Mohammed al-Otaibi. He said 'the head of state security called me and they have an assignment. They are asking for anyone from your delegation for... a top secret mission'. It would last four-five days. Consul-general al-Otaibi then spoke to a staff member whom he told that security staff of the ambassador had contacted him to say that 'there is an urgent training in Riyadh... The issue is very important and developed rapidly'. They agreed the staff member would catch a flight at 8 or 9pm next day.

On Saturday 29 September, after Jamal's impromptu Friday morning visit, reportedly the Istanbul chief-of-station of Saudi intelligence Ahmed al-Muzaini (officially a military attaché at the consulate and a diplomat) and another attaché (maybe al-Qarni) flew straight to Riyadh from Istanbul's satellite Sabiha Gökçen Airport on the Asiatic side at 2.31pm for consultation with his superior, vice-president of Saudi intelligence major-general Ahmed al-Asiri, *Sabah* reported. Other staff, involved in sweeping the consulate for bugs two days before, also travelled to Riyadh.

Military attaché Al-Muzaini flew back on Saudia flight SV263 ('SF263' in the UN report) to Istanbul afterwards on 1 October, going through Atatürk Airport customs lugging a large suitcase after his 48-hour trip and exited the terminal at 4.02pm (all captured on leaked CC-TV), with his colleague, delivering Riyadh's orders to the Saudi consul-general Mohammed al-Otaibi. The first forward team of three Tiger Team soldiers also arrived on this Saudia from Riyadh on Monday 1 October at Atatürk Airport.

While Jamal was still in London with his friend Azzam Tamimi, the four men set to work immediately. They were joined by four further staff, including Muflis al-Musleh. The forward trio of operatives went to the consulate at 7pm, an hour and a half after checking in, and returned to the Wyndham Grand at 10.40pm, shortly after take-off of Jamal's Turkish Airlines plane.

At 5.30pm al-Muzaini took a Saudi consular BMW on a reconnaissance trip to Belgrad Forest 25 minutes to the north of the consulate, caught on (later leaked) CC-TV footage at 6.28pm at its gated entrance in the woods. Reconnaissance was also made at Yalova, across the Bosphorus on the Asiatic side of Turkey, 1 hour and 15 minutes by car south from the consulate. Near Yalova, in the city of Termal, one of MBS's friends owned a palatial villa with a deep well in the garden.

Upon arrival at the consulate, the general among the trio of soldiers, major-general Mansour Abahussein (who travelled on a diplomatic passport from Riyadh in a traditional white *thaub* robe and a patriotic red-and-white-blocked head *ghutra*), had made a preparatory call to this friend of MBS's. All these details were also leaked later and confirmed in the UN report. Abahussein asked him 'how far the house was from Istanbul, and Ghozan responded "The bridge has been opened. It takes one hour and fifteen minutes to get there via highway. It takes forty five minutes from the airport." He asked "Is there anyone there?" Ghozan replied: "No, there is nobody. Just a caretaker"' (detail 84).

Abdulaziz al-Ghumuzi, Saad al-Qarni and another spoke at 9.48pm and discussed the Tiger Team operation. 'They will have something to do on my floor in the office... Their work inside will take two or three days' (detail 85).

Oblivious of all this activity, Jamal arrived back at his Istanbul apartment early in the morning on Tuesday, a little groggy from his cold and the four-hour red-eye flight. At 4.57am he went downstairs again in a black t-shirt and faded jeans looped with a leather belt to wait outside for a minute or so to meet his fiancée. Just before take-off from Heathrow, he had texted her at 10pm, 'I'm on the plane right now, I'm coming home to you. In love, loving and passionate.' She arrived with a purple scarf wrapped around her hair – once in Kemalist Turkey a reason for being denied access to schools and universities, working for the government, a passport, but now a sign sympathetic to Erdoğan's

AKP – and in a long coat. Jamal let her in through the security door of the building while she carried a plastic bag in her left hand.

Later they went out again together and he had changed into a blazer, shirt and grey trousers. While out, he called the number of the Saudi secret-service officer he had been given to say he wanted to come in that day for the paperwork. Some forty minutes later, near 11.50am, the officer, still masquerading as a consular clerk, called back and told him yes the papers were ready and he was welcome to come and collect at 1 pm.

Jamal's thirty-eight-year-old fiancée Hatice Cengiz, a PhD student at the Fatih Sultan Mehmet University, Istanbul, heard Jamal on the calls while they were out. She said she didn't realise he meant to go to the consulate that day and she decided to join him on this trip, too, as she had on the first one. She had skipped university to be with him for the rest of the day. The apartment needed more furniture and they could shop afterwards.

They returned to the apartment's entrance lobby at 12:17pm, talking animatedly, holding hands and smiling, Hatice almost cradling Jamal's arm. Jamal briefly let her hand go to flip his card past the pad to open the door. Almost half an hour later they left once again hand-in-hand walking along the new plantings on the side of the road to the security gates of the complex.

At 12:42pm they passed the tall glass-and-brown-metal guards' house, filing one by one by its yellow metal railing through a turnstile for pedestrians, Hatice briefly getting caught off-balance. They both snaked past the gate and turned left and crossed thc road to hail a taxi for the 30 minute drive to the consulate. It was to be Jamal's last journey. All their movements were captured on the CC-TV (later leaked) angled from the road at the frontage of the entrance.

While he was no longer 'that hesitant [about their] second trip', Jamal again did not think Hatice should come inside the consulate with him. But he did agree to do the same as during the first visit to the consulate when she waited outside to drop him off at the airport.

The plan was no different – for her to wait outside. He gave her his mobile phones. They contained sensitive messages, information and numbers he didn't want to take into the consulate. If he didn't come out after a few hours she should contact the authorities, he said. He didn't give her more precise instructions than those.

Hatice said she would wait outside, near a supermarket 20 yards from the roadblock and the entrance to the consulate. 'Fine, my darling', he replied, and turned towards the security guards, who frisked him briefly before he walked to the door of the covered walkway to the consulate's public area.

She circled around a little and bought chocolate and water for Jamal, waiting patiently.

By 4pm her mood changed to panic and she called someone close to her who checked and said the consulate had shut its doors to visitors at 3.30pm. She went up to the guard outside – a Turkish man, she thought – who did not know who Jamal Khashoggi was and told her that there was 'no one inside and everybody had left'. She then rang the consulate from her mobile phone, and the Saudi officer who answered her call came outside after a few minutes and said he had 'checked all the rooms and there was no one inside; so it was pointless for [her] to wait'.

This made no sense. Anxiously, Hatice contacted Turan Kişlakçi, director of the Turkish-Arab Journalists' Association. Though Jamal hadn't given specific instructions for her to call Kişlakçi – nor had he prewarned Kişlakçi that he was visiting the consulate that day to say he might be at risk – Turan was an old friend of Jamal's whom he had known for a decade and a half. He had made Hatice's first introduction to Jamal. A lively, enthusiastically-gesticulating, bearded, bespectacled, serious-looking forty-five-year-old Turkish man with a Pakistani graduate degree, Turan dressed in stylish suits, and had gone to Hatice's father on behalf of Jamal to discuss the marriage. Turan was in a meeting, however, and she couldn't get through.

Though Jamal hadn't instructed her about this either, at 4.41pm she also called Yasin Aktay, personal advisor to the Turkish president, former

MP and vice chairman of the ruling AKP, and also a close friend of Jamal's. Erdoğan, in fact, was a friend, too. Aktay knew the exact time she called because he took a screenshot of the call. Her name on his phone came up as 'Hatice Kaşikçi', the Turkish spelling of Khashoggi.

Jamal hadn't specifically given her Aktay's number to call that day but eight or so days earlier Jamal hadn't felt well enough to attend a talk and was hospitalised. It had worried Hatice and she had asked him whom to call in case of an emergency – Jamal had given her Aktay's number as a close friend. She also rang a number of Arab friends of Jamal's in Istanbul.

She persisted with Turan, calling 'four or five times', and was rewarded when she finally got to speak to him at 5pm.

'Turan', she said in distress 'come to the front of the consulate, Jamal is missing'. He asked whether she had called Yasin Aktay, and then he also called Aktay in Ankara himself.

Hatice's call to Aktay was bull's eye. Aktay called the Saudi ambassador Waleed Elkhereiji who said 'that's awkward' and asked for ten minutes, 'I'll call the consulate and see what happened and will call you back'. When Elkhereiji didn't call back, nor responded to a text and another phone message, Aktay realised this 'was beyond his power'.

Something far bigger was taking place. He called a Saudi peer of Jamal's for an assessment who fumed he had told Jamal 'many times' never to enter the consulate, Aktay later told the UN rapporteur, Agnes Callamard. This mutual Saudi friend told Aktay to call the president immediately. Aktay left a message for President Erdoğan with his office, as he was tied up in a senior party-committee meeting in the capital.

Hatice meanwhile had also called the police. She said that Jamal was being held or that 'something bad' had happened – as President Erdoğan would later describe it.

The alert to the president was sufficient to wake up Turkey's security forces with a sharp jolt and make them start a feverish search for Jamal. Handed Aktay's message by a secretary during the top-level meeting, Erdoğan instantly realised its significance and took Jamal's disappearance from Turkish soil very seriously. He promptly ordered 'that all measures be taken' to locate 'his friend' – the word he used to describe Jamal in later press conferences. Aktay contacted Hakan Fidan, the head of the Turkish secret service MİT, and his deputy, and told them what the president had said. He also contacted the Istanbul police who involved Istanbul's chief prosecutor, Irfan Fidan.

A major cross-agency investigation was swiftly opened at 5.50pm Erdoğan would later personally confirm. At that point his officials, he said, still thought Jamal was inside the consulate.

MİT and other Turkish authorities urgently called their opposite Saudi numbers. No answer. They also feverishly started to go through masses of footage of the wireless MoBeSe system, a Turkish CC-TV network of over 400 HD cameras around Istanbul with close to 500 staff maintaining and analysing its data. At least six CC-TV cameras were positioned at the front of the consulate and another seven covered the back entrance. Investigators traced back every car – there were twenty six of them – and person entering or leaving the consulate that day.

As night fell, Hatice was still walking up and down outside the consulate's roadblock at 5.33pm. And at some point after 5.50pm the police showed her a CC-TV security-still taken from the street at 1.14pm to confirm it was Jamal going into the consulate, asking her – 'is it him?' Next day, after a terrible night, Hatice rushed back to the consulate and went to the police station in the Fatih district near their home to give a statement, and hand Jamal's iPhones over – he liked to use new technology – as well as his laptop, and some of his clothes and things like hair.

However quick off-the-mark the Turkish secret service MİT and police had been after the terse presidential ukase, theirs proved to be a rear-guard action to catch up with the nineteen Saudi plotters. Almost three quarters of an hour before Erdoğan's kick-off, Gulfstream HZ-SK1 had landed at Atatürk Airport at 5.15pm. It had picked up the first six of the Saudi team, including the man involved in the decision to kill

Jamal – brigadier-general Maher Mutreb.

The soldiers and their luggage had gone through Atatürk Airport Genel Havacilik private-jet terminal's routine boarding procedure 5 minutes before the Turkish investigation was opened. Mutreb was travelling on a diplomatic passport and two others on government passports, which meant that they themselves and their luggage were dealt with under the private-jet-terminal's diplomatic 'free passage' rules. Some of the luggage of the other four soldiers was opened for sight inspection and the men headed to their private Gulfstream IV, which spirited them away at 6.20pm when Turkish authorities were only half an hour into hastily getting their heads around events at the consulate.

On 27 March 2019, al-Jazeera would show CC-TV of a partially obscured black Mercedes van driving up to a jet and claim that Mutreb and the operatives were inside to board their jet, implying that Jamal's body parts could have been loaded up from the van. But the Qatar channel didn't explain how airport security would have allowed the van, or its unscreened luggage, access to the airport parking area for all jets even if it had diplomatic status and even if the CC-TV captured the right moment.

The team-leader of the Saudi operation major-general Abahussein was in a hairier spot by this time. He was on the second Saudi Gulfstream with six of his men. Though he also travelled on a diplomatic passport and a jet under diplomatic clearance, by now it was touch and go.

The police and MİT, the Turkish secret service, were on full alert and getting up to speed. The Saudi team-leader knew this because the operative at the consulate who had taken Hatice's call at 4pm and told her to go home had given him the first warning of detection. The next one was the call a few minutes after 4.41pm by the Saudi ambassador, Waleed Elkhereiji, to consul-general al-Otaibi inquiring about Jamal in order to report back to Yasin Aktay. It sounded the alarm for the operation to wrap up.

A few minutes after the ambassador's call, Maher Mutreb and Salah

Tubaigy left the consul-general's residence at 4.53pm (caught on CC-TV). Mutreb and the other five operatives went to the airport going through security between 5.44 and 5.49pm to board the getaway jet. Forensics expert professor Tubaigy went to the consulate to check on progress there of al-Hawsawi and Saif al-Otaibi, the cleaning team. They would leave the consulate at 9.40pm for the second jet. Riyadh also had its plan in place on how to stall Turkish officials and diplomats asking for clarification. They would simply not return calls, like the ambassador, until instructed to do so.

At Genel Havacilik private-jet terminal, Turkish officials were now on high alert. The officials had been told Jamal was being kidnapped and likely on the jet, the June 2019 UN report would state – whereas the first jet had not been inspected. They now demanded to the see the passenger manifest of the second jet and followed diplomatic protocol beady-eyed while searching the non-diplomats, their luggage. The jet was searched by sight for Jamal by intelligence officers posing as airport staff. Professor Tubaigy and the operatives left at the consulate, al-Hawsawi (who had come down from the residence earlier on) and Saif Alotaibi, arrived at Genel Havacilik at 7.40pm but wouldn't get through security until 8.28–29pm. The consul-general's-residence disposal team, major-general Abahussain, al-Arifi, al-Bostani and al-Zahrani, would arrive at 8.24pm and not go through security until 9.44–46pm. It had only taken Mutreb and the others minutes from arrival at the private-jet terminal to get through security and for the plane to leave the runway 35 minutes after.

Would Turkish authorities dare to ground the sitting-duck jet flying under diplomatic clearance, or prevent its four non-diplomatic passengers from boarding?

5

Tysons Corner

Nothing happened. As the Turkish search team didn't find Jamal or anything else untoward airport authorities cleared the second Gulfstream for take-off at 10.46pm. Separately, the contingent of four Saudi secret service agents stationed at the consulate left unhindered on commercial flights, as did the final two Saudi operatives a little after midnight.

Despite having been a key fixture in Saudi Arabia's grand palace-corridors of power, Jamal had relied on Erdoğan's security clout to deter his own former royal patrons. How could it have come this far?

The first wedge driven between the royal palace and Jamal Khashoggi had been a 2016 ban from public speaking and writing, including social media, imposed by Riyadh while Jamal was still living in the kingdom. Remarkably, the ban had little to do with any criticism he might have had of the Saudi government, its policies, the royal family, or indeed MBS himself (or religion). It, in fact, had nothing to do at all with any critique of Saudi Arabia itself, the royal family, or MBS himself.

Rather, the ban was imposed because of Jamal's criticism of the new president-elect Donald Trump. He had called him 'contradictory' at an obscure energy conference held by think tank The Washington Institute. The conference had taken place at the US capital two days after Trump had won the 8 November 2016 election. Billed as a 'commentator' by the organisers, Jamal said Saudi Arabia should form 'a bulwark against' Trump. He also doubted that Trump really understood that 'supporting Putin' meant supporting Iran.

It was all quite interesting, yet hardly likely to keep Donald Trump or his periphery awake at night while they were celebrating. Moreover, the Institute was a distinguished, stolidly-scholarly think tank of the kind that rarely creates waves or headlines. The furthest Jamal's words got to were two lines in the middle of someone's blog post – a long way from Fox News where the president-elect might have noticed them.

Instead, however, Riyadh took Jamal's opinion as if the nation's future was on the line. The Saudi government saw the vain and volatile billionaire and soon-to-be president as their mark and feared Jamal's views might be seen as those held among the royal elite – or, at any rate, something very important was at stake. Stung, Saudi Arabia not only forbade Jamal from public speaking and writing but it went the extra mile. It also issued an official press release to distance itself from him: 'Jamal Khashoggi does not represent the government of Saudi Arabia or its positions at any level'. Riyadh seemed to be making a giant mountain out of a Trump molehill. It was baffling as Jamal had by this time no longer any official position in Saudi Arabia to speak of.

Yet it seems that what Jamal knew in connection with Donald Trump was so sensitive to Riyadh that it was not enough that he was shut up and sealed off. Jamal's credibility also had to be struck down at all costs. There seems little doubt that a direct thread had started to unspool from the kingdom's precipitous decision to gag Jamal – one which was to end with the decision to execute him on 2 October, almost two years later to the day.

A year later, in US exile fifteen kilometres from Washington, DC, in Tysons Corner, Fairfax County, Virginia, where Jamal owned a condominium from his US embassy time, Jamal was finally free again to speak and write publicly. He was invited to write pieces for the online edition of the *Washington Post*, for example. One of these, on arrests regarding women's rights, would be included in the print edition on 23 May 2018 as an op-ed column, another one was to be printed posthumously two weeks after his disappearance.

In his first online piece under the *Post* banner Jamal wrote on 18 September 2017, 'I have left my home, my family and my job, and I am raising my voice. To do otherwise would betray those who languish in prison. I can speak when so many cannot. I want you to know that Saudi Arabia has not always been as it is now. We Saudis deserve better.' Jamal was later to write one piece a month for his *Post* blog, sometimes two. His *Post* editor Karen Attiah said that the online traffic generated by his first piece in Arabic superseded expectations: it 'spiked in traffic', which led to her request for more pieces from her new writer.

Jamal had opened a Twitter account in January 2016 with a last tweet in November that year on what he had said about Trump. Written in Arabic, he now resumed it gaining 1.72 million followers across the Arabic-speaking world. In a year and a few months he tweeted over 54,100 times and followed 753 people, including KBS and MBS's top media aide Saud al-Qahtani, but not MBS himself.

Jamal's self-exile in 2017 was well-timed, as one might expect from a well-informed man – he had been warned to leave said his Turkish friend Turan Kişlakçi. He escaped with two suitcases to his condo in Tysons Corner during Ramadan (27 May to 25 June in Riyadh) a couple of months ahead of MBS's Ritz Carlton purge of leading Saudi princes and officials of November 6, 2017, which side-lined the entire clan of the previous king, King Abdullah. It was also the month when MBS first became crown prince on 21 June, and news of the stealthy, cruel unseating of the previous crown prince in a night of (virtual) long knives buzzed around the palace.

Jamal Khashoggi, however, was still on the fence on 4 July whether to return to Saudi Arabia or not when his friend since 2001, Maggie Salem Mitchell, director of the Qatar International Foundation, hosted a dinner at Clos Maggiore in Covent Garden, London. At the wood-panelled restaurant with abundant ivy on the walls, branches with flowers in the courtyard, as well as a magnificent wine list including rare vintages of Château Pétrus, he discussed his dilemma: 'To keep quiet, to sit in his house in Jeddah and smoke cigars... or to go to Istanbul or the US.'

The Ritz Carlton purge itself was to ensnare one of Jamal's richest royal patrons – the colourful, talkative entrepreneur, vegetarian, fitness-fanatic and lover of stylish sunglasses Prince Alwaleed bin Talal, one of King Salman's nephews through Munaiyir – founder-King ibn Saud's sixteenth wife. He owned at various times part of Murdoch's News Corporation, Disneyland, Lyft, Citibank and also luxury hotels such as the Mövenpick chain. Until his release on 28 February 2018 and the payment MBS extracted from him, Prince Alwaleed was one of the world's richest billionaires – even in Saudi Arabia.

On the whole, Jamal's *Post* blogs presented an even-handed tone when critical of the desert-kingdom's new policies, and indeed were occasionally laudatory. He was a monarchist and did not consider himself a writer for the 'opposition' but rather thought of himself as an 'independent writer.'

While still in Saudi Arabia in June 2017, he had, for example, submitted an application for a fellowship at the prestigious Woodrow Wilson Center in DC. It described a book project 'to explain American life to the Saudi reader and Arabs in general', which would be an 'eye-opener' on 'schooling, educational reform [and] control of public funds' as well as mortgages (housing being the problem that affected most ordinary Saudis, given royal ownership of most of the land). He proposed travelling to US rural towns and describing how town meetings worked and the elections of mayors and governing boards.

To be fair, Jamal had also used his blogs to comment directly on the crown prince, the most powerful man in the oil-rich kingdom after the aging and infirm King Salman, his father. Jamal seemed to be a dedicated monarchist who worried MBS might be a latter-day Louis XIV. In private he was far more candid. In one of the first emails he wrote to Karen Attiah, his editor at the *Post*, he said he never imagined his Saudi Arabia would be filled 'with intimidation, lies, and hate' like Egypt. And he had also continued to criticise Donald Trump – lastly in his blog of 28 August 2018 on the relevance of the Muslim Brotherhood – for not correcting 'Obama's mistakes.'

6

The Attack

When Jamal walked towards the front door of the consulate from the road block for his 1pm appointment, he was a little late. It was 1.14pm and from the covered walkway he expected to go right to one of the three windows in the public section to get his two marriage documents while waiting on the bench of three fabric-covered chairs with comfortable padding. Instead, he was asked whether he would 'take tea' with the consul-general, Mohammed al-Otaibi.

Jamal uneasily accepted the invitation with an 'edge' in his voice. It was not totally impossible that the consul was star-struck – the reception on Friday had been very warm. Special treatment would have befitted someone of his high status in Saudi society, given his closeness to former and present king and crown princes. The same had after all happened when KBS had invited him up to his private office in the US embassy the year before. If he upset the consul general, he might not get his papers today or for long time. He could only accept the invitation or he might as well leave.

Jamal was ushered into the second-floor office of the consul general, a mahogany-parqueted and panelled room, with deep green leather club chairs and sofas, leather-covered tables, neon lights, and a very large green, pristine Saudi national flag. He would have had little reason to fear al-Otaibi, an ordinary career diplomat charged with sorting out applications, other formalities, and the day-to-day running of the consulate.

Jamal, however, was not the only stranger in the restricted area of the consulate. As if in the opening sequence of a James Bond movie, ten of the fifteen operatives of the Saudi hit squad that had assembled in

Istanbul were waiting for him in the five-storey building. The soldiers had arrived separately in the morning between 9.50 and 11.03am in civilian clothes. In addition to brigadier-general Mutreb, professor lieutenant-colonel Salah Tubaigy, the head of forensics in the kingdom's interior ministry, was present in the building. The others were major Badr al-Otaibi, lieutenant al-Harbi, sergeant-major Waleed al-Sehri, Turki al-Sehri, al-Balawi, Saif al-Qahtani, and brigadier-general al-Madani.

While waiting for Jamal, Mutreb and Tubaigy were talking and Mutreb asked the team, has 'the sacrificial animal' arrived. At 1.13pm, the answer finally came – 'He has arrived' (detail 91). The plan unfolded like a well-oiled machine.

Most of the fifteen soldiers had taken part in the operations of the 'Rapid Intervention Group', *Firqat el-Nemr* or Tiger Team, a group of fifty specialist soldiers acting as 'field operatives' formed in 2017 to kidnap, detain, or even torture, Saudi citizens after MBS's appointment as crown prince. Those caught by the group were forced to sign non-disclosure agreements about what had happened to them, on penalty of 'full responsibility'. The 'tigers' were drawn from very different parts of the Saudi secret service to bundle specialist areas of expertise for maximum efficiency.

The fidelity of the Tiger Team members had been repeatedly tested and rewarded in previous assignments. The team derived its name from the nickname of their leader 'Tiger from the South', though his new moniker from being the spokesperson of the Saudi-led coalition in the Yemen war was 'The Beast'. MBS himself had chosen major-general al-Asiri, 'The Beast', to form the 'spinal cord' of the Tiger Team, and attached a further five whom he trusted most from his personal security detail. But other members of the team were trained in the latest spy technology.

The current assignment of the fifteen was different from any they had done before. Contrary to Saudi law, custom and Islamic observance, today's target was not meant merely to disappear to Saudi Arabia. The hit squad were going to terminate their quarry.

The trap had been set with tight military precision. No sooner had Jamal entered the consulate at 1.14pm then the second Gulfstream HZ-SK1 took off at 1.47pm, flying directly to Istanbul. It aimed to remove from Turkey the first evidence and members of the hit-squad. It's flight path had been prepared at 10.30am, close to the time when Jamal rang 'Sultan', the consulate's secret-service agent, to confirm that he would visit the consulate. It was filed at 1.30pm after Jamal had entered the consulate. The jet arrived empty and the pilot only stepped out of the cockpit briefly while the jet refuelled (captured on CC-TV leaked to Qatar's al-Jazeera on 27 March 2019).

Step two was to deal with the forty four non-Saudi staff at the consulate and the consul-general's residence. Some had already been told not to report for work that day. Lunch hour was the same for everyone who worked at the consulate, and started at 12.30pm. Of those at the consulate some were given the afternoon off with the plausible reason that an important visitor would arrive. Others, such as Turkish drivers, were told to stay in their rooms as there would be an inspection from Riyadh. Those in the residence were told not to report or not to leave because of an engineer visiting. The loyalties of the Saudi staff in the building could be relied upon. With families back in Saudi Arabia, they'd be too terrified to speak out of turn. A number of staff members were then instructed to clear their offices on the second floor. This floor would remain out of bounds over the following days while the consulate's interior was being cleaned at 11am.

It was a simple matter to disable the hard disk of the Saudi-operated (but Turkish-installed) CC-TV within the consulate, which they did – President Erdoğan would officially say they 'destroyed' it, intelligence officers used the word 'removed' in leaks to the media.

Despite this precaution, Mutreb and his team had been filmed by thirteen cameras outside the consulate while walking towards the door of the building. The footage would later be leaked to the world press by 'anonymous official sources'. Mutreb arrived at 9.55am in a tailored suit, wearing it as if a uniform, and another tall and big team member bounded in smiling at 11.03am in a loud blue check shirt and jeans with two smaller team members – one with a hoodie and another with a white-red jumper and dark jacket.

Taken on its own, that early-morning footage was hardly suspicious. The team members had filed in independently over the course of two hours and were indistinguishable from ordinary Saudis attending the consulate's weekly walk-in hours from 9am to 3.30pm.

Jamal Khashoggi's fate was now sealed behind closed doors in a secure building surrounded by Saudis. A diplomatic mission is territory whose boundaries the host nation is not permitted to 'penetrate' under diplomatic law and it is blind-sided if the guest nation so wishes – which they invariably do. The inability to access the Ecuadorian embassy kept Julian Assange from being arrested by British police for seven years, until Ecuador's president decided to expel him on 1 May 2019. What was about to take place at the Istanbul consulate would never be known to the outside world. Or so Riyadh and the elite Saudi hit-squad thought.

But in Turkey, and elsewhere, diplomatic missions sometimes manage to have foreign ears. Unbeknownst to the Saudis, intelligence officials from at least one spy agency recorded every sound and every word spoken during the Saudi operation.

When Jamal entered the consul general's office, one of the team grabbed his arm and Jamal exclaimed 'Release my arm! What do you think you are doing?'

He now recognised Maher Mutreb, his former London-embassy colleague. No doubt he also knew that Mutreb accompanied MBS on his trips abroad. When they were both stationed in London they had been friendly.

Jamal had been personal advisor to Prince Turki bin Faisal when he was Saudi ambassador to the United Kingdom, 2003-5, and to the United States, 2005-7. Those years were fraught for Saudi Arabia. The secret links between Saudi's toxic, ultra-conservative Wahhabi brand of Sunni Islam and 9-11 were becoming public knowledge as first detailed in Craig Unger's *House of Bush, House of Saud* and Michael Moore's documentary Fahrenheit 9/11. Fifteen of the nineteen suicide hijackers were, after all, Saudis.

Mutreb was first secretary of the embassy, doubling as station-chief of the Saudi secret service, and Jamal and he had worked together further to the fall-out of 9/11 for Saudi Arabia. Mutreb would at times join Jamal and others for Friday prayers and tea afterward in Mayfair.

Jamal realised his fears had come true. Hatice had asked the week before, what might happen. He said he didn't worry about being arrested, but he reckoned he might be 'interrogated… asked to return home, or maybe… pressured to return home'.

This morning, over breakfast, Jamal had however said confidently 'they can't do something like that in Turkey.' His body language had been relaxed this time, Hatice said, and had none of the anxiety of the previous Friday.

Yet Jamal – a survivor of Saudi palace rip currents – lacked the foreboding that, in fact, MBS considered him so urgent a liability that even his death was an acceptable outcome of the operation. At a different time he had told her – 'If I were an undesirable, they would have cut-off my pension'.

Mutreb told Jamal curtly that he had to return to Saudi Arabia: 'You are coming back'.

Mutreb tried again, bluffing, 'We will have to take you back. There is an order from Interpol. Interpol requested you to be sent back. We are coming to get you.' Jamal simply replied that 'there isn't a case against me. I notified some people outside; they are waiting for me; a driver is waiting for me.'

'Let's make it short', Jamal was told repeatedly while he admitted that it was only Hatice waiting outside (UN detail 94). There followed 7 minutes of quarrelling and a heated Skype call to Saud al-Qahtani, the crown prince's closest aide, known in dissident circles as the 'Saudi Steve Bannon'. His other nickname was 'Lord of the Flies', after the swarm of social media trolls he commanded to attack adversaries. The Skype call streamed on for 7 minutes to Riyadh.

Jamal also knew al-Qahtani well. Shortly after his self-exile from Saudi Arabia, al-Qahtani had called him in Virginia and given praise for public statements in support of the crown prince's reforms, including the decision to let women drive. The surprise reform was first announced on 26 September 2017. 'Keep writing and boasting', al-Qahtani had added in October. He had offered a high-level job in the royal court, or in a Saudi think tank, Jamal could take his pick. Al-Qahtani had said suavely 'Oh, Jamal, come home, you miss being here'.

Mentioning these offers to friends, Jamal had said, 'I won't fall for that... I don't want to end up in jail.' He was not far off. It was all feigned by al-Qahtani. In September 2017 the crown prince told Jamal's colleague, the head of Saudi broadcaster al-Arabiya Turki Aldakhil, in confidence that he would go after Jamal 'with a bullet' according to later leaked US intercepts.

Jamal had in return politely challenged al-Qahtani on colleagues who had been rounded up or arrested. A friend who was in the same room witnessed the tension despite the cordial tone of the conversation with al-Qahtani, 'I saw how Jamal's hand was shaking while holding the phone'.

Saud al-Qahtani was, in fact, the very person who had imposed the public appearance ban on Jamal after the election of Donald Trump. On 21 November 2016, Jamal spoke between 5 and 6 pm on 'Fighting Terrorism' at the World Police Conference (WPC) held at Doha's top hotel, the space-ship-on-the-sea Sheraton Grand, Qatar, among a glittering cast of leading CEOs, former prime ministers, and former functionaries such as Jean-Claude Trichet and Lord Kerr, Britain's highest career diplomat. Jamal was billed as CEO of Prince Talal's shuttered al-Arab channel and had repeated on Twitter the anti-Trump warning he had issued at the DC think tank days after Trump's win. It was weeks before MBS's scout, energy minister Khalid al-Falih, headed for Trump's transition team led by Jared Kushner to flash Riyadh's billions.

Al-Qahtani had called him in a fury to say he was 'not allowed to tweet, not allowed to write, not allowed to talk'.

'You can't do anything anymore – you're done', al-Qahtani had barked tersely at Jamal over the phone.

Jamal's torrent of tweets ended abruptly, as did his seven-year-long weekly column in *al-Hayat*, the London-based Arab paper owned by MBS's nephew Prince Khalid bin Sultan, a grandchild of founder King ibn Saud's and former deputy under MBS's father when he was still minister of defence.

A few months on, while MBS was manoeuvring in the background to become his father's crown prince, Jamal had travelled to London in April 2017 to stay for three weeks with Nawaf Obaid, a fellow former advisor to Prince Turki. He mooted his plan to move to the US to his friend. But al-Qahtani called Jamal during this London sabbatical and said warmly all would be forgiven once he returned home. Obaid, who told the *Washington Post* this, said it was part of al-Qahtani's 'hot-cold approach' to Jamal. The thaw with Saudi's highest media-intelligence official evidently hadn't lasted long when Jamal wrote his application to the Woodrow Wilson Center, DC, in June and packed his two bags again for Tysons Corner.

This time, al-Qahtani dropped all pretence of charm. Jamal was told he was being kidnapped and would be taken back to Saudi Arabia by force.

'You can't do that,' Jamal replied apprehensively, 'People are waiting outside.' 'People' was a generous term, as at this point only Hatice stood between him and the hit-squad.

At some point following the conversation with al-Qahtani four officers attacked Jamal. During a further 4 or 5 minutes, the soldiers held him in a vice and restrained him. Jamal groaned and repeatedly pleaded, 'I can't breathe'.

The death-squad had at most four hours until Gulfstream jet HZ-SK1 would land, and after killing Jamal they needed to disappear Jamal's body as best they could.

Some two hours after Jamal had entered the consulate, six vehicles left the consulate's compound back entrance, all ostensibly going in different directions on different routes. Two arrived at 3.09pm at the residence of consul-general Mohammed al-Otaibi, who lived a few hundred yards away.

The consul-general's private home was a far more imposing affair, built like a miniature palace, its pediment crowned with the Saudi emblem of golden crossed swords and a palm tree. A Saudi flag flew outside and, flanked by two guard cubicles, one next to a ramshackle tall car port, a wall with dark green heavy metal inserts traced with big gold rivets, like those on the doors of the consulate, screened the residence from prying eyes. Here, too, Turkish employees had hastily been told to take the day off.

The biggest of the consular vehicles, a Mercedes Vito van with tinted windows and plates 34 CC 1865, pulled into the consul-general's garage. Three of the team were captured on (later leaked) CC-TV carrying two very big round but light plastic bags, and rolling five large suitcases through the front door of the consul-general's home at 3.19pm. The other consular car, an Audi with number plates 34 CC 2464 parked in its place in between the two guard houses flanking the garden wall. Earlier in the morning five of the Tiger Team had driven up in consular Mercedes 34 CC 3071 at 11.08am in preparation for what would happen in the afternoon – major-general Abahussein, major al-Arifi, al-Bostani, al-Hawsawi, Khalid al-Otaibi.

Neighbours of the residence, which is situated next to a popular restaurant, reported that for the first time ever there had been a barbecue that afternoon next to the pool in the large fenced-in garden of the residence. The neighbours had speculated what the barbecue was for, it was reported later in the Turkish press.

On 4 March 2019, an al-Jazeera documentary would reveal leaked information that the consul-general had had a Tandoori oven installed in the garden of his residence in the middle of September 2018. Tandoori ovens can reach temperatures of 1000 degrees, the top temperature commonly used to cremate human remains. A Turkish newspaper reported on 5 March that a police report stated 32 portions of raw meat had been ordered for the consulate that day by the team.

At 4.51pm a relaxed brigadier-general Mutreb was captured on CC-TV leaving the consul-general's residence with two men. An hour later he went through airport security at 5.58pm, 22 minutes before taking off in the first Gulfstream IV. And at 7.37pm two more men left the residence in a Mercedes, followed at 7.48pm by several others who climbed into the Mercedes Vito van.

The operation had run smoothly and, as they were exfiltrating, the hit squad would not be needing their hotel rooms after all. They paid their hotel bills and cancelled the reservations for the rest of the week before heading to the airport. Only the first trio who arrived on Monday had actually stayed the night in their hotel rooms. The other twelve had merely used them as a parking space for their gear.

At 6.20pm Gulfstream IV HZ-SK1 took off from Atatürk Airport and headed to Cairo. After spending twenty-five hours on the ground there, it flew on to Riyadh. Six Saudi security forces were on board, led by Mutreb. They all went through security at the same time between 5.44 and 5.49pm.

Gulfstream IV HZ-SK2 left Istanbul four hours later. It skirted the border between Iraq and Iran, favouring the Iraqi side, and crossed the Persian Gulf, landing in Dubai at 2.30am. The following morning, it flew on to Riyadh. Seven Saudi security operatives were on board. Three came through security at 8:28pm and four followed three quarters of an hour later at 9.44pm. In all thirteen members of the Saudi death squad departed on these two flights. The final two would leave Turkey on Turkish Airlines flight TK144 to Riyadh, going through security at 0.18am for boarding through the main terminal and a scheduled take-off at 1.20am.

The audacious plan to disappear Jamal had been pulled off like clockwork by the team of highly skilled military, right under the noses of the Turkish authorities.

It was the Saudi equivalent of operation Neptune Spear in which US navy SEALs captured and killed Jamal's former intelligence friend Osama bin Laden on hostile territory. Unlike that widely televised operation, however, the strike against Jamal Khashoggi was meant to remain a deep secret, known only to the death squad and a small number of people in Riyadh.

Then everything began to go wrong, not least of all for the man who had ordered the operation.

7

The Crown Prince

Until the murder of Jamal Khashoggi, Crown Prince Mohammed bin Salman or MBS had been the darling of the West where he was seen by pundits and governments alike as a desperately-needed reformer in a country stuck in the Middle Ages and run in increasingly geriatric succession by the sons of King ibn Saud – a man who had died in 1953. MBS had opened cinemas and restricted the powers of the religious police. Women were allowed to drive and visit sports stadiums. On 19 March he had even relaxed the rule that Saudi women wear a black *abaya* covering their face, promulgating that it was not a matter of sharia law. The first public concert featuring a female singer had been held. His 2017 shakedown of the starchy generation of older princes was unorthodox but understandable, it was argued, as the kingdom was suffering from the low oil prices and needed cash.

Dynamic MBS planned to diversify the economy, moving Saudi Arabia away from its slavish dependence on oil, even setting up a $200bn investment plan in solar energy with Japanese Softbank, the subject of Jamal's last-ever tweet. He also spent an awful lot of money buying Western arms. Tantalisingly, he toyed with the idea of privatising the state oil company Saudi Aramco, the world's most profitable company, in order to plug the gaping hole in the royal coffers of the desert kingdom. Although it would only float 5 per cent of the company, the West had been excluded from owning part of the company ever since nationalisation in the seventies (from then owners, the US oil companies Texaco, Exxon and Mobil). Every investor salivated at the prospect of owning shares in this unbeatable company.

But by Saudi royal-succession rules, MBS should not have been even close to a position of royal power in the first place. Saudi Arabia was founded in 1932 under King ibn Saud. After he died in 1953, he was supposed to be succeeded in turn by all his surviving sons. He had forty-five sons, thirty six of whom survived him. Six of them had indeed become king.

Among the still surviving sons there was, for example, the relatively spruce seventy-six-year-old Prince Ahmed, with whom King Salman shared the same mother. He was one of the youngest children of ibn Saud and his thirty-first son. And when King Salman ascended the throne in 2015 as the sixth ibn Saud son to become king, he had picked his youngest half-brother, the also septuagenarian Prince Muqrin, to become his crown prince and first deputy prime minister. This was in readiness for a seventh son of ibn Saud to become king after Salman – King Muqrin. Or so it seemed.

But after just three months, King Salman replaced Muqrin with his nephew Prince Mohammed bin Nayef. Bin Nayef was the first crown prince in his fifties since 1982. For connoisseurs of Saudi palace intrigue, he was also the son of Prince Nayef, who had died in 2012, Prince Salman and Prince Ahmed's brother. Their mother was Hassa al-Sudairi, the tenth of ibn Saud's twenty four wives. Salman's choice of Nayef's son strengthened the Sudairi succession line. She had no fewer than seven sons, who together had formed a powerful block amongst the thirty-six surviving sons – Salman and Ahmed were the last two 'Sudairi sons' alive.

In June 2017, this second crown prince was also sacked by royal decree, however, and replaced with Mohammed bin Salman, King Salman's own son. MBS had already been appointed as deputy crown prince under Crown Prince bin Nayef.

Born in 1985, MBS was the eldest child of King Salman's third wife Princess Fahda bint Falah. Several of King Salman's other sons, who studied overseas to perfect foreign languages and earn advanced degrees, spent time outside the royal cocoon and built impressive résumés. One became the first Arab astronaut, another a deputy oil minister, yet another the governor of Medina Province. MBS, however, was exclusively educated in Saudi Arabia and did not speak English as fluently as they did, although he understood it well.

Rachid Sekkai, who taught him English and later worked for the BBC, said he toyed with a walkie-talkie in class and was more interested in playing in the garden and cracking jokes with his brothers and the guards. When the chance came to visit America, he refused to go to the US embassy for a visa to be finger-printed 'like some criminal', according to a State Department cable.

While his father was still governor of Riyadh Province (and highly feared), MBS was brought up in a palace that was built like a fortress. After a private education, he studied law at King Saud University in Riyadh, graduating fourth in his class. Another prince of the same generation said he got to know him during high school when one of their uncles held regular dinners for the younger princes at his palace. He recalled MBS being one of the crowd, saying he liked to play bridge and admired Margaret Thatcher.

At the age of twenty four, MBS became an advisor to his father Prince (then) Salman. Other political appointments followed and when his father became second deputy prime minister and defence minister, MBS stayed on as his father's private advisor. Prince Salman became crown prince in 2012, then king in January 2015, naming as one of his first appointments MBS as deputy crown prince and his minister of defence. The latter gave MBS a lot of sway in the West with arms procurements.

It was in his new capacity as minister of defence that MBS first wielded Saudi executive power.

In neighbouring Yemen, the rebel Houthi militia of the Shiite Zaidi sect and forces loyal to the former president, Ali Abdullah Saleh, who had been ousted in 2012, took the capital city Sana'a in 21 March 2015 and proclaimed themselves the official government of Yemen. Saleh's Sunni successor Abdrabbuh Hadi was in power in the principal port of

Aden, however, while al-Qaeda and Isis (Daesh) also gained control of parts of Yemen. The Houthi then marched on Aden and Hadi fled on the 25th, finding refuge in Riyadh, where he is understood to be languishing under house arrest.

In retaliation, MBS organised a Sunni coalition of the Gulf states and began air strikes on Houthi positions and imposed a naval blockade. Interestingly, he did not inform the head of the National Guard, Prince Mutaib bin Abdullah, when the first air strikes flew over. Prince Mutaib was one of the royals ousted from all offices in the 2017 Ritz Carlton purge.

Having total command of Yemeni airspace, MBS expected a quick victory over the Houthi and, consequently, the restoration of the Hadi regime which he then could take credit for. At the start of the war, he was often photographed visiting troops and meeting with military leaders. But as the campaign reached stalemate and turned into a war of attrition, his appearances grew rare. As a military leader, MBS took frequent holidays, putting himself out of contact for days on end.

Instead of a quick victory, civilian casualties mounted, and MBS drew growing criticism from human rights groups, while diplomats pointed out that the death toll for Saudi troops was higher than the government acknowledged publicly. The prolonged war and the Saudi-led blockade also led to a famine. Half of the war-torn country's population – fourteen million people – were on the brink of starvation and it was estimated that 85,000 children died from malnutrition.

In order to counter these negative headlines and keep tighter control over the conversation inside and outside the kingdom, MBS had established the Centre for Studies and Media Affairs under his right-hand man Saud al-Qahtani to propagate a positive spin on the Yemen war in Washington. The Center hired numerous Washington and London-based lobbying and public relations firms to assist in the PR campaign. When the *Economist* dubbed him the 'architect of the war in Yemen', MBS's sly response was that he was waging war on Islamic terrorism.

While oil prices were dropping, MBS paid for the costly war by slashing the state budget and freezing government contracts in the name of austerity. He cancelled the bonuses that made up one third of the salaries of government employees, having to reinstate them seven months later in the face of public anger. For himself, however, he could not resist buying a 440-foot yacht, the Serene, from a Russian vodka billionaire for $500 million. Fearing assassination, he was said to sleep on board.

He also bought Château Louis XIV near Versailles, France, the world's most expensive home with a $300 million price tag. This modern palace was built by Saudi property developer Emad Khashoggi, a cousin of Jamal's. The Leonardo da Vinci painting 'Salvador del Mundo' cost him $450 million in the most expensive art sale in history – it was rumoured to be berthed on the Serene. And before the murder of Jamal Khashoggi, MBS was planning a £4 billion takeover bid for Manchester United, though the Glazer family said they had no immediate intention of selling the club.

Even before he became crown prince in 2017, it quickly became clear that MBS was on a mission to ease aside his predecessor, Crown Prince bin Nayef, who, as a competent long-time hard-line counterterrorism expert, had good connections in Washington and the support of many of the senior royals. The White House saw an early sign of the ambition of the young prince in late 2015, when – breaking protocol – MBS delivered a soliloquy about the failures of American foreign policy during a meeting between his father King Salman and President Obama.

Given Saudi Arabia's crusty echelons of power and its crown cascading down aging and infirm brothers, many young Saudis admired MBS as a dynamic representative of their generation who addressed some of the kingdom's problems in a forthright manner rather than in the traditional piecemeal way. The country's controlled news media lent a helping hand by building up MBS's image as a hardworking, businesslike leader less concerned with the trappings of royalty than his predecessors – his profligacy was one of the secrets blanked in the Saudi media on palace orders from the Centre for Studies and Media Affairs. The old guard among the royal family, however, saw him as a power-hungry inexperienced upstart who didn't understand the consequences of upsetting the apple cart.

Early in 2016, Crown Prince bin Nayef retired to his villa in Algeria. Previously he had taken hunting holidays there, but this time it was different. He stayed away for weeks and was often incommunicado. Even CIA Director John Brennan, who had known him for decades, had trouble reaching him. A diabetic, bin Nayef was also suffering from the prolonged effects of injuries from an assassination attempt where an al-Qaeda suicide bomber detonated a bomb surgically implanted in his rectum. Crown Prince bin Nayef was, in actual fact, avoiding the predations of MBS, (then) the deputy crown prince, who had his eye on the royal succession.

King Salman did not sit on the side lines either. He had already united his own court with that of his son when he ascended the throne, and handing MBS control over access to the king. In April 2015, King Salman had also made MBS head of the lucrative Saudi Aramco oil company, the chief engine of the economy. MBS replaced Khalid al-Falih, who became energy minister.

In December of the same year, MBS announced as minister of defence the formation of a military alliance of (Sunni) Islamic countries to fight Islamic terrorism. Counter-terrorism had long been the province of Crown Prince bin Nayef, but the new alliance gave no role to him or his interior ministry. When MBS listed the countries of the alliance, a number of them said they knew nothing about it, or were waiting for information before deciding to join. By not intervening, the king made it clear that MBS had his tacit approval here, too.

In April 2016, MBS launched his ambitious plan for the future of the kingdom's economy, called Vision 2030. The plan sought to increase employment and improve education, healthcare and other government services, and move the economy away from reliance on oil. A National Transformation Plan, laying out targets for improving government ministries, came shortly after. It also called for transparency and accountability, indirectly admitting that they had been missing before.

A luxury beach resort was planned for the Red Sea coast between al-Wajh and Umluj where women would be allowed to wear bikinis in the pool and beach areas. Twenty two islands would see hotels with Donald Trump style bling spring up, adding a projected $6 billion to Saudi GDP. Over $2 billion was invested in an entertainment authority MBS established. This government branch staged live music concerts, comedy shows, wrestling matches and monster truck rallies. A large sports, culture and entertainment complex was to be built, along with a theme park.

Any criticism of the relentless rise of MBS was silenced by phone calls to Saudi journalists telling them they had been barred from publishing, and sometimes from travelling abroad. One Saudi journalist published an article about MBS on his website, the Riyadh Post, where he said that the prince's popularity was based on a 'sweeping desire for great change' and the hope that he would 'turn their dreams into reality'. But he said: 'If you fail, this love withers quickly, as if it never existed, and is replaced by a deep feeling of frustration and hatred.' The website was blocked the next day.

While still deputy crown prince to bin Nayef, MBS also made well-publicised foreign trips to Europe, the Middle East and Washington, where he stayed at the Georgetown home of Secretary of State John Kerry. In September 2015, dinner at Mr Kerry's house ended with MBS playing Beethoven on the piano for his host and other guests. He attended the G20 summit in November 2015, leading the German secret service to predict bluntly in a leaked report that Crown Prince bin Nayef would not become king. Then in May 2016, Secretary of State Kerry was a guest on MBS's yacht, the Serene, and in June 2016, the two men shared an *iftar* dinner, breaking the Ramadan fast.

MBS's influence in Washington was aided by Sheikh Mohammed bin Zayed, the crown prince of Abu Dhabi, deputy supreme commander of the United Arab Emirates Armed Forces, and possibly the richest man in the world with $1.3 trillion at his fingertips, who was a favourite of the Obama administration and a respected voice in the Sunni world. Both princes shared an innate hostility to Shia Iran and the Muslim Brotherhood, whose Islamic populism they considered direct threats to their hereditary form of government post-Arab Spring. It helped that the sheikh also had a personal antipathy towards Crown Prince bin Nayef.

From the moment his father became king, MBS had no time to lose to establish his power base as the seventy-nine-year-old's health was deteriorating. King Salman had a stroke from which he had not fully recovered before he ascended the throne and was suffering from Alzheimer's.

The *coup de grace* was prepared on 17 June 2017 when King Salman issued a decree restructuring Saudi Arabia's system for prosecutions that stripped Crown Prince bin Nayef of his long-standing powers of overseeing criminal investigations. He was then placed under house arrest, while those loyal to him were purged.

Still bin Nayef refused to give up his claim to the throne. But during an end-of-Ramadan celebration at the palace the crown prince was led to a separate room to 'meet the king'. However, court officials – including MBS's henchman al-Qahtani – took his phones and wore him down into the night as he grew tired, suffering from diabetes and the effects of the terrorist attack on him. Then the king met alone with the exhausted bin Nayef and asked him to step down. To the other princes it was meanwhile broadcast by rumour that he had abdicated because of his addiction to painkilling drugs. Bin Nayef was relieved of all his functions and removed from royal succession. In a final humiliation the former crown prince was forced to pledge public loyalty to his successor when MBS became crown prince on 21 June 2017.

Donald Trump was one of the first who phoned to congratulate him. The two had a special bond. A month after Trump's election in 2016 the high-level Saudi delegation close to MBS had met with Trump's transition team, and MBS was one of the first to issue an invitation for a full-blown state visit to Riyadh – which happened with much pomp and circumstance on 20-21 May 2017.

The 2016 Saudi delegation, led by energy minister Khalid al Falih, had shrewdly concluded about the Trump team that 'The inner circle is predominantly deal makers who lack familiarity with political customs and deep institutions, and they support Jared Kushner'. Relations with the Obama White House had been frosty, but Trump's team offered an opportunity to burnish the Riyadh-DC relationship with a golden glow. Al-Falih had met with Kushner and talked about spending hundreds and hundreds of billions on deals and more deals. They also offered their clout to help resolve the Israel-Palestine crisis, a set of negotiations dear to Jared Kushner's heart and later labelled as the 'deal of the century' by Trump.

On 4 November 2017, MBS had made his public move against his aged royal adversaries. He ordered hundreds (estimates run between 200 and 500) of senior princes, wealthy businessmen, politicians, clerics and government officials to be detained at Riyadh's palatial 492-room Ritz-Carlton hotel and its gentleman's-only spa with two extravagant staircases winged in grand curves leading to a domed pool area, all with an explosion of azure and aquamarine framed in gold and white above.

The detainees were relieved of their functions and only released after they gave up billions of dollars to a new anti-corruption committee set up by the crown prince. It was run by Saudi prosecutor general Sheikh Saud al-Mojeb who said the guests received 'the same rights and treatment as any other Saudi citizen'. Bank accounts were frozen and the hotel's internet and telephone lines were disconnected while they remained under house arrest. MBS's aide Saud al-Qahtani was also part of the corruption negotiation team inside the Ritz Carlton.

Two brothers of the powerful Bin Laden family, related to Osama and part owners of the privately-held Binladin construction group, were given a room in the Ritz Carlton. The group had to-date built everything for the Saudi government and was now engaged with MBS's vision 2030. The brothers were left watching TV but had to hand over their 36.2 per cent share on 26 April 2018. The group would also change its name. Bakr, Osama bin Laden's half-brother, transferred his 23.58 per cent on the same date, but remained in custody at a different place. As leader of the firm he had rebuffed an approach by MBS in 2015 to become a board member. Riyadh would finally release Bakr in January 2019 to alleviate international pressure building up as a result of the Khashoggi affair.

Prince Ahmed, MBS's uncle and the king's remaining Sudairi brother, had been tipped off hours before MBS's Ritz Carlton plot began. He barely escaped to live in self-imposed exile in London in a £50 million home. Although Prince Ahmed had been removed from succession in 2012, he remained highly influential as a heavy-weight candidate for the throne among ibn Saud's remaining children. His Sudairi-ibn Saud claim was like gold to silver compared to MBS's and it had no doubt been wise to run before the hotel scythe landed.

Senior royals who weren't purged bitterly complained that MBS used his power as chief of his father's royal court to block their access to King Salman during the Ritz Carlton months. With some further tacit encouragement from his father, MBS then set about restructuring the intelligence agencies, another Saudi power base sceptical of him.

Outside the kingdom, MBS started a new round of confrontation in the first month of his appointment as crown prince. In June 2017, he led a blockade of Qatar, funder of al-Jazeera, the more successful pan-Arab rival to Saudi broadcaster al-Arabiya. MBS alleged that the Gulf state was supporting Shia terrorism from Iran. Qatar denied this, though the tiny gas-rich state admitted that it had provided assistance to some Islamist groups such as the Muslim Brotherhood. Yet it said it did not support militant groups linked to al-Qaeda or Isis (Daesh).

It was a subtle point to make. Riyadh mistrusted the Muslim Brotherhood and how it had surfed the populist Islamic wave that gripped the Middle East. After the Arab Spring, the brotherhood hijacked Egypt's first-ever elections following President Hosni Mubarak's unseating by popular revolt. The Muslim Brotherhood's

President Morsi had soon set about to restore dictatorial powers for himself in the image of Iran, but in such a calamitous fashion that he was soon generally hated and had been deposed in a coup led by Abdel el-Sisi with the Egyptian army and Saudi help.

Like the war against Shia-governed Yemen, the Qatar blockade continued to drag on. It was effectively nullified by imports from Iran, Qatar's Shia neighbour across the Persian Gulf, and Sunni Turkey. Turkey's support for Qatar annoyed MBS immensely.

Although 70 per cent Sunni, Turkey had resisted Saudi Wahhabism – which had spread in opposition to the sultan – for centuries and tended to ignore the Shia-Sunni divide in its foreign policy, striking a pragmatic rather than dogmatic course. President Erdoğan had just survived his own army putsch and populist Islam was his power base rather than the army. Iran and Qatar were Erdoğan's natural allies whereas el-Sisi's army-backed dictatorship in Egypt was a natural fit with the Saudi and UAE camp.

Early in 2018, given the gathering weight of international headlines against him, MBS had decided to brush up on his overseas image with a lavish tour projecting his brand of youthful Saudi Arabia.

In the UK, he met Prime Minister Theresa May, Queen Elizabeth and Prince William. Then he flew on to the US where he visited Washington, Hollywood and Silicon Valley, meeting President Trump, Bill and Hillary Clinton, Henry Kissinger, Michael Bloomberg, George W. Bush, George H.W. Bush, Bill Gates, Jeff Bezos, Oprah Winfrey, Rupert Murdoch, Richard Branson, Mayor Eric Garcetti of Los Angeles, Michael Douglas, Morgan Freeman and Dwayne Johnson. He also met with prominent Jewish groups and garnered almost universal praise.

Meanwhile one former courtier with a monthly blog on the *Washington Post* website, was also making plans to restart his life, career and family in Istanbul – Jamal Khashoggi.

8

Weight in Gold

Although a Saudi commoner and not a royal, very little was one dimensional about Jamal Khashoggi once one looked behind his amiable, academic demeanour. He belonged to the highest echelons of the Saudi elite orbiting and serving the apex of the Saudi royal family. He was also one of the few Saudis who fit into the village-like matrix surrounding global leaders and billionaires.

Those who knew Jamal on the pundit circuit agreed with him and said that he did not fit the profile of a rebel at all. Only on 17 January 2016, he had written in Qatar's English language newspaper *The Peninsula*, 'Today I criticise … the liberals.' He chastised them for attacks on 'religiously committed persons or those who care about Gaza strip'. He chided the liberals for using 'the same tactics' as their opponents. Cancelling out the argument, both sides would accuse each other without foundation 'of being conspirators, or of being in the Muslim Brotherhood, or part of the alleged conspiracy of the American-Qatari-Turkish alliance.' Rather than being a polemicist, Jamal ventilated moderation and debate in public, even after his exile. He didn't blow up in vituperation.

He was deeply attached to his country and, as an exile in the US, he missed his friends and family there, if not his life in the highest royal circles. He was at best a lukewarm critic of the kingdom. Joyce Karam, the Washington Bureau Chief of London-based Saudi paper *al-Hayat* and a long-time friend, judged, 'He is not exactly Saudi opposition'. 'He always walked a fine line, you know, sometimes agreeing with Saudi policies and sometimes disagreeing with it.' In fact, because of his tendency to circle the centre, some Saudi critics living outside Saudi Arabia feared that Jamal had never really given up his intelligence work for the palace.

Barbara Slavin, Iran expert at the Atlantic Council, a sixty-year-old DC think tank, said he was 'very intelligent, pleasant, thoughtful' and 'was telling [MBS] that if you keep putting people in prison for even modest criticism you will defeat the whole purpose of [your] reforms'. Mike Franc, director of DC programmes at the prestigious Hoover Institute told the *Atlantic*, 'I don't recall he ever said anything mean about a person – even MBS. He never uttered a nasty word about him'.

But there was also a puckish side to Jamal when speaking in secret to more radical minds on the extreme side of the spectrum. He had a lively WhatsApp conversation exchange of over four hundred texts, pictures and videos with twenty-seven-year-old activist Omar Abdulaziz, who lived in exile Canada, and whose family in Saudi Arabia was harangued as a result. In these, Jamal called MBS 'Pac-Man' and a 'beast'. To Abdulaziz he quietly pledged over $30,000 of his own money to further plans of spreading information to young activists in Saudi Arabia in secret.

Jamal Khashoggi had twice been the editor-in-chief of *al-Watan* (The National) one of Saudi's top-three newspapers. Unlike his equivalents in the US or Europe, his job was not to publish news awkward to the regime. In the hermetically-sealed kingdom, one job was to sequester any intelligence that the king did not wish to see dispersed to his Saudi subjects. Newspapers in Saudi Arabia are privately owned, but effectively semi-government institutions. They are guided by the palace in Riyadh which can fire top leadership. 'There could be some criticism with red lines for the media', in the words of London-based Saudi exile, Yahya Assiri, a former air force officer, graduate of Kingston University, and media commentator.

Nonetheless, Jamal did twice lose his editorship. This was not because he had failed in his duty to the government and crossed red lines, but due to the pressure on the palace of Saudi Arabia's powerful ultra-conservative clerics. They disliked Jamal's laxness towards their rigid Wahhabi-strand of Sunni-Islam.

If anything, outwardly Jamal was a Saudi grandee and mandarin, and, as a writer, more of a cultural commentator than a Western-style newshound with an unyielding need to airing the truth.

Even after his editorships, Jamal continued to be privy to secret information through his exceptional contacts and close friendships within the rarefied stratosphere of the Saudi royal family. Jamal knew the opaque inner workings, processes and political alignments of the influential yet impenetrable top of the Saudi royal family inside out. According to some reports, Jamal even had the rank of 'advisor to the royal court' to the previous king, King Abdullah. He certainly told his friend Turan Kişlakçi he 'had worked four or five years for the government'. To foreign reporters he was a godsend, a Kremlin-watcher who could read power shifts and meanings from the courtly pageantry swirling around marble buildings and Louis XV chairs that passed for Saudi politics. To anyone seeking to play, derail or understand the kingdom, he was worth his weight in gold.

One particularly sensitive area for Saudi Arabia was a longstanding strategic concern of Riyadh about its nuclear capability. Or rather, the lack thereof. As opposed to its rivals for influence in the Middle East, Saudi Arabia merely had plans. Iran had an operational nuclear reactor since 2011 and Turkey had started building one in 2018 – many other Middle-Eastern states also had advanced plans for reactors. And a nuclear reactor formed the threshold to nuclear weapons. Israel had already bombed the reactors in Iraq and Syria out of existence for that reason in, respectively, 1981 and 2007.

But Iran's nuclear programme was the one that got away. The Shia-fundamentalist country was so close to developing its own atomic bomb that the Obama administration had desperately tried to force Iran to abandon its nuclear-weapon strategy. It did so through severe sanctions that made Iran agree to a 2015 nuclear carrot-and-stick treaty, the Iran Nuclear Deal. In the deal Iran agreed to use nuclear power only for civilian ends and permitted stringent verification and monitoring by the Atomic Agency. Not forever, but for a period of time at any rate.

This treaty did not sit well in Riyadh. For almost a decade, nuclear capability was the most-desired military asset the Saudi government did not yet possess in its ample arsenal. This was true for King Abdullah as much as King Salman.

Enter Michael Flynn. Unbeknownst to many – except presumably the US intelligence services – Michael Flynn, Donald Trump's first pick for national security adviser, was warming up the Trump transition team in November 2016 to the idea of selling nuclear technology to the Saudi royal family under the header of a scheme called 'The Iron Bridge'. Dating back to 2015, it was a scheme hatched by retired US generals and six US nuclear power companies in a consortium called IP3. The consortium specifically aimed to build some 40 nuclear installations in Saudi Arabia.

Flynn's official appointment lasted all of twenty four days, as he turned out to be a liar and confessed to the felony of perjuring himself under oath to the FBI. Flynn had also conceded that he had been on the payroll of IP3 and had made sponsored trips to Saudi Arabia as early as 2015 – failing to disclose the latter detail on his White House security clearance.

Yet by the time of Flynn's mayfly decline and fall his lies no longer mattered. The 'Iron Bridge' scheme had been woven through the new warp threads of Trump's White House. The scheme suited the transition-team-Trump outlook on many levels.

Resuscitating moribund traditional industries had been one of the core planks of the Trump campaign and those around him. It played well with hamburger-and-fries voters, not least septuagenarians like himself. Coal, for example, didn't stand much of a long-term chance against the price drops in renewable energy, or the cheap oil from fracking. Even coal-gobbling behemoth India started to switch away from it. In 2017, the price of solar power precipitously halved to \$40/mwhr in India and would drop further, whereas coal cost at least

$60 and would only go up in the future. Yet Trump's campaign promises to save the mineral did wonders for the US coal industry. Peabody Inc., the world's largest private-sector coalminer, emerged from its 2016 bankruptcy buoyed by Trump's election promises.

In the case of nuclear-power, Trump's passion for an out-dated industry teetering on the brink of bankruptcy worked out slightly differently. With sunshine available in abundance for solar power in the Middle East, selling expensive, capital-intensive 1970s nuclear technology to Saudi Arabia made no obvious sense. Indeed, MBS and his energy-minister al-Falih were already placing a $200bn bet on solar power. Except, however, for the important fringe benefit that a nuclear power infrastructure was the required stepping-stone to owning a nuclear arsenal.

What Flynn and his fellow generals at IP3, in effect, were trying to cash in on before the sun set on the US nuclear-energy industry was selling the dream of an atom bomb to Saudi Arabia. The 'deal makers' now in charge in of the White House levers saw an eager, rich client who could afford headline-making amounts and a local US industry in financial trouble. It was a deal made in heaven.

Trump's closest friend, confidante, fellow septuagenarian, fellow billionaire with close ties to the Middle East, Tom Barrack, a Lebanese American, also got actively involved in the 'The Iron Bridge' and wrote the Trump administration white paper on it of 21 March 2017. In the document he proposed that he would be given ambassadorial or special envoy status to see it through. On 19 February 2019, House Democrats would publish a report exposing the whole scheme with the help of whistle-blowers. The report made its social network, and its hairy skirting of US criminal federal law, a matter of public record.

But 2015 was not only the year of Obama's Iran Nuclear Deal, it was also the year when King Salman ascended to the throne with MBS in tow. The retired generals who founded the IP3 consortium (and paid for Michael Flynn to visit Saudi Arabia that year) had clearly sensed an opportunity in Riyadh. In charge of Saudi procurement was a new minister of defence, the son of the previous minister of defence, King Salman. MBS was a thirty-year old with a hunger for successes that would lead him to royal succession.

And it seemed in 2016 with the surprise election of Donald Trump that Saudi Arabia finally all of a sudden also had the very pliable partner from whom to acquire the basic technology that opened the door to the world's most devastating weapon. When Saudi energy minister Khaled al Falih, MBS's predecessor at Aramco, met Trump's son-in-law Jared Kushner in November 2016 his mission was about far far more than cultivating goodwill after the frosty relations with the Obama administration.

Things snowballed quickly. On Trump's Inauguration Day, Michael Flynn texted, 'we are good to go' and instructed IP3 'to put things in place'. By a lucky break, Angela Merkel cancelled her visit to DC on 14 March. Jared Kushner swiftly manoeuvred MBS into the slot that had freed up and his father-in-law received MBS in the Oval Office. The three of them covered 'The Iron Bridge' as part of a package of $200 billion 'investments' over 4 years by Saudi Arabia.

Money was in the air. Three days later the IP3 generals proposed to MBS that IP3 buy Westinghouse, the leading but bankrupt US nuclear power company, in 'partnership' with Saudi from Toshiba, the IP3 member that owned the company. Nor did MBS make any bones about what he had in mind all along. A day after the letter, Saudi Arabia's defence minister MBS said on CBS's 60 Minutes, 'if Iran developed a nuclear bomb, we will follow suit as soon as possible.'

On 20-22 May 2017, Riyadh pulled out all the stops and Donald Trump was received like a king in Riyadh on his first presidential visit abroad. Donald Trump was decorated by the king with a gold necklace of a Saudi order, appeared to curtsy, opened an anti-terrorism centre with the king and Egypt's president el-Sisi who had flown in, shook a flustered cutlass at far more enthusiastic royals and princes during a traditional Saudi sword-dance. With great ceremony, he also signed an immediate $110bn spending deal rising to $350bn over several years.

Secretly, the Trump administration also issued seven authorisations to US companies to share nuclear intelligence, two of them weeks after the assassination of Jamal. Al-Falih and MBS's new friend and Donald Trump's senior advisor in charge of the White House 'Office of American Innovation', Jared Kushner, oiled the wheels.

Later that year, by coincidence, Jared Kushner's family's imperilled fortunes were rescued from being wiped out on 3 August 2018 by Brookfield Asset Management. Two days earlier, on 1 August, Brookfield had purchased bankrupt nuclear-power plant builder Westinghouse for $4.6 billion from IP3 member Toshiba. The Kushner company was at risk of bankruptcy through defaulting on a $1.4 billion mortgage repayment plus accrued interest that was due in January 2019 on 666 Fifth Avenue in New York. Brookfield, however, paid $1.1bn for a 99-year lease in cash, which saved the Kushners by the bell. Of Jared Kushner the crown prince reportedly boasted in 2017 that 'he was in his pocket.' IP3 member Toshiba was similarly grateful. It had filed for bankruptcy of Westinghouse on 31 March 2017, as Westinghouse's mounting losses were risking Toshiba's own survival.

Did Jamal Khashoggi's views on the matter, then, tangle with Saudi Arabia's nuclear plans? As a long-standing palace insider, few Saudis could match his insight on Riyadh's defence and energy policies. After all, it was his criticism of Trump at an energy conference a few days after the US presidential elections that had led to his speaking ban.

Although MBS is at times portrayed as a green and impetuous leader, in wanting nuclear arms he was certainly no outlier in the kingdom. Quite the opposite. In 2008, King Abdullah and the US had still signed an accord in which the kingdom agreed not to enrich uranium itself if it ever built nuclear reactors. In effect, King Abdullah had promised not to make a nuclear weapon as enrichment of uranium is the *sine qua non* for any country wanting to make its own bomb.

But, ever since Iran's nuclear reactor started up in 2011, Riyadh had made clear that it had changed its mind about the 2008 accord. It wanted nuclear weapons the moment Iran had them. While the Iran nuclear deal was being thrashed out in Geneva by the Obama administration, Jamal Khashoggi was wired into the palace structure resisting it. Riyadh and Jamal hated Obama's July 2015 deal in equal measure. A major bone of contention was that Obama's deal authorised Iran to enrich its own uranium. Admittedly, this was only for the lower grade of enrichment for civilian use, but it meant that the US had allowed Iran an installation it had denied its ally. It spat in the face of Riyadh.

When King Salman, and the new minister of defence MBS, took over the reins on 23 January 2015 they also took charge of Saudi Arabia's strategy to thwart any deal in Geneva, except on the strictest terms. But the new king and his son failed. On 15 July 2015, the day of the deal's announcement, Jamal would politely tweet from Riyadh 'reality forces us to be against'. It seemed like hectoring compared to the oasis of calm that was Riyadh's official response. From the safety of Virginia, Jamal wrote on 3 January 2018 in his *Washington Post* blog what he really thought of Obama's deal. In a blunt throw-away line he said that the palace had not performed its duty 'to short-circuit the Iran nuclear deal'. He didn't accuse the crown prince by name, but the whole piece was about MBS.

Yet, four months after Jamal's *Post* piece, Donald Trump would land MBS a mammoth home victory when he ripped up Obama's nuclear deal on 8 May 2018. It was exactly what the Riyadh-elite, to which Jamal belonged, always wanted. Playing the long game had got MBS two flies with one blow of his cheque book.

This time the Washington DC's motive was not to block enrichment of uranium by Iran, stop nuclear proliferation, and, hence, ease Saudi Arabia's concerns about an Iranian nuclear bomb and growing power in the region. This time it was about paving the way for doing a $350bn-plus deal with Saudi Arabia. The Trump, Barrack, Kushner troika were pulling IP3's 'Iron Bridge' scheme to sell nuclear technology and Trump had removed the Iran Nuclear Treaty roadblock to the deal being placed.

The consortium's original scheme had included the sale of enrichment facilities, but in November 2017 MBS had merely opened the bidding process for a modest number of two nuclear reactors (not liking half measures, MBS said he was planning a total of sixteen). Other competitors, such as Russia, China and France, had started circling.

Jamal Khashoggi was also entirely on board with Riyadh throwing its weight around in the Middle East to counter Iran's influence. He supported MBS's Yemen war as it meant Saudi resistance to the spread of Iran's regional power. As a Saudi patriot he feared Iran as much as anyone in the palace – it was why he mistrusted Donald Trump in his comments days after the election. In fact, he compared MBS's powergrab negatively to the veto power of Iran's ayatollah: 'MBS is now becoming the supreme leader', he told the *New Yorker*'s Robin Wright.

When the new king and MBS let Obama's Iran deal pass in July 2015, the Obama administration did give the young, ambitious new Saudi minister of defence something very important in return – support and airforce bombardments of Iran-backed Houthi rebels in Yemen. Jamal had approved of these attacks whole-heartedly. He had coined it the 'Salman Doctrine' – strikingly flattering praise for MBS's hawkishness – a strategy whereby Saudi Arabia would 'lead and take initiative' while the US 'provides logistical and intelligence support when needed.'

When Jamal was banned from the media in November 2016, it happened at an embryonic moment for the Saudi relationship with the new team in the White House. Yet by the time Jamal exiled himself in the US in the summer of 2017, the nuclear relationship between MBS and Donald Trump had been forged successfully. The reassuringly warm bath of the Saudi media prevented Jamal's words – and those of far more strident dissidents – from inciting unrest among the king and crown prince's thirty-three million subjects. Did it really matter as much as then that Jamal had a blog in the Jeff Bezos-owned *Washington Post*, even if the *Post* was one of Trump-pet figures of hate, or a Twitter feed, and said edgy things at times?

What drove Riyadh, nonetheless, to order a highly unusual, high-risk rendition with a license to kill in October 2018 when the Trump administration was on board and a rock-steady ally?

9

Saudi Secrets

The son of a merchant, Jamal Khashoggi was born in Medina, the second holiest city in Saudi Arabia, on 13 October 1958 to a well-connected family. Medina in the sixties, when he was a young boy, had many more historic religious buildings not yet bulldozered as a consequence of Wahhabism's contempt of idolatry. His family roots were Turkish and his grandfather Mohammed Khashoggi had moved from the city of Kayseri, in Anatolia, to the Hejaz region of the Arabian Peninsula when both were still under Ottoman rule. Khashoggi, or *kaşikçi,* is the Turkish word for spoonbill, a bird with the spoon-shaped beak related to the ibis.

Mohammed became personal physician to founder-King ibn Saud, a status that allowed his family to achieve prominence. Mohammed was the father of late billionaire arms dealer Adnan Khashoggi, the middleman in Reagan's Iran-Contra scandal in the 1980s. Adnan was also once neighbour of Donald Trump and sold him a $200-million yacht. By coincidence, Jamal's patron Prince Alwaleed had later bought the yacht from Trump and rented it out to the makers of James Bond movie Never Say Never Again as the villain's lair. Jamal's aunt Samira was the first wife of Mohamed al-Fayed, the former Egyptian owner of Harrod's who had been refused a UK passport on account of not being 'a fit and proper person'. (To his friend Turan Kişlakçi Jamal disowned his family's connection to Adnan, however.)

After receiving his primary and secondary education in Medina, Jamal Khashoggi went to the US to study business administration at Indiana State University, graduating with a bachelor's degree in 1982. His first wife was Rawia al-Tunisi. They had two sons, Salah and Abdullah, and two daughters, Noha and Razan – his two daughters were in the US in October and were visited by Maggie Salem Mitchell for support. They were all educated in America and three of them took US citizenship, while Salah, the eldest son, became an investment banker in Saudi Arabia.

Following his graduation, Jamal returned home to Saudi Arabia, where his first job was managing a group of bookshops. By the mid-1980s, however, he was writing for English-language newspapers such as the *Saudi Gazette* and *Arab News*. From 1991 to 1999, he worked as a foreign correspondent in such countries as Afghanistan, Algeria, Kuwait, Sudan, and in the Middle East, reporting on the First Gulf War.

To the outside world he became at this time well-known for his interviews with Osama bin Laden. Bin Laden had been a prominent member of the mujahideen resistance against Soviet-Russia's push into Afghanistan. He was funded by the Saudis and Americans – spear-headed by the Bush family – who were seeking to stem the spread of Communism by proxy. It was only after the Russian withdrawal from Afghanistan in February 1989 that bin Laden gradually turned on his American backers through forming al-Qaeda, a new resistance movement aimed at routing the influence of his US supporters after he had successful ousted the Soviets.

It was as foreign correspondent that Jamal had become the go-to asset for the Saudi and US intelligence services and impressed powerful Saudi royals such as longstanding intelligence chief Prince Turki bin Faisal. He was a foreign correspondent in Afghanistan, Algeria, Kuwait, Sudan, and other Middle Eastern countries. During his time in Afghanistan, Jamal came to visit Osama bin Laden, first at his hideout in the Tora Bora mountains, later in Sudan. He was one of the few links (if not the only one) to bin Laden that the Saudi and US intelligence services had.

It was his big career break. According to a report by *Washington*

Post columnist David Ignatius, 'Khashoggi couldn't have travelled with the mujahideen that way without tacit support from Saudi intelligence, which was co-ordinating aid to the fighters as part of its co-operation with the CIA against the Soviet Union in Afghanistan.' His uncle Adnan Khashoggi meanwhile sold guns to the Afghans – paid for by the Saudis and Americans. At the time, Jamal was privately critical of (then) Prince Salman, MBS's father, head of the Saudi committee for support to the Afghan mujahideen, as he was funding Wahhabi extremist groups that were undermining the efforts of the other guerrillas.

Even before his meetings in Soviet times with bin Laden, Jamal had had a personal interest in political Islam. After the Iranian revolution in 1979 that ended the reign of the shah of Persia and led to the rise to power of Ayatollah Khomeini, he began attending Islamic conferences and meetings in Indiana and became very religious for a while. Jamal admitted that as a young man he had joined the Muslim Brotherhood, the reformist movement begun in Egypt in the 1920s. At the time, however, the brotherhood was supported by Saudi Arabia and it was not seen as an act of rebellion.

He had since renounced the movement. He would not have been able to work for the palace otherwise. To his friend Turan Kişlakçi he said that 'in the 1990s, I left because I thought there was no room for intellectuals in the religious community'.

He accepted Saudi Arabia's strict adherence to Wahhabism, however, and did not criticise the linkage to the royal family as such. His fiancée Hatice Cengiz, said he sketched to her his move over thirty years from 'Islamist', to 'intellectual', to 'sympathiser' of Mohamed Bouazizi, the Tunisian street-vendor. Bouazizi's death by self-immolation catalysed the Arabian Spring and the Muslim Brotherhood's attempts to carry over religious populism into democratic votes in the Middle East akin to the division between the IRA and Sinn Féin during the Troubles in Northern Ireland.

Jamal had first met bin Laden, who was Saudi by birth, in Jeddah in the early 1980s. They were the same age, in their mid-twenties.

'Osama was just like many of us who became part of the Brotherhood movement in Saudi Arabia,' Jamal said. 'The only difference that set him apart from others, and me, he was more religious. More religious, more literal, more fundamentalist. For example, he would not listen to music. He would not shake hands with a woman. He would not smoke. He would not watch television, unless it was news. He wouldn't play cards. He would not put a picture on his wall. But more than that, there was also a harsh or radical side in his life. I'm sure you have some people like that in your culture. For example, even though he comes from a rich family, he lives in a very simple house.'

In Afghanistan he got to know bin Laden better. He was impressed by his enthusiasm and devotion. In 1987, this gave him his first scoop.

'I interviewed Osama – a gentle, enthusiastic young man of few words who didn't raise his voice while talking,' he said. They discussed the condition of the mujahideen and what bin Laden was doing to help them. 'I did not know him thoroughly enough to judge him or expect any other thing from him. His behaviour at that time left no impression that he would become what he has become.'

Al-Qaeda, the Sunni-Islamist terror organisation, was founded in 1988 as the Soviets were withdrawing from Afghanistan. Bin Laden talked of spreading *jihad* through central Asia.

Jamal wrote a large two-page piece on al-Qaeda for *Arab News*, headed on the left page with a beaming bearded Jamal posing with a rocket-propelled grenade launcher (not a 'rifle' as a *Post* article had it) and on the right page with bin Laden smiling and looking down, both surrounded by pan-Arab youths. There was no talk of attacking the United States or Europe. When Jamal first met his friend Barnett Rubin, now a senior fellow at NYU, at the US consulate in Jeddah a year after the Russians withdrew he gave him a copy of the article.

Bin Laden and Jamal met for the last time in the Sudan. This was in 1995, the year its president, Omar al-Bashir, had just reinstated Sharia law and was in the sixth year of his three-decades-long dictatorship.

'Osama was almost about to change his mind and reconcile and come back to Saudi Arabia,' Jamal said. 'It was a lost opportunity.' A year later, in early 1996, President al-Bashir started secret negotiations with the CIA to either expel or extradite bin Laden in return for lifting US sanctions against Sudan.

New Yorker writer Lawrence Wright, who wrote *The Looming Tower* and knew Jamal for well over a decade and a half, said that Jamal had warned bin Laden when the latter stated he wanted to drive the US from the Arabian Peninsula: 'Osama, this is very dangerous. It is as if you are declaring war. You will give the right to the Americans to hunt for you'.

Although Jamal had been asked to try to persuade bin Laden to renounce violence and failed, he retained the ear of powerful members of the ruling house. He was surprised when bin Laden announced he was declaring war on America in 1997 and shocked by the attacks on 9/11. He gave up the idea of creating an Islamic state in Saudi Arabia. 'I think we must find a way where we can accommodate secularism and Islam, something like what they have in Turkey,' he said later.

When bin Laden was killed in 2011, Jamal wrote on Twitter: 'I collapsed crying a while ago, heartbroken for you Abu Abdullah [bin Laden's nickname]. You were beautiful and brave in those beautiful days in Afghanistan, before you surrendered to hatred and passion.'

The rewards for loyalty to the Saudi royal family during the turbulence in Afghanistan were great. In 1991, Jamal had become editor of *al-Madina*, one of Jeddah's oldest newspapers, and in 1999 Jamal rose further to become the deputy editor-in-chief on *Arab News*, the biggest English language daily in the kingdom, and a key interlocutor for western journalists with the Saudi royal family, whose formal apparatus was often incomprehensible to outsiders. He also became a go-to source for foreign journalists trying to understand the rise of Islamism and Islamist terrorism.

Four years later he became the editor-in-chief of the leading Saudi daily *al-Watan*, a paper on the liberal spectrum in the kingdom. But here he fell afoul of Saudi Arabia's deeply-conservative religious sectarianism. After less than two months, he was dismissed by the Saudi Arabian ministry of information because he had allowed a columnist to question the fourteenth-century Islamic scholar ibn Taymiyyah, who was the founding father of Wahhabism. Such rebuffs from religious conservatives were to mark the remainder of his career as an editor.

As a result of this *faux pas* Jamal escaped into quasi exile in London and became diplomatic adviser to the urbane Prince Turki bin Faisal, grandson of Saudi Arabia's founder. Maggie Salem Mitchell, director of the Qatar Foundation International, who befriended Jamal around this time, recalled that in order 'to save his life, [the Faisals] got him out of the kingdom'.

Ten days before 9/11, by remarkable coincidence, Prince Turki had abruptly resigned as Saudi-Arabia's top intelligence chief for twenty-two years, despite a new four-year extension given months earlier. His return from the cold as Saudi ambassador to Britain a year and a half later was fortuitous for Jamal.

Prince Turki was promoted to Washington two weeks after 7/7 in London, when the bibulous cigar-smoking then ambassador to the US, Prince Bandar bin Sultan, suddenly left as he was implicated in the mysterious planes with Saudi royals that departed for Riyadh despite the US-wide flying ban for any aircraft after 9/11. Prince Turki and Jamal now sparred closely to direct popular fury in the United States away from the kingdom and cover over tracks. During all these years Jamal mingled freely with American, British and Saudi intelligence officers.

In DC, John R. Bradley wrote in the *Spectator*, the Pentagon thought so highly of Jamal that they included him and two other Saudis in top-secret talks about regime change under which the US would govern Saudi Arabia and its oil reserves via an appointed council of Saudis. This retaliatory invasion was in the end angled at Sadam Hussein in Iraq, who had no involvement in 9/11 but did sit on considerable oil reserves. King Abdullah must have thought as highly of Jamal's discretion and loyalty as the Pentagon to allow talks to proceed that put his own dethronement in the hands of a commoner. Evidently Jamal's efforts had helped the neocon threat bounce off of the royal family.

As a reward, the palace permitted Jamal to return to *al-Watan* as editor in 2007. But he was dismissed a second time three years later, this time for himself criticising the kingdom's harsh Islamic rules. It was the last time he had direct influence over developments in Saudi Arabia.

'The clergy. They didn't like me,' he said. 'They didn't like the way I ran the paper. Totally lobbied against me and they got me out. I miss journalism and I think it's a very interesting time in my country. I see change, and I would like to be part of that change.'

Jamal, said Hatice Cengiz, told her that he was initially forbidden to write about the Arab Spring as Riyadh was fearful the Obama administration was about to foment an uprising in Saudi Arabia. He was also not allowed to write about the el-Sisi coup in Egypt in 2013, which he deplored. When the bans were relaxed he continued to freelance, living off his royal pension. Jamal published three books, including, in 2016, while still living in Saudi Arabia, a study of the Arab Spring. The other two were on Saudi's dependence on foreign labour (2013) and US relations (2002).

Jamal now contributed regularly to the Arab media and foreign broadcasters. In 2015 he agreed to become editor-in-chief of a new news channel based in Bahrain, al-Arab. Backed by Jamal's sponsor billionaire Prince Alwaleed bin Talal and partnered with US financial news channel Bloomberg Television (which also co-owns Haberturk TV in Turkey), it was meant to be a rival to Qatar's al-Jazeera. However, it was closed down by the Bahraini government on its first day after the new channel aired an interview with a member of its Shiite opposition. Maggie Salem Mitchell recalled saying to Jamal, 'Dude, what did you think was going to happen?'

Jamal was a regular political commentator for MBC, BBC, al-Jazeera, and Dubai TV. And between June 2012 and 18 November 2016, his opinion columns in London-based newspaper Arab-language *al-Hayat* (Life), aimed the Saudi and Arab diaspora, were regularly shared on the website of Saudi-owned news channel al-Arabiya. He also wrote for two other London-based Saudi-sponsored papers, online *majalla.com* (magazine.com) and *Asharq al-Awsat* (The Middle East).

As *al-Watan* editor Jamal's position had been akin to that of Turki Aldakhil, who ran al-Arabiya while MBS was establishing his power as the new crown prince. The Saudi media were a primary means of the Saudi royal family to maintain control over the kingdom. Even after his resignation as editor and the accession of the new king, Turan Kişlakçi recalled that Jamal retained the backing of MBS when he rose to power under his father in 2015 – they liked it when Jamal theorised in 2015, for example, about the 'Salman Doctrine'.

Not that the Western-style press is wholly free from being used for government purposes. On 8 February 2019, for example, the CIA would leak the intercept of the top-secret conversation in September 2017 between al-Arabiya's Turki Aldakhil and MBS. During this conversation, MBS, the CIA source leaked, had said he would go after Jamal 'with a bullet'. The question was as much here why the CIA would leak this, as whether premeditation to murder was implied by MBS's use of the word 'bullet' and Jamal's subsequent death inside MBS's consulate in Istanbul.

After originally supporting the war in Yemen in 2015, once in exile Jamal became critical when it dragged on (voicing the opinions of other high-level Saudis who had previously held the reins of power), and also of the human cost and conduct in the war. An anonymous source said that he had met Jamal at the end of September who disclosed to him with great reluctance that, 'he was getting proof that Saudi Arabia had used chemical weapons. He said he hoped he would be getting documentary evidence.' Reportedly the source was an academic. This rumour was not backed up by any further evidence.

In June 2017, Tysons Corner, Virginia, had changed. When Jamal had bought it while working at the Saudi US embassy with Prince Turki, it was still a sleepy place. But since then it had become a commuter satellite-town with its own metro stop on Washington DC's Silver Line. Nonetheless, despite being the corporate base for Freddie Mac, Hilton, Booz Allen, USA Today, Jamal's refuge was at-one removed from the epicentre of US power, much like he himself now was outside the royal palace.

Jamal took occasionally a pro-Qatari stance in his *Washington Post* blog and he was to have been a guest speaker at the Gulf International Form's inaugural conference at the National Press Club in Washington, DC, on 16 October 2018, which was funded by the Qataris.

While pushing the envelope as a contrarian, Kristian Coates Ulrichsen, fellow for the Middle East at Rice University's Baker Institute for Public Policy, estimated that in his pieces Jamal did not really want 'to see the crown prince fail; rather, he felt the Crown Prince and those around him were making mistakes, and was hoping that they would be able to learn from them.'

Unbeknownst, in fact, to his *Washington Post* editor Karen Attiah, it was revealed in December by her colleagues on the paper's news desk that Jamal's blog entries were at times shaped by Maggie Salem Mitchell, the director of Qatar Foundation International.

Maggie and Jamal agreed between themselves to keep this cooperation 'discreet'. She would propose topics, draft material ('So do you have time to write it?', he contacted her early in August 2018), and prod Jamal to take a harder line against the Saudi government. It did mean Jamal crossed the bright red line of independence in journalism.

The *Post*'s op-ed team later conceded they were unaware of this influence. When asked, Maggie Salem Mitchell, the director of the Qatar Foundation and Jamal's friend since 2002, said she did it to help him succeed in the US as his English was limited. Attiah agreed that his idiomatic English was poor. She had made the initial approach after someone had given her Jamal's WhatsApp but soon realised 'that he was thinking in Arabic, and writing what he could in English, and I would try to fill in the spaces of what he meant. It took a bit of work'.

Maggie Salem Mitchell tried to make Jamal feel welcome, she said, as he had left his wife and family behind and was lonely. She went clothes shopping with him ahead a talk at a Brookings Institution's forum in New York (16-18 September), in the first months of his self-exile. 'We're in Men's Wearhouse, and I was like, "Jamal, maybe you should get two jackets ... one casual, one." He said, "Maggie, I'm a minimalist. I don't want to have a lot of things".'

They both drove to New York together with a Doha acquaintance of hers and her partner Mike Franc, a director at the Hoover Institute, and helped Jamal prepare for a BBC interview at the forum along the way. His Saudi accent prevented him from saying the word 'Orwellian', which he specifically wanted to use. 'We had this stupid belly laugh, all of us trying to get him to say Orwellian', Franc recalled in the *Atlantic*. For Jamal this became central word. A month later, on 13 November 2017, he told the BBC World's Hard Talk that he was 'worried for my country, my children and grandchildren – one-man rule is always bad, in any country'.

On the Saturday before his death, Jamal said on BBC-24's Newshour about the PLO conference he had just attended, 'An event like that would be difficult to hold today in the Arab world because we are retreating from freedom in most of the Arab countries. Most of the Arab world is currently collapsing, for example in Libya, Syria and Yemen and has no interest in discussing Palestine because they have miseries of their own. Then in countries like Saudi Arabia, my country, or in Egypt, they have no interest in those kinds of issues that motivate and rally the people because they want to subdue them instead.'

That evening he had dinner with Daud Abdullah, a former editor and translator at the Abul Qasim Publishing House in Jeddah and the director of the Middle East Monitor which had organised the conference, as well as other colleagues and attendees of the conference, in a Turkish restaurant in Bloomsbury. Two days later, he flew back to Istanbul.

10

Exodus

Jamal's self-imposed exile in 2017 came at a cost – just as it did when he escaped to London in 2002. Not only was he unable to go back to Jeddah and his friends, this time he was no longer part of shaping the future of Saudi Arabia. In addition, his third marriage ended as a result of his exile to the United States.

During this difficult time, Hatice and Jamal first met two days before Trump handed the home victory to MBS on 8 May 2018 by ripping up the Obama Iran deal that Riyadh hated so much and that Jamal himself had castigated MBS for. Trump had been signalling this for a couple of months and no doubt they talked about it. Jamal was a speaker at the five-star Istanbul Marriott on new security arrangements in the MENA (Middle East and North Africa) region at the al-Sharq Forum, a think tank set up by the energetic former director general of Qatari-based al-Jazeera. Hatice got in contact with Jamal and said she had been following him closely as a PhD-student for his insights and wanted to interview him. It was at this conference that Turan Kişlakçi had introduced them to each other (in an interview with the *Financial Times* in August 2019 Hatice, however, said she walked up to Jamal 'during a coffee break and introduced myself; I said to him that I wanted to interview him for a political website').

Despite the fact that only 0.5 per cent speak Arabic in Turkey, quite exceptionally, Hatice spoke the language fluently. She came from Bursa – the automotive and silk capital of Turkey, two hours to the south of Istanbul – from a large conservative family which was originally from Armenia. She was the second child of five, attended a local religious state-school called *imam hatip* (which Atatürk permitted after outlawing the *madrasas* common elsewhere in the Muslim world) for women and was taught Arabic to read the Koran and its commentaries. This is not uncommon in Erdoğan's Turkey. The Turkish Diyanet (directorate of religious affairs) – whose budget quadrupled under Erdoğan to promote Hanafi-Sunni Islam, Turkey's majority denomination – employs official state preachers and a third are women, while a sizeable number rank higher than imams.

She then studied for three years at Sunni-Islam's most prestigious university in the Middle East, al-Azhar University in Cairo, Egypt, where the four Sunni denominations are taught. She spent a lot of her spare time reading widely and returned to Turkey in 2006 to jobs as a tourism guide. But, having won a place at Istanbul University's Theology Department in 2010, she followed her further religious studies up with a Masters at Sabahattin Zaim University and lived in Oman from 2016-2017 for research into its 'inter-sectarian' model – its half-Sunni half-Shia population lives together peacefully unlike anywhere else in the Middle East – followed by her current PhD in history at the Fatih Sultan Mehmet University.

Istanbul University ranked fourth in Turkey, but the latter two institutions dangled at the bottom of the Turkish university league table, well past the 100 mark. Nonetheless she wrote her first essay for the magazine of Turkey's Foreign Policy Institute, a prestigious think tank headed by a man dubbed at its 40th anniversary 'our diplomacy guru' by Mevlüt Çavuşoğlu, Erdoğan's foreign minister. She dreamt of being an academic and investigative journalist.

There wasn't much time for the interview and Jamal and Hatice had but a short meeting at the Marriott. She emailed him later in the US that she regretted she hadn't been able to get the interview published as his public profile was modest in Turkey. But she emailed the piece to him and he 'liked it very much' and wrote 'that it was valuable that she cared'.

'Hatice, it doesn't matter. I appreciate your efforts, I appreciate it. When I next come to Turkey we can talk longer.' 'Our meeting is a start',

Jamal had playfully added.

Hatice responded whether he might be able to expand the interview and 'to talk in more detail'.

In return, he suggested that they should meet again when he was back in Istanbul. From this second meeting, she continued conducting formal interviews with him and their relationship blossomed quickly alongside.

In his personal life, Jamal said, he 'felt great solitude' and longing for Saudi Arabia. He was 'so isolated' from everything in the US and didn't know what was happening to his friends in the Saudi government. Hatice sensed a 'great political and emotional loneliness'. In fact, he didn't want to tell his family in Saudi Arabia how depressed he was.

'Night after night I am in the US, on my own, and I watch the developments in my country. Being single causes me real pain and I cry. But I don't want to tell this to my children', he said to her.

He also said that after his last marriage had broken up for political reasons due to his self-exile, he had decided he 'wanted to get married again'.

'Suddenly, I saw a completely different human being, and then a special, direct dialogue began', Hatice recalled. They started to include the future in the things they discussed. Whenever Jamal was feeling down, Hatice would cheer him up and remind him of what lay ahead.

Their conversations intensified. Hatice was connected to senior policy circles in Turkey, and so was Jamal. He had longstanding friendships with leading people in the Turkish media but also knew senior politicians close to President Erdoğan and had many Turkish friends. In the words of Hatice, he also had 'a friendship with the president', and met at least once with him during their months of growing closer together.

Jamal came to Istanbul in July where they met a musical event and before he left Jamal told Turan that he wanted to marry Hatice. They called each other regularly. In August Jamal was back, speaking every Friday at Turan's Turkish-Arab Journalists' Association and where their relationship started in earnest. She found him 'wise', 'mature' and a 'beautiful person'. He was gregarious, energetic and in love with life, and they shared a deep intellectual interest in the politics, religion, history and culture of the Middle East. He appreciated her thoughts on the sectarian Sunni-Shia divide and how to bridge its violent antagonism.

'No kebabs' for him, observed Hatice. Istanbul as the former heart of the Ottoman empire, had a long and refined gastronomic tradition, and Jamal enjoyed eating fish and always 'tasted the best things in restaurants'. 'He was upset if he didn't eat well.'

After returning to the US in August, Jamal texted with exhilaration, 'I came home safe and sound. I want us to be together as one'. He also wrote to her, she said, 'no one has loved me like you do.'

Meanwhile, still in August, Hatice went to the nearby Fatih Marriage Office to find out what marriage formalities applied to Jamal as a Saudi citizen. She was told about the two forms he needed and that they could only be certified in Turkey at a diplomatic mission or in Saudi Arabia, Jamal's home country. Hatice also told her conservative Turkish family – they hailed from Bursa, Turkey's fourth largest city – of their marriage plans. Jamal's friend Turan Kişlakçi went to her father to ask for her hand on his behalf: 'you go and talk to him', Jamal had said to Turan.

Hatice's father was not keen, however. He had reservations about the age difference and Jamal's health, but came around in the end. He would give his blessing if they observed all the correct civil-marriage formalities under Turkish law, not those of a religious marriage only. Later, standing in front of the consulate on his vigil, Turan would express his irritation about this. The formalities Hatice's father had in mind also included the traditional Muslim *mehr* (dowry, *mehir* or *başlik parasi* in Turkish) for the bride – an apartment in her name, or at any rate one they would co-own. It was meant 'to safeguard his daughter' he told Turan. But, when all his conditions were accepted, he agreed to meet the thrice married Jamal on either 8 or 9 September and gave his consent to the marriage. Within twenty days of proposing, Jamal had 'met my parents and bought an apartment for us. He was practical', Hatice told the *Financial Times* in July

2019.

On 10 September, Jamal's son Abdullah arrived in Istanbul for a visit to his father and the three of them met for the first time at Turan's Association. Here Jamal told Hatice he had four children from his first wife, who lived in Dubai. He also said he had been divorced three times including his most recent marriage that had ended less than a year ago for political reasons. 'It didn't matter to me', Hatice later said.

They went to buy their engagement rings that day, and Abdullah told his siblings that his father had a new fiancée and a new home in Turkey.

No doubt the Khashoggi family weren't the only ones to learn about the surprise news if they were being wiretapped by Saud al-Qahtani's Centre for Studies and Media Research the way al-Qahtani had secretly monitored even high-ranking royals – such as Crown Prince (then) Prince bin Nayef. It was around this time that Saudi officials began to exchange ideas about Jamal's rendition according to US intelligence intercepts. GCHQ in Cheltenham also picked up that 'something was going' at this time.

There was not much time left that month to get organised as Jamal had at least three commitments. He had been far more excited about the nuptial festivities than she was and asked what they should wear for the wedding. But she had responded, 'let's take care of practical matters first.' Hatice preferred simple convenience over elaborate and costly celebrations, particularly when there was so much suffering in the world, she said – it was perhaps a difference from Saudi custom, and one of the things Jamal liked about her, she told *Sabah*.

They decided first to start with finding a place where to live and, then, to get married. Jamal 'loved people, the crowds, the noise' and wanted to live in Fatih (conqueror), the historic district of Istanbul and heart of the former Ottoman, Byzantine, Roman empire. But Hatice was less keen on life in cramped, winding streets with crumbling ancient architecture.

On 25 September Jamal completed on their apartment in 'Castle 2' of the Topkapi Europe Residences in the Zeytinburnu district, just outside the ancient Roman walls of Constantinople built by emperor

Theodosius. Located in this bustling but dishevelled working-class district, the new residences were nonetheless an oasis of calm. It was an elegant luxury regeneration development completed in 2016 with large, brown-metal windows, wide balconies, landscaped gardens, CC-TV, gated security, tennis courts, indoor pools, a fitness centre and sauna. As often in Istanbul, the development's historical references rioted – it was built on almost the exact location where Mehmet the Conqueror had breached the St Romanus gate with a giant cannon called 'Basilic'. This technological innovation finished what was left of ancient Rome in Asia and the gate became known as cannon gate, or 'Topkapi', but in Zeytinburnu the term amicably conjoined 'European Residences' for marketing purposes.

The ample apartment with three bedrooms, ensuite bathroom, balconies, and a large sitting room and kitchen was totally modern yet within easy reach of all government buildings, and had distant views on the ancient sights such as the Hagia Sophia, mosques, and, way in the distance, Topkapi Palace, the famous seraglio of the sultans and former heart of the Ottoman empire. Sultan Mehmet had chosen the place when he put up his encampment on a bluff, yet the nineteenth-century Ottomans renamed it Topkapi Palace as an honorific, regardless of the fact that the bluff overlooked the Bosphorus and was far removed from Topkapi itself.

More practically, perhaps, it was near the new seventh Istanbul campus of Hatice's latest alma mater, Fatih Sultan Mehmet University, and 15 minutes from CNN Turk, Fox TV and other media.

'Open the curtains', Jamal had said to Hatice excitedly. From the windows, you could see the Fatih Mosque, another Mehmet landmark.

'I'll go and pray there when we are married and have tea with your father.' He was excited by the prospect of breakfasts in Fatih, whose many minarets reminded him of the buildings of his youth in the holy city of Medina. He spoke often nostalgically about missing Eid, the end of Ramadan, in his home town.

Although the apartment was built to an exceptional standard, its price was relatively modest at just over $250,000, particularly after the pounding the Turkish lira had taken at the hands of President Donald Trump. It is not clear how well-off Jamal was, but his salaries had no doubt been substantial over the years, and he continued to be paid a royal pension. In addition, there was incidental income.

On 2 December 2009, for example, a businessman who called Jamal 'uncle J' transferred $100,000 into his account in order to interview Malaysian President Najib Razak on 14 December for *al-Watan* (sarawakreport.org). The interview was designed to help create an elaborate smokescreen of gold-plated Saudi respectability around Razak's slush fund and piggy bank of well over $10bn. Called Malaysia's sovereign-wealth fund '1MDB', it paid for Razak's wife's lavish purchases of jewellery, houses and handbags, as well as massive electoral bribes. Jamal himself wasn't aware of the fraud and just took the interview, but on 9 May 2018 it shattered Malaysia's ruling party's uninterrupted rule since independence in 1957. In December the scandal further ensnared Goldman Sachs with a $6bn law suit and a criminal investigation, causing a 30 per cent drop in its share price.

As a result of Turkey's economic malaise, Erdoğan's government had dropped the requirements for citizenship by three quarters to a quarter of a million dollars, and Jamal could technically apply for Turkish citizenship at the same time as purchasing their apartment. But, he said, Riyadh already called him 'the Turk' and he feared they would come after him more if he applied for Turkish nationality. He worried, in particular, that something bad might happen to his eldest son Salah, the banker in Jeddah.

Instead of remaining based in Virginia as an expat – where Jamal had a few weeks ago applied for his US citizenship and was waiting for the paperwork to go through – he was changing his home-base a second time and now planned to spend much more of his life in Istanbul. It was a huge emotional step away from his homeland and also one that could have immediate practical consequences. Saudi Arabia doesn't grant multiple nationalities without permission from the king. Under Saudi law his nationality could be cancelled with the click of a button once he naturalised elsewhere.

In between waiting for the deeds to the apartment to arrive and Jamal's hectic cosmopolitan schedule, they had started to order furniture for the moment when they would live together as husband and wife.

By Friday 28 September, two days after the deeds came through and the day Jamal would leave for London, he decided to make things official. At 9.53am Jamal and Hatice stepped into the Fatih Marriage Office together and the marriage official gave Jamal the list of documents he needed to get married. It was no more than 10 minutes or so from the apartment. Jamal, suffering from his cold, chewing gum, seemed a little distracted. He was wearing a yellow jumper and red baseball cap and carried a brown coat with him. Hatice wore a scarf and long coat and her satchel hung around her shoulders. They sat down at a desk with an official and Hatice got up again to busy herself with a number of forms from a stand. She gave some to Jamal and kept some herself, and which they all discussed. It was all later leaked on CC-TV and discussed in-depth on Turkish TV. The purpose,

An hour and a half after the Fatih Marriage Office consultation, Jamal and Hatice would also make the 30 minute journey to the consulate with the papers for the unannounced visit. They had deliberated for a little while whether to go. Jamal told Hatice he was worried 'something might happen'. In the end, he said 'Let's go'.

For the second consular visit after his early morning return on Tuesday, Jamal no longer felt worried. In the taxi drive to the Saudi consulate their mood was high-spirited and they talked about light-hearted matters. Jamal wanted a US-style two-door fridge but Hatice had already ordered a standard one. She called the company from the car to change the model without success. Jamal had joked about it and they both laughed.

To Hatice and Jamal, their marriage was only a few rubber stamps away. Papers in hand, they might go from the consulate back to the Fatih Marriage Office to apply for the marriage license. In the evening, they would tell friends and family and pick the date for the civil wedding ceremony before Jamal had to leave again for the US on 10 October.

Hatice planned to wear white. Jamal had asked her the week before, 'do you want children?' As he already had two sons and two daughters and two grandchildren, she wasn't sure what he wanted himself, and she had simply replied, 'if Allah doesn't want me to, I don't need to have children'.

11

'Certain circles'

Just before Hatice and Jamal met through Turan Kişlakçi, Turkey had begun the construction of its first nuclear reactor on 3 April 2018 by Russia's Rosatom. Regardless of the international inspections it had agreed to, Turkey seemed to have stolen a march on Saudi Arabia. Like Iran, it was one step closer to the bomb. From May 2018, Jamal Khashoggi also reappeared on the radar of the royal palace. From that month, after a half year lull, MBS's aides kept inviting him back to Saudi Arabia to take up a role as advisor.

The thrice-married Jamal instead would marry a Turkish wife, and would renounce in effect his Saudi nationality by applying for a US passport. And he was moving closer to President Erdoğan developing their acquaintance. Why did Erdoğan have any interest in non-Turkish speaking Jamal unless, it was because Ankara considered Jamal a crucial asset in thwarting Saudi Arabia's plans?

Could Jamal have stuck a sharper needle into the eye of his former employer while Riyadh's nuclear catch-up was entering another make-or-break phase? Earlier, on 7 March 2018, MBS had said that Turkey was part of the 'triangle of evil', together with Iran and extremist religious groups. The Saudi embassy in Ankara paddled back on MBS's words the next day and blamed the messenger for getting it wrong, but the words summarised the position in Saudi Arabia quite well.

After the Arab Spring, Erdoğan had fostered two lines of regimes reliant on populist Islam/the Muslim Brotherhood: Tunisia, Libya, Egypt, Sudan along one line and Syria, Iraq, Iran along another. In between this sandwich lay Saudi Arabia.

The Saudi royal family perceived any religious populism as an existential threat, whether Sunni or Shia. The 1979 fall of the shah as absolute monarch (and owner of oil revenues) in Shia Iran was the most egregious example, followed closely by the 2010 Arab Spring, which ended the authoritarian regimes of Sunni Egypt, Libya and Tunisia, and half-Sunni Yemen and bolstered Turkey's lines of regional power. As recently as 2014, and still under the previous king, King Abdullah, Jamal's royal patron, Saudi Arabia had classified the Muslim Brotherhood as a 'terrorist organisation' and the king decreed a twenty-year prison sentence for anyone belonging to a 'terrorist group'.

MBS was, therefore, certainly no Saudi outlier with regards to Turkey. Riyadh had stopped seeing eye to eye with the country from the moment Erdoğan rose to power in 2003, harnessing popular Islam aided by the Muslim Brotherhood into his increasingly authoritarian rule of over a decade and counting.

More to the point, perhaps, Turkey used to be a sleeping giant checked by its army. But Erdoğan projected Turkish power well beyond its borders despite a modest military budget of $18bn that was dwarfed by Saudi's $64bn. Apart from challenging MBS's blockade of Qatar, Turkey had opened military bases in Qatar and Somalia and had been in talks with Sudan's brotherhood-linked dictator Omar al-Bashir of three decades, before the Sudanese army removed him in May 2019 following popular protests. Routing Saudi power in the region and spreading the political arm of the Muslim Brotherhood were two prongs of Erdoğan's foreign policy.

Jamal was a godsend for Erdoğan to have on side, particularly after the Iran Deal was kyboshed by Trump. On May 22, at a fast-breaking *iftar* meal with ambassadors, he said 'We do not accept re-igniting issues, including the Iran nuclear deal... The main threats against our country and region are nuclear weapons.' Jamal's insights could be invaluable in giving teeth to what Turkey does 'not accept'. For decades Jamal had enjoyed Saudi royal patronage, been involved in Saudi intelligence, entrusted with Saudi's vital secrets, been authorised to develop close relationships in the

US and Europe, and embedded deeper and deeper in Riyadh's secretive palace culture. Jamal knew where the palace was divided.

Not that Jamal had gone over yet and become part of Ankara's security carapace. It was still witching hour in September. Even in exile Jamal had faithfully kept the royal palace abreast of developments in his life that affected the kingdom – as if to signal that his public criticism of MBS had no bearing on his patriotism as a Saudi national. When, for example, he was approached by an FBI agent working for the victims of 9/11, he contacted KBS, the Saudi ambassador in the US, and expressed his loyalty to the kingdom and said he would impart 'the innocence of my country and its leadership'. Whatever 9/11 secrets he knew were safe with him.

The palace had always trusted Jamal. Ordinarily, giving a journalist access to state secrets means reading about them in the paper the next day, or at least spreading them around as media gossip. But Jamal's discretion and skill were so trusted in Riyadh that, even after his time in the US and UK embassies with Prince Turki had ended, he took diplomatic meetings on behalf of the Saudi government. It was his friend Azzam Tamimi of London's Finsbury Mosque who had recalled that Jamal had attended an international top with Hamas in Beirut on behalf of the palace's foreign ministry.

Asked by *Haberturk* (Turkish News) about Jamal and the 'many secrets he knew of the absolute monarchy' in Saudi Arabia, Turan Kişlakçi replied to that aciculate question that he had challenged Jamal on this closeness to the palace as consultant, and to Prince Turki (who is considered to have an air of intellectual superiority by his royal relatives, and as a result not well-liked). Turan pointed out to Jamal 'that is secret service and you are a journalist'. Jamal, however, had responded unapologetically about this blurring of opposing lines.

'There is part of the palace that at times would like to exclude the religious and the conservatives. I am part of it, and I am glad I am part of it. I have used it to make a difference, particularly to the PLO.'

On 15 November, in a further rare glimpse through the heavy walls of the royal palace itself, Saudi prosecutor general Sheikh al-Mojeb would lift the lid of secrecy on the official motive behind the Tiger Team rendition of Jamal.

MBS's top-aide and Jamal's media-supervisor Saud al-Qahtani, the chief prosecutor's office stated, had briefed members of the team that, further to his Centre's intel, Jamal Khashoggi had been 'co-opted by organisations and states hostile to the kingdom and that the victim's presence outside of Saudi Arabia represents a threat to national security'. The deputy-head of Saudi intelligence, major-general al-Asiri, had for this reason ordered the rendition on 29 September, and brigadier-general Maher Mutreb, Jamal's former London-embassy colleague, attended the al-Qahtani meeting as a key member of the team.

With another piece of the 'Iron Bridge' scheme falling into place in May, MBS intended to award the tender for the first two nuclear power plants in early winter 2018. Right at this time, the Arab-speaking Hatice had made contact with Jamal. What would happen with his insight, know-how and skill in Turkey while delicate US-Saudi negotiations about nuclear power were imminent? It did not seem as if Jamal was thinking of living a secluded life in marital bliss with his young new wife. They looked more like an ambitious power couple. Were the secrets and palace know-how Jamal was privy to safe, or were they on the verge of leaking away from the Saudi sphere of influence into the orbit of an opponent with an interest in denying Saudi Arabia's longstanding hopes?

In his address, al-Qahtani had given the palace's answer to that question to the Tiger Team members present at the rendition meeting.

When brigadier-general Mutreb yelled 'Traitor! This is what you deserve!' while Jamal was being grabbed, he dropped an unmistakable clue as to what was really behind the cold-blooded murder of his former media and secret-service colleague in London.

Jamal's significance was not lost either on Vladimir Putin, a world leader who viciously hunted down journalists inside his own country and took lethal aim at people he considered intelligence risks outside Russia's borders.

President Putin would take the opportunity to offer his personal view on the Khashoggi affair on 18 October at a conference in Sochi – the Valdai Discussion Club, Russia's state of the union for top officials and oligarchs.

Leaking what was in Russia's intelligence files, he pointedly said about Jamal's *curriculum vitae*, 'As far as I can judge this man is to a certain extent part of the Saudi elite. In some way or other he was connected to certain circles in power'. Disregarding the fact that the world media considered Jamal's journalism the cause of his assassination – plain and simple – the very well-informed Putin observed obliquely instead, 'It is hard to say, what is going on there.'

Putin had previously brought up the subject of 'traitors' on 3 October – the day after the torture and assassination of Jamal Khashoggi, and the same day on which MBS was to protest publicly and in person his innocence of Jamal's fate to Bloomberg in the evening.

On that day Vladimir Putin was taking part in a midday Q&A session at the Russian Energy Week conference in Moscow. But he had all of a sudden veered off topic and launched into a vitriolic broadside. It seemed so random at the time that his outburst made headlines around the world. Seated next to Vladimir Putin at the Q&A session and looking serene was Khalid al-Falih, MBS's trusted energy minister.

'Imagine' Putin fumed, pulling a disgusted face, 'suddenly someone goes and betrays your country. What do you think about him?… He's just a scumbag, and that's it.'

The word Putin spat out at the conference attended by oil-and-gas state ministers and CEOs of oil companies was '*poldonok*', a boorish Russian swear word.

The aim of his sudden outburst was on the face of it the former-GRU spy Sergei Skripal even though in October, this affair had drifted to the backburner of the news cycle.

Putin had also commented that some 'are pushing forward the theory that Mr Skripal is almost some kind of human rights defender.'

It was an odd theory to bring up eight months after the fact. Sergei

Skripal was a retired mid-ranking former Russian spy living in very modest circumstances in sleepy Salisbury. He had never gone on the record for anything, let alone human rights. At best, he had become in 2018 a mute symbol for human rights.

Jamal Khashoggi was, however, a long-standing member of the Saudi intelligence community and knew secrets only available to the highest circles of the Saudi royal family. The *Washington Post* blogger with his 1.7 million Twitter followers, could also definitely be 'pushed forward' as a human rights defender because that is exactly how the Middle-East rumour-mill labelled him in the first 24 hours of his disappearance.

Jamal Khashoggi may not have been well-known enough in the Anglophone or Turkish media to stop the presses, but his disappearance was already big news on 2 October for Arab mass-media outlets such as al-Jazeera, the Qatari-owned broadcaster. Its media-team deeply rated the Saudi commentator's measured support for Qatar against the actions of his own government. Against MBS, Jamal also supported greater freedom of expression in the Middle East and saw the Muslim Brotherhood as a symptom of a popular demand rather than as a terrorist organisation whose very existence was nefarious like al-Qaeda or Daesh/Isis.

On this point not only Qatar, Turkey and Bahrein agreed with Jamal. Rex Tillerson, Donald Trump's secretary of state, former CEO of ExxonMobile and hardly a barn-storming hippy, concurred. Rejecting the classification of the brotherhood as a terrorist organisation as 'problematic', Tillerson stated on 14 June 2017 that elements of the organisation had become a legitimate part of governments 'by renouncing violence and terrorism.' He used Turkey and Bahrein as examples.

When Putin spoke on 3 October, the Turkish and international media still imagined that Jamal might be alive, but officials in Riyadh knew better. There was a reason why none of the frantic phone calls that Turkish authorities made to their Saudi counterparts after 5.50pm on 2 October remained unanswered.

12

3 October

Already in late August/early September, US intelligence had intercepted communications by Saudi officials discussing a plan to capture Jamal. In fact, quite a few people in the US intelligence community were aware of it. The secret information had been disseminated to relevant US government agencies and was contained in reports that were routinely available to people working on US policy toward Saudi Arabia. Jamal was a US resident and, under standing government order ICD19-'Duty to Warn', US intelligence services were obliged to warn him of impending danger.

'Capturing him, which could have been interpreted as arresting him, would not have triggered a duty-to-warn obligation', a former official told the *Washington Post*. 'If something in the reported intercept indicated that violence was planned, then, yes, he should have been warned.'

Did the Saudis intend to arrest Jamal (which would be lawful, and there would be no duty to warn incumbent on US intelligence personnel), or plan violence, torture, or to kill him (all of which unlawful)? Trump-administration officials reviewed the intercepts and decided not to tip off Jamal about the developing Saudi plans. Given Jamal's *Post* connection and the military-aspect of the planned Saudi rendition, it was difficult to see what persuaded the Trump administration to spread the news to its own agencies but not to include Jamal himself in their alert if only to err on the side of caution regarding the fourth estate. But that is what they did.

As to whether he might be arrested during a consular visit to obtain certification of his marriage documents, Jamal had talked about this with his friend and fellow member of the Turkish-Arab Journalists' Association, Turan Kişlakçi. They had met on Wednesday and Thursday the week before his first consular visit in order to prepare for a talk the week after at the Association's premises.

Jamal had no worry on that front: 'I'm not afraid, because there is no official investigation against me. On the contrary, recently, [Crown Prince] Mohammed bin Salman asked me to be his adviser, and I refused, saying this is against my country and region's interests.... The most they can do is interrogate me. And I can give them answers, I have nothing to hide.' Jamal evidently assumed his support to Omar Abdulaziz in Canada was invisible.

In actual fact, on 3 October when asked by Bloomberg, 'Is he facing any charges in Saudi Arabia?', MBS's answer was surprisingly evasive about the man assassinated the day before in his consulate.

Pressed by the Bloomberg team, 'So he might be facing charges in Saudi Arabia?', MBS ignored the question again and repeated what he had said before, 'If he's in Saudi Arabia I would know that'.

There was a reason why MBS was carefully hopping between facts. In a later leaked conversation he had with top White House staff in daily contact with Trump, and whose aides would be keeping up with what he said on Bloomberg around this date, MBS told these officials Jamal was a 'dangerous Islamist', a crime in Saudi Arabia carrying a prison sentence. That very week, economist Essam al-Zamil, a friend of Jamal's and critic of the crown prince's proposed sale of 5 per cent of Aramco, was charged with joining the Muslim Brotherhood, providing information to foreign diplomats, and inciting protests. But MBS wanted to project concern about what happened to Jamal.

At that moment, those standing outside the consulate, including Kişlakçi, knew next to nothing, however. Kişlakçi said, 'We believe he's still inside. There was no sign that he was taken out in a black car or something. Maybe they are interrogating him'. According to Kişlakçi, 'His fiancée's father pressured him to get the relevant documents to initiate the official marriage process in Turkey. His trusted Saudi friends in the US gave him assurance. He was confident in what he was doing.'

But al-Jazeera, the TV station based in Qatar, was now reporting that Jamal had been abducted. Some seventy thousand tweets were discussing his disappearance – though many said they doubted Saudi involvement, alleging a conspiracy between Turkey and the Muslim Brotherhood to defame the kingdom.

Others, though, were already pointing the finger at MBS. One commentator wrote: 'If news of abducting Jamal Khashoggi is true, it will be one of the biggest follies of Mohammed bin Salman. The man has an international standing and reputation. It will not go unnoticed.'

Another, quoting a source who claimed to be close to the royal court, said that Jamal had indeed been abducted and was smuggled into Saudi Arabia arriving there in the early hours.

'If it is true, it is would be difficult to imagine Turkey standing idly by while Mohammed bin Salman is playing with its sovereignty before the world,' the tweet read.

Hatice Cengiz was now beside herself with worry and spoke to the media.

'I don't know what has happened to him,' she said. 'I can't even guess how such a thing can happen to him. There is no law or lawsuit against him. He is not a suspect, he has not been convicted. There is nothing against him. He is just a man whose country doesn't like his writings or his opinions.'

The Turkish government still had no answers what had happened with Jamal either. A Turkish security official was quoted as saying they were in discussion with the Saudis and believed that Jamal was still being held in the consulate.

Further to the questions, Saudi Arabia sent a statement to Associated Press, saying 'Mr. Khashoggi visited the consulate to request paperwork related to his marital status and exited shortly thereafter. The government of Saudi Arabia follows up diligently on any reports related to the safety of any of its citizens and will continue to follow up on these reports'.

Turkey's concept of what had happened in the consulate was confirmed by President Erdoğan's own office and contradicted the Saudi statement. 'According to the information that we have, this Saudi citizen is still in the Saudi Arabian consulate in Istanbul,' said Ibrahim Kalin, Turkey's presidential spokesperson on 3 October at a press conference.

'We don't have any information to the contrary. We continue to follow this issue closely.'

Echoing MBS's statement to Bloomberg on 3 October, Saudi authorities issued a statement flatly denying Jamal was being detained, and claiming that he 'visited the consulate and exited shortly thereafter'. It was technically true.

Meanwhile the *Washington Post* issued another statement concerning the fate of its blogger in the night of 2 October.

'We have been unable to reach Jamal today and are very concerned about where he may be,' said Eli Lopez, a senior Global Opinions editor at the online newspaper. 'It would be unfair and outrageous if he has been detained for his work as a journalist and commentator.'

Press calls and emails to Saudi missions in London, Washington, and Istanbul yielded no further information about Jamal.

After the Saudi radio silence to inter-government telephone calls on the evening of 2 October, the Turkish government tried to apply pressure behind the scenes.

Hakan Fidan, Turkey's powerful secret-service chief rang the 'head of the Kingdom of Saudi Arabia' in the following days, asking for Jamal's return. Non-aligned Turkish website jonturk reported in March 2019 the rumour that Fidan and MBS had had a stormy exchange in which Fidan asked for Jamal's body and MBS abruptly ended the call saying that he would put Fidan on his black list.

The official stance of Saudi Arabia slightly shifted, with the state-run Saudi Press Agency providing an official update at 5.14am in the morning of 4 October: 'The consulate has confirmed that it is co-ordinating with the brotherly local Turkish authorities in the follow-up procedures to reveal the circumstances surrounding the disappearance of citizen Jamal Khashoggi after having left the consulate building.'

Next Saudi ambassador Elkereiji was summoned to the Turkish foreign ministry to clear up the matter. Despite Aktay's call on 2 October Elkereiji told the Turkish deputy foreign minister that he had no information about the missing journalist. 'We are investigating,' he said. 'I will convey any information we get.' In Riyadh a Saudi under-secretary spoke to Turkish ambassador Erdoğan Kök.

The Saudis used the situation to cause further confusion with some officials leaking that Jamal never entered the consulate and others saying he entered and then left. In effect, they were implying that Hatice Cengiz, who had dropped him off at the consulate, was confused at best or making it all up to cause trouble at worst.

The Turkish police continued their work on the case. 'The missing persons department has launched an investigation upon the application of Jamal Khashoggi's family,' reported the Kemalist opposition newspaper *Sözcü* (The Advocate). 'Police teams have launched a broad investigation to find Khashoggi, primarily analysing city surveillance footage.'

There was still the suggestion of sweeping access to the Saudi consulate sanctioned by the palace. In the wide-ranging Bloomberg interview of 3 October MBS had already given his personal promise to allow such access. Calling Jamal a friend to indicate his close personal interest in the matter, MBS said, 'Yes, he's not inside.' This was not a lie, but what followed would neither happen according to the letter nor the spirit of his words. He guaranteed that, though the 'premises are sovereign territory', he would 'allow [the Turkish government] to enter and search and do whatever they want to do.'

Social media users were not convinced, however, and continued to say – as the Turkish government did – that Jamal was being held at the Saudi consulate.

Others speculated he had been smuggled back into Saudi Arabia. Jamal's personal website, to which Hatice had access, bore a banner headline saying: 'Jamal has been arrested at the Saudi consulate in

Istanbul!'

Again, the Saudi Arabian authorities issued a statement denying (truthfully, albeit economical with the truth) he was being detained. Supporters of MBS continued arguing that the whole story had been made up to smear the kingdom.

Hatice, Jamal's fiancée, was adamant, saying: 'We want to know his whereabouts. Where is Jamal? We want him to come out of the consulate safe and sound.'

She subscribed to the theory that he had been kidnapped. 'If that's not what happened, where is Jamal?' she asked. 'Right now we have no information. As a missing person, he is in danger.' She said that the Turkish authorities were working hard to locate her fiancé and wanted to believe that he had not been smuggled out of the country.

'I want to be positive, I want to be hopeful,' she said. 'I hope that Jamal is in Istanbul.'

Karen Attiah, Jamal's editor at the *Washington Post*, said the newspaper had still not been able to reach him.

'We have inquired about Jamal's whereabouts, and expressed our deep concern, to both Turkish and Saudi officials,' she said.

On Friday 5 October, the *Post* printed a blank column in the paper to show solidarity with their missing blogger. It bore Jamal's byline and photograph, and was headlined: 'A missing voice.'

A note from the editor read: 'Jamal Khashoggi is a Saudi journalist and author, and a *Washington Post* Global Opinions contributing columnist. Khashoggi's words should appear in the space above, but he has not been heard from since he entered a Saudi consulate in Istanbul for a routine consular matter on Tuesday afternoon.'

Clutching at straws given Turkey's and Saudi-Arabia's stance on investigative journalism, the *Post* called on the crown prince to 'do everything in his power to ensure that Mr Khashoggi is free and able to continue his work'.

In an editorial, the newspaper said: 'Mr Khashoggi is not just any commentator. Over a long career, he has had close contact with Saudi royalty and knows more than most about how they think and function. His criticism, voiced over the past year, most surely rankles Mohammed bin Salman, who was elevated to crown prince last year and has carried out a wide-ranging campaign to silence dissent while trying to modernise the kingdom. Among those in his prisons for political speech are clerics, bloggers, journalists and activists. He imprisoned women who agitated for the right to drive, a right that was granted even as they were punished.'

The *Post*'s editorial board also made a direct appeal to MBS: 'The crown prince has been all over the US preaching his vision of a more modern Saudi society, breaking out of the stale old religious codes and practices, opening up to foreign entertainment and investment. If he is truly committed to this, he will welcome constructive criticism from patriots such as Mr Khashoggi.'

Journalists from Turan Kişlakçi's Turkish-Arab Journalists' Association meanwhile staged a protest outside the Saudi consulate in Istanbul.

'We demand the immediate release of Jamal Khashoggi, who we think is being "hosted" at the consulate building in Istanbul, or the revealing of his whereabouts,' said Kişlakçi. 'If they do not release him we will stand here for weeks and months. We will stage the same demonstrations of solidarity not just here but everywhere in the world.'

The New York-based group Human Rights Watch took a keen interest. Middle-East director Sarah Leah Whitson said: 'If Saudi authorities surreptitiously detained Khashoggi it would be yet another escalation of Crown Prince Mohammed bin Salman's reign of repression against peaceful dissidents and critics. The burden of proof is on Saudi Arabia to produce evidence for its claim that Khashoggi left the consulate alone, and that Saudi agents have not detained him.'

At this point, however, MBS seemed to hold all the cards. Without further information the media cyclone would soon pass.

13

'Friends'

In the Bloomberg interview of Wednesday night 3 October, Crown Prince Mohammed bin Salman had volunteered part-definitive part-vague information on Jamal's whereabouts.

'If he's in Saudi Arabia, I would know that,' MBS had answered confidently. It was impossible to verify.

Yet, contradicting the words of Jamal's fiancée who had been waiting outside the consulate's front door, MBS said, 'My understanding is he entered and he got out after a few minutes or one hour'. But he also equivocated about this, adding, 'I'm not sure'.

'We are investigating this through the foreign ministry to see exactly what happened at that time'.

Amiably, he directed subtle responsibility for the fate of his 'friend' (his own words) Jamal at Turkey. 'We hear the rumours about what happened,' said MBS. 'He's a Saudi citizen and we are very keen to know what happened to him. And we will continue our dialogue with the Turkish government to see what happened to Jamal there.'

The crown prince used the rest of the Bloomberg interview both to brandish his profile both as a new broom and as a conservative, while dispatching any criticism of him personally as a consequence of the machinations of the kingdom's enemies.

'I didn't call myself a reformer of Saudi Arabia,' he said. 'I am the crown prince of Saudi Arabia and I am trying to do the best that I can do through my position.'

He addressed the arrest of women's rights activists in his kingdom and accused them of espionage. It was the same blame-the-foreigner strategy that the profiles in support of him used on social media.

'They have connections with agencies of other countries,' he said, naming Iran and Qatar. 'They have a network, connection with government people, leaking information for the sake of these other governments.' The activists, who had been calling for women's right to drive, had not been formally charged and were denied contact with their families following their arrest five months earlier, or so he said.

MBS also addressed Donald Trump. On exactly the same day Jamal was lured into the consulate and assassinated, the US president had, in an extraordinary statement, said at a political rally in Mississippi:

'We protect Saudi Arabia. Would you say they're rich? And I love the king, King Salman. But I said "King – we're protecting you – you might not be there for two weeks without us – you have to pay".'

Donald Trump's statement was so curious that it became instant global news. Like Vladimir Putin's unscripted reflection on 'traitors' the next day, it was an uncanny coincidence.

In response, MBS was adamant to Bloomberg that the Saudi royal family were no puppets of the US. He smoothly brushed off Trump's comment.

'We believe that all the armaments we have from the United States of America are paid for, it's not free armament,' said MBS, focusing on Trump's suggestion that the US paid for the Saudi military. 'So ever since the relationship started between Saudi Arabia and the United States of America, we've bought everything with money.' Warmly MBS went on to express his delight with fellow billionaire Donald Trump.

Trump had registered eight companies in Jamal's town, the Saudi beach resort Jeddah, after MBS's $500 billion bonanza to turn Saudi Arabia's Red-Sea coastline into a holiday destination and shortly after launching his presidential campaign. Trump already had a hotel bearing his name in neighbouring UAE.

'I love working with him,' MBS gushed about his new-found billionaire friend of March 2017. Like Jamal, Trump was a critical friend, though, and MBS said, 'You know, you have to accept that any friend will say good things and bad things. If you look at the picture overall, you have 99 per cent of good things and one bad issue.' He had sounded a lot more measured about friend Jamal, but the Bloomberg journalists left it at that.

Then, on Friday night at around 11pm, everything changed with a media leak to a young PhD student at Brown University's Watson Institute in Washington, DC. It was the first semi-official sign that, whatever had happened to Jamal Khashoggi, it was not good – 'and by not good, I mean terrible.' Selim Sazak, a smiling, pleasant-looking, round-faced, well-dressed 2015 Fulbright scholar and researcher at NATO, posted these words on Twitter ('studies things that blow up', according to his handle until May 2019). He said that a senior Turkish official had told him this.

Instead of a hostage situation or a rendition of Jamal, his words placed the events at the consulate in an entirely different category. They were taking on the appearance of a secret execution by a state of one of its citizens on hostile soil of the kind that had happened almost seven months ago to the day in Britain when Russian secret-service agents sought to assassinate Sergei Skripal and his daughter. Britain had not been able to prevent the attack in Salisbury, and nor had Turkey known about the strike against Jamal it seemed from Sazak's words. Many more leaks by Turkish officials would percolate hereafter, all similar in that they were highly suggestive but not necessarily forensically detailed.

Who else knew more? US intelligence knew at least as early as the beginning of September that Jamal's rendition was being mooted. So did GCHQ in Cheltenham. Had either of those two shared information with others?

'We were initially made aware that something was going in the first week of September, around three weeks before Mr Khashoggi walked into the consulate on 2 October, though it took more time for other details to emerge', a 'highly placed' intelligence source leaked to a British Sunday paper on 29 October.

The Saudi memos intercepted by GCHQ circulated in Riyadh

around the time Jamal and Hatice decided to get married, Hatice went to the Fatih Marriage Office around 7-8 September and Jamal's son Abdullah learned about, as well as met, Hatice for the first time on 10 September in Istanbul. He contacted the Khashoggi family back home in Saudi Arabia and told them about Jamal's new engagement to a Turkish woman. As the marriage, Jamal's application for US citizenship, and the rendition memos concurred, the conclusion seems inescapable that the palace worried betrayal of thirty years of trust was but a matter of time and that action had become imperative.

Either way, the GCHQ intercepts of the rendition left little to the imagination that force would be used against Jamal by the Saudis. 'These details included primary orders to capture Mr Khashoggi and bring him back to Saudi Arabia for questioning. However, the door seemed to be left open for alternative remedies to what was seen as a big problem', the senior British intelligence source leaked.

What did these intercepts actually mean to people working in British intelligence – or US intelligence for that matter? Intelligence gatherers are 'in pursuit of information, rather than evidence'. They don't find a neat email with a blue-print, arrows, operatives and goals. It is a game of inferences and statistics. 'There is rarely a definitive point at which "enough" intelligence has been harvested.' 'There comes a time when an intelligence service or operative simply has to make a stab at assimilating what all this means.' This is what the UN delegation concluded having gone through intelligence intercepts with the benefit of hindsight (detail 39).

GCHQ had intercepted Jamal's rendition information in early September from the 3 quintillion bytes steaming around the world every day. It caught GCHQ's fine-grained cyber net to identify threats to the UK. 'FIVE EYES coverage of the world is pretty impressive. The alliance is electronically promiscuous – if I can put it like that. It hoovers up gigabytes of stuff each day that is then fed through their computers looking for patterns,' said a senior security expert with No 10-level clearance and daily experience with secret intelligence reports interviewed for this book.

In other words, intelligence services have to act 'in anticipation of an event' as the UN report stated. British intelligence had to anticipate and pursue information that fit into a pattern of behaviour. It is clear that the contents of the intercepts raised fears that London could be targeted as a location for Jamal's abduction in the way the Russians had used London for their unfinished business with former KGB colonel Litvinenko (and Salisbury for former GRU colonel Skripal). Although it might never happen, this was the event it worried about. Jamal had made is self-exile very public on 18 September 2017, and wrote critically about the Yemen war in which the UK arms industry supplied billions worth of weapons to Saudi Arabia (£4.7bn-worth would be stopped by the Court of Appeal on 20 June 2019). After his intelligence posting at the Saudi embassy in London and years of writing for London-based Arab publications, Jamal was a regular visitor to the UK. He had stayed for weeks when he was first contemplating moving to the US or Turkey in April 2017 and also in July that year when having dinner at central-London's Clos Maggiore restaurant.

While some intelligence fears and patterns may prove to be chimaera, such as the Weapons of Mass Destruction in Iraq, the Saudi rendition plot of Jamal was, in fact, real and trigger-ready. In Riyadh, the Saudis were actively looking for a suitable foreign location to deploy their rendition team against Jamal. 'The fact that a team was put together and operational within 48 hours tends to point to a "Special Operation" scenario, with core team members already appointed and in place, ready to act whenever the order comes. Such a level of preparation is unlikely to have occurred otherwise.' This is what the UN delegation concluded in its report having reviewed the forensic evidence and interviewed experts (detail 199).

The first red flag for British intelligence was hoovered up as early as 24 September when the Middle East Monitor put on the website of its PLO conference, 'A late addition to the line-up of speakers is Jamal Khashoggi, Saudi journalist and the former editor-in-chief of al-Arab

News Channel'. Jamal's presence at the high-profile conference could not do anything else but lock London into the rendition matrix GCHQ had uncovered earlier in the month.

Was this, then, the moment British intelligence assimilated all the information at its disposal and decided to act and prevent another Skripal-style attack from happening? According to the senior security expert with no 10 intelligence experience interviewed for this book, it would have prompted an immediate interdiction. 'I have no doubt that our people would have known that something by the Saudis might be going down in London and suggested that the dirty work should be done elsewhere. That's how it works.'

Meanwhile, British intelligence continued to be on high alert about the feared cloak-and-dagger operation on British soil. Anything could happen during this four-day visit. First, Jamal flew into Heathrow on Friday late afternoon. This would have been another set of flags. Since four fifths of the 9/11 attackers were Saudi special attention is paid to who goes where when. From Jamal's Turkish Airlines flight details and his hotel reservation at the Ambassador Bloomsbury hotel by the PLO conference organisers, it was clear that he would be in Britain for four days from Friday to Monday evening. 'Air travel is subject to a whole load of checks since 911. Saudi spooks would alarm the system pretty damn quick', said the senior expert interviewed for this book.

Other red flags soon appeared like poppies on a field. The first movement was of two Saudi secret-service personnel travelling to Riyadh on Saturday at 3.15pm, shortly followed by others at 5.15pm (UN detail 81). *Sabah* reported that al-Muzaini, the Saudi chief-of-station in Istanbul, had travelled back to Riyadh from Istanbul's Sabihah Gökçen Airport. The Turkish government paper had CC-TV grabs of him arriving at the departures lounge at 2.33pm. Everything remained peaceful, however, on the London-front from Friday to Sunday and nothing happened. But things started moving again on Jamal's last day, Monday 1 October, when he was due to fly out at 10pm in the evening on Turkish Airlines.

To start with there was al-Muzaini, the Saudi secret-service whose flight back to Istanbul was for Monday. On his Saudia flight SV263, leaving Riyadh at 11.10am and arriving at 3.25pm in Istanbul, were also three members of the Saudi Tiger Team – major-general Abahussein, lieutenant al-Arifi and intelligence officer al-Zahrani – with at least one additional consular security staff member who had left for Riyadh on Saturday (detail 82, S'F'263 there) as well. The Saudis had pressed the nuclear button after all as British intelligence feared and were in pursuit of Jamal, who was still in London.

'On 1 October we became aware of the movement of a group, which included members of [the Saudi secret service] to Istanbul, and it was pretty clear what their aim was', the highly-placed British source told the Sunday paper. MI6's response was immediate. 'Through channels we warned [Saudi intelligence] that this was not a good idea', the source said. The attack plans, whatever they were exactly, would have to be stopped was the message. Nothing happened and Jamal left Heathrow unharmed. The crisp warning seemed to have been heeded.

But suddenly further flags started popping up while Jamal was on the plane. There were three flights of lower-level Tiger Team operatives with flights arriving two hours before Jamal's Turkish Airlines plane touched down at 4am in Istanbul – lieutenant al-Bostani, MBS security team member al-Hawsawi, MBS royal guard Khaled al Otaibi. Then there was the flight plan and passenger manifest with the nine Tiger Team operatives on the first private jet heading to Istanbul, first filed with the European Organisation for the Safety of Air Navigation at 8.30pm, and amended an hour later at 9.23pm to insert diplomatic cover subject to Eurocontrol rules (UN detail 86). The passenger manifest included to two people who were linked to Jamal through his work for Saudi intelligence – brigadier-general Maher Mutreb and major Badr al-Otaibi (detail 87) – and four linked directly to MBS.

By the time of Jamal's departure, it was virtually certain that while any Saudi plan to plan an attack on British soil had been nipped in the bud, Jamal was likely going to be attacked somewhere in Istanbul. As would be the case. 'Subsequent events show that our warning was ignored', the Sunday paper's intelligence source observed.

Although British intelligence couldn't have known this, the UN delegation's access in 2019 to recordings inside the consulate of secure telephone calls made clear that – seizing the moment – Saudi intelligence was indeed poised to strike, picking the theatre of its rendition plot on Friday afternoon just before Jamal was heading for Heathrow. But it was not London where it would take place but Istanbul. The selection was down to sheer opportunism rather than long-standing planning to capture Jamal there.

The first call to alert Riyadh of Jamal's consular visit was made by Istanbul Saudi security attaché Saad al-Qarni without orders precedent to do so that Friday. He said, among other related things, to Maher Mutreb at 2.27pm while Jamal's plane was still taxiing, 'we did not receive any letter from our service regarding whether there is any problem or not on him' (detail 27).

When questioned in the UK Parliament on the 29 October report in the Sunday paper, foreign secretary Jeremy Hunt replied, 'But, I did not know about this attack.' He had previously said 'It is not possible for a foreign secretary or indeed any minister to comment on intelligence matters.'

British intelligence's decision to inform the Saudis but not their US colleagues would have been congruent with the decision of Trump administration officials not to forewarn its resident of the impending plot. If GCHQ had shared that 'alternative remedies' for 'a big problem' had become a fact on the ground, the Trump administration would almost have no escape from its duty to warn Jamal. At least from September, Trump intelligence staffers were sailing into potentially very tricky legal territory by not sharing with Jamal its internally widely circulated intel that Saudi Arabia was about to make a move.

The decision to keep information from a US resident would look curious if something did happen and it ever came to light – even if no one would ever believe that President Trump's verbal attack on Saudi

Arabia the day after the rendition were somehow connected through real-time knowledge. The US excuse wrote itself if Jamal vanished without a trace after his rendition – which is after all the point. In case of a lawful arrest, there was no duty on the US intelligence services to pre-warn a US resident. And who would know for sure in the case of a ghostly disappearance?

But the optics would be less good if the rendition came to light. At worst, it would start to look like tacit approval of the rendition of a US journalist by the Trump administration.

As the latter situation obtained, Trump officials were in the end forced to defend themselves from breaching US government order ICD19. Their excuse, cast in serpentine language, boiled down to the argument that it wasn't clear whether Jamal would be lawfully arrested or illegally detained or killed. Jamal himself had repeatedly asked Saudi officials in the US whether there was a Saudi warrant for his arrest, which suggests that he had a good grasp of the far-reaching implications of such a warrant had on his safety abroad.

Apart from many other things, there was no upside for US intelligence to share its August/September intercepts with NATO ally Turkey. Nor in embarrassing MBS, an otherwise enthusiastic ally of the US and President Donald Trump, who was nurturing an order book of $350bn with the kingdom. On NBC's Meet the Press on 26 June 2019 Donald Trump would inflate this figure to '$400 to $450 billion over a period of time' and diminish the importance of the Khashoggi affair by saying 'It has been heavily investigated... I have seen so many reports', prompting the presenter to say 'you'll overlook some of this behaviour'.

There was also the Kurdish situation in Turkey's neighbour Syria where the US and their NATO ally were on opposing sides.

And there was the fact that President Erdoğan had seriously irked Trump by not releasing Andrew Brunson, a US pastor Turkey held captive since the military putsch against Erdoğan in the summer of 2016. He had been charged with being a member of the Gülenist Terror Group (FETÖ) in Izmir province and spying for them and convicted to three years imprisonment. Following Trump's angry tweets against Turkey on the subject of Brunson, there was little love lost in Washington for the obstinate Erdoğan who refused to release the pastor. Earlier Trump had imposed drastic sanctions that made the Turkish lira plummet by 45 per cent in August 2018.

One suggested reason (by *Forbes* writer Melik Kaylan) for Erdoğan's intransigence in the Brunson case was the corruption file the US were gathering for sanctions against specific Turkish people under the 2012 Magnitsky Act. They included Erdoğan's confidants and family members. More to the point, the file included phone-taps of President Erdoğan himself telling his son to stash away millions of Euros around the house. The phone-taps had been certified as admissible evidence in a 2017 court case against a Turco-Iranian trader called Reza Zarrab. According to the *Forbes* writer, Erdoğan had no intention of budging until his associates and family members were taken off the US sanctions list which made them financial pariahs.

14

Cui Bono?

In order to reconstruct the causes of past events, Karl Marx stipulated 'who benefits?' – as did lawyers in ancient Rome, *cui bono*? Setting aside the question whether or not they interfered with events around Jamal Khashoggi's rendition, the leader of one country certainly both benefitted from the furore that ensued and had a very effective policy of causing the US to tailspin.

When Vladimir Putin spoke about the Khashoggi case at the Valdai Discussion conference of 18 October in the Black-sea beach resort Sochi, he echoed Donald Trump's own official response. Vladimir Putin declined action or sanctions against Saudi Arabia when asked this question by Raghida Dergham, a former colleague of Jamal's at Saudi-funded newspaper *al-Hayat* where he had his column until 2016. Putin agreed with Trump that more facts were needed about Saudi governmental involvement before taking measures against the kingdom as a whole.

'We first need to wait for the results of the investigation' to conclude who is behind the assassination, Putin said.

'How can we, as Russia, start to harm our relationship with Saudi Arabia without knowing what really happened?'

Putin went on to draw a comparison between Jamal and the poisoning in Salisbury with *novichok*, the top-secret state-of-the-art Russian chemical nerve agent, of Sergei Skripal, his daughter, detective sergeant Nick Bailey, Charley Rowley, as well as the agonising death of Dawn Sturgess, a little over two months earlier in Britain.

Complaining bitterly about US and European sanctions against

Russia over the Salisbury *novichok* attack he argued, 'There's no proof with regards to Russia, but steps are taken.' The *novichok* sanctions against Russia were unfair, unjust and unfounded in other words. There was no solid proof that either he, his associates, or Russia, had anything to do with the top-secret state-of-the-art poison. Or at any rate, not more proof than there was in the Khashoggi case.

The facts in Jamal's case were really no different from the Skripal one, he claimed. 'Here, people say that a murder happened in Istanbul, but no steps are taken [against Saudi Arabia]. People need to figure out a single approach to these kinds of problems', he said exquisitely needling the West. It wasn't equitable for the US and UK to blame Russia for the deployment of a secret Russian-state nerve-agent on foreign soil. 'Enough evidence' was required Putin said, pleading for justice for Russian behaviour.

Other countries without a free media formed a chorus line behind Putin's complaint that the Skripal sanctions against Russia were unfair. A Chinese media outlet helpfully connected the dots made by the Russian president. Eager to make clear that 'citizens' rights' were no more than a cudgel of West democracies to bully other countries around the world, the Chinese outlet commented sourly that it 'shows that there are double, even multiple standards for the West's human rights diplomacy'.

In a further dig Putin went on to say that, 'the US bears a certain responsibility' for the assassination of Jamal Khashoggi.

Putin clarified that he really did mean genuine responsibility rather than merely moral responsibility: 'we can see that complicated processes are also taking place within the US elites', he spelled out. The US had had a part in the events.

Drily he concluded, 'I hope America will not go as far as Saudi Arabia did.' If it wasn't a slip of the tongue, it was a peculiar throwaway comment. He had said moments ago there was 'not enough evidence' that Riyadh was behind Jamal's assassination, whereas now he seemed to imply Saudi Arabia was the culprit.

Russia worked closely with Turkey. It was already building Turkey's first nuclear reactor in Akkuyu. And another long-term Putin objective was to peal Turkey away from NATO and draw Erdoğan ever closer into the military orbit of Moscow.

Or as, the *Moscow Times* wrote on 15 April 2019 in a candid appraisal, 'Without firing a single shot, deploying a single tank or using a single internet troll, Moscow can soon destroy the unity of NATO by removing a key country from its military network.'

The prize the *Moscow Times* referred to was Turkey's out-dated air-defence system. As a NATO member, Turkey had committed itself to a minimum of 100 F-35 fighter jets from Lockheed at $70 million each. The Turkish air force had already taken possession of the first one on 17 June 2018, though their F-35 wasn't allowed to leave the US just yet. But it was available for training Turkish fighter pilots. The deal was worth $8bn and up to 7 per cent of F-35 parts would be made in Turkey since it was one of the eleven countries investing in the state-of-the-art fighter jet.

But Erdoğan was at the same time looking to update Turkey's antiquated anti-air defence and had ordered China's FD-2000 missile defence system in 2015. Since that would be tantamount to handing secret F-35 data to China, the Obama administration had kyboshed the Chinese deal and forced Turkey to reopen the air-defence tender. Aggravating his NATO partner again, Erdoğan had thereupon picked Russia's long-range s-400 system. It meant that secret F-35 data would now be shared with Russia instead of China once Turkey got the fighter jets.

The Trump administration was pressuring Turkey to cancel the order for the s-400 system and pick a NATO supplier, either the US Patriot system or the Franco-Italian Eurosam. But, unlike the Obama administration, it had been spectacularly unsuccessful.

Three weeks after Turkey started the drip drip of fly-on-the-wall details of the assassination, Erdoğan's defence minister Hulusi Akar confirmed that Turkey's order for four s-400 units at $2.5bn from Rosoboronexport, Russia's main arms-export agency, would go ahead.

The s-400s would be on Turkish soil from October 2019. As a countermove, the Trump administration then struck back on 1 April 2019 and halted the delivery of all F-35s to Turkey.

As opposed to the US, having excellent relations with President Erdoğan, and detailed knowledge of anything that goes on in Turkey and Istanbul in particular, was crucially important to Russia. Its one and only warm-water shipping and naval route ran from the Black Sea through the Bosphorus to the Mediterranean. This maritime route was so strategically important to Russia that, when the EU looked close to bringing Ukraine into its fold, Vladimir Putin didn't think twice about occupying Ukraine's Crimea and its Black-Sea ports for both commercial and military reasons.

Helping Turkey was not only good for business and military strategy, it would also destabilise the dysfunctional relationship between the Trump administration and Congress, and put pressure on the US relationship with Saudi Arabia. The Mueller investigation laid bare on 18 April 2019 how astutely Russia operated. It gathered secret intelligence on Hilary Clinton which it filtered to the Trump campaign via Julian Assange's Wikileaks on 16 March 2016, promptly after Donald Trump asked for it publicly during a campaign stunt on 3 March. Russia's swift response at minimal effort had created towering waves for three years and counting, not least once again through the proof of Russia's actions detailed in the Mueller Report of May 2019. Donald Trump himself reignited the issue on 13 June as to whether he would accept damaging information on a Democratic candidate from a foreign power: 'It's not an interference. They have information. I think I'd take it.'

15

Thunderbolt

On 6 October, at 11pm the Turkish government followed up its leak to PhD student Selim Sazak with the first climactic leak to international-news agency Reuters. Turkey's 'we don't have any information' stance was replaced from one day to the next with 20/20 vision. How was that possible?

'The initial assessment of the Turkish police is that Mr Khashoggi has been killed at the consulate of Saudi Arabia in Istanbul,' two anonymous Turkish officials told the news agency. 'We believe that the murder was premeditated and the body was subsequently moved out of the consulate.'

Suddenly the fact that Turkey thought (and therefore had precise information on what had gone on inside the consulate) that Jamal's fate was premeditated murder hit the international media like a thunderbolt.

Hatice Cengiz was aghast and found the new twist to the story hard to believe. She tweeted, 'Jamal was not killed and I cannot believe he was killed!' She later added that she was waiting for official confirmation from the Turkish government of the leaks by its officials.

The *Washington Post* editors gave the news report credence in Saturday's paper of 6 October. 'If the reports of Jamal's murder are true, it is a monstrous and unfathomable act,' said Fred Hiatt, the *Washington Post*'s editorial page editor. 'Jamal was – or, as we hope, is – a committed, courageous journalist.'

Suddenly, over the course of a few hours, Saudi Arabia was on the back foot. Saudi officials continued to claim that Jamal entered the consulate but left shortly afterwards. But they released no CC-TV footage to back up the claim.

'Entries and exits into the embassy, airport transits and all camera records are being looked at and followed. We want to swiftly get results', President Erdoğan officially told Reuters himself on Sunday. But he also moved his language away from Jamal being detained at the consulate – the version his spokesperson Ibrahim Kalin had previously presented. 'I hope we will not be faced with a situation that we do not want,' he said, describing Jamal as 'a friend' and 'a journalist I have known for a long time' – it was not clear whether they could communicate in the same language since Jamal spoke no Turkish.

He had added, 'My expectation is still positive'. Erdoğan's words allowed Turkey to reel back from the information Turkish officials had leaked 'unofficially' to Reuters, but were not the truth in hindsight. There was no 'positive' outcome for Jamal and Erdoğan knew it when he spoke those words.

Erdoğan's personal advisor, Yasin Aktay, however, heralded to the Saudis what would later become Turkey's new public version of the events at the consulate. He presented a hunch to CNN Turk – no longer owned by CNN but bought in March 2018 with a state loan by AKP-cheerleader, the Demirören group, also owner of Turkish newspapers *Milliyet* and *Hürriyet* – 'My sense is that he has been killed. The Saudis are saying we can come investigate, but they have of course disposed of the body.'

He threatened, 'There is concrete information; it will not remain an unsolved case. If they consider Turkey to be as it was in the 1990s, they are mistaken.'

The information leaked to Jamal's friend Turan Kişlakçi of the Turkish-Arab Journalists' Association who was a further degree removed from Ankara officialdom, went yet another step further in contradicting what Ankara had said so far.

'It is certain that he was killed,' he said, reporting that 'lower officials' had leaked to him that Turkey had evidence that his friend had been murdered in a 'barbaric' way, made to 'faint', and 'dismembered'. The officials had told him, 'make your funeral preparations'.

The Turkish authorities had not yet officially produced any proof to support claims that Jamal had been assassinated. Unofficially authorities were leaking that details of their investigations would be made public in the days ahead. Nor had President Erdoğan publicly challenged Riyadh. Turkish diplomats were trying to keep the fallout 'under control' behind the scenes. Saudi Arabia and Turkey could still find a solution together. That is to say, Ankara would agree to sweep the new information Turkey had about Jamal's assassination under the carpet as long as the Saudi terms were right.

Saudi Arabia could assume Turkey knew certain things for a fact. Security officials would have access to all available surveillance data from 5.50pm on 2 October: CC-TV, airport data, consular phone records, consular car movements, etc. But they also knew the Saudi attack itself had been strategically excellent. Everything had depended on avoiding that disparate pieces of information from these sources came together too soon for their opposite numbers. And all Saudi operatives including the local secret service staff tainted by the operation had safely been exfiltrated from Istanbul to Riyadh.

It was hardly suspicious for consulate intelligence chief al-Muzaini to fly to Riyadh for a briefing on a Saturday and back on the Monday. It was also perfectly normal for six Saudi men to fly in from Riyadh. Every day some 147 flights passing through both Riyadh and Istanbul off-loaded Saudis. Even if Turkish intelligence had made a point of tracking the Saudi intelligence chief's movements, it would still have been impossible to connect the six other arrivals to him – or indeed to Jamal. It would only be obvious if you possessed the cyber capabilities that the UK and US shared through the Five Eyes Alliance (dating back to 1941). 'The difference in reach and analytical power between Five Eyes and the next best is huge', said a senior security expert with No 10-level clearance interviewed for this book.

For Turkish officials the nine men on the Gulfstream would be as invisible as if they had arrived on one of the many scheduled flights from Riyadh. The arrival of Saudis on a private jet run by Prime Aviation, the largest private jet company in the Middle East with 70 per cent of the market, was hardly a reason for anyone to sit up and take notice.

However, nine operatives arriving on one private plane did have one operational disadvantage. It made detection very easy once Turkish officials knew a hostile Saudi operation was taking place. Arriving on a single jet would make it a race against time for the Tiger Team not to get caught as it was logical for Turkish officials first to match entry data from all private jets arriving from and departing for Riyadh with camera surveillance at the consulate. It would be a mountain of work to do the same with pictures of all Saudis arriving on the hundreds of commercial Riyadh flights over the previous days. It was important to delay that moment of detection for as long as possible.

While the single-jet arrival may have upped the stakes of the gamble, it did mean that the Tiger Team could time their Istanbul arrival with Jamal's within half an hour. Since it was a theoretical possibility that the six earlier Tiger Team arrivals might already be tracked by MİT, the Saudis checked in at different hotels to make it more difficult to make a connection between the three sub teams.

And indeed, once Turkey had made the match between the first team member's face driving through the non-public back-gate of the consulate but arriving through the public entrance and the same face on the private jet, they knew they had located the Saudi strike team. The airport's passport, CC-TV and manifest data would quickly tell MİT that the Saudi team had nine members. Identifying the jet would lead to the discovery that the Gulfstream IV on which the nine men arrived earlier in the morning was still waiting on the tarmac at Atatürk Airport's Genel Havacilik private-jet terminal. Not only that. Seven men were due to fly out of Istanbul on the same jet.

In a frantic rush, a Turkish team was dispatched to inspect the Gulfstream thoroughly and to make sure Jamal wasn't being smuggled out of the country. Officials also carefully checked all the luggage on board. They cleared the plane for take-off nonetheless. It was on the runway 60 minutes after the seven operatives went through airport security. This marked a delay of 25-30 minutes compared to the departure of the first jet, of whose existence the Turkish investigators were not yet aware.

Through the Turkish data trail, the idling plane on the tarmac was clearly linked to the operation – the Saudi strategists must have realised this and maybe planned it as a 'sitting duck' to divert attention away from the more important getaway jet. The sitting-duck's flight plan was filed at 8.30pm London time, but cancelled and refiled at 9.23pm – while Jamal's Turkish Airlines plane was taxiing to its Heathrow runway – under diplomatic clearance. It would make it almost impossible for Turkish airport authorities to prevent the plane from taking off – unless Turkey wanted to wanted to create an international incident.

This was the second private Gulfstream that landed in the afternoon and took-off almost immediately. It was trail-free, at least until it would be boarded for take-off by members of the Tiger Team linked to the operation by having arrived on the 'sitting duck' earlier in the morning.

Invisible to the Turks until then, this second Gulfstream IV bought time for a safe escape. Passenger manifests at Atatürk's Genel Havacilik private-jet terminal were provided on a form in hand-writing, and last-minute filing may have provided additional time cover. Once the operatives' passports were scanned at airport security an alert might be tripped, but Turkish authorities would still not know which plane they were on until the hand-written manifest was entered into the airport's databases.;

Many incriminating items were taken back home on this jet, Turkish authorities later leaked unofficially. In the team's luggage were scalpels, two syringes, scissors, three staple-guns, two defibrillators, one signal jammer, ten telephones, five radios and wireless intercoms for the radios. Even boarding a private jet with items might cause delay, but not if you are a diplomat and have safe passage. Brigadier-general Maher Mutreb, the man who had made the decision to kill Jamal, was on this jet and travelled on a diplomatic passport.

Certainly the getaway jet took one of the shortest routes out of Turkish airspace from Atatürk Airport in around 45 minutes. The 'sitting-duck' jet would idle for another four hours on the tarmac, made a stop at Nallihan between Istanbul and Ankara, and then skirted along the longest arc through Turkish airspace for almost two hours heading for Dubai.

The fact that, once Turkish intelligence had made the first match through CC-TV around the consulate to the arrival jet, they also knew that all nine men on the Gulfstream IV were hostile operatives had another consequence. It also meant that they would start to track all their movements around Istanbul against the visual data of MoBeSe.

It was the collated data of the nine men and this pan-Istanbul CC-TV that would then lead Turkish intelligence to the names of the other six operatives on the team once they boarded the 'sitting duck' jet to travel back with the one member who had arrived on the same plane earlier in the morning – pathologist Salah Tubaigy. Although possible, it was unlikely that they would have been able to get these six names any earlier from visual matches with commercial arrivals given the amount of visual data. Their passports, once scanned through security, could now be linked to arrival data on commercial flights of the previous days and matched with footage around the consulate and the airport and the movements of the men through MoBeSe.

By matching up entry and exit data, there was also a data trail for Turkish officials to the 'getaway' Gulfstream because six of the original nine would leave on this hitherto unassociated jet. The trail to this jet would start either when their passports were scanned by Genel Havacilik's private-jet airport security or when the jet's passenger manifest was filed. The risk level would depend on the moment this data was available for actual analysis by MİT.

Here the Saudi timing worked optimal in favour of their tight operational schedule. The six including Mutreb had gone through security 5 minutes before the Khashoggi investigation started at 5.50pm.

This left the men 35 minutes till take-off and another 45 minutes to get out of Turkish airspace. It was enough – Turkish intelligence hadn't yet connected all the dots on the evening of 2 October. The Gulfstream IV that had left Riyadh when Jamal called to confirm his consular appointment was treated like any business jet at Atatürk and took off without problems.

From the arrival data of the nine men, MİT would also be able to conclude that – as only seven of them departed on the 'sitting duck' – two operatives were still at large after both jets had left Turkey. These men left for Riyadh on a commercial flight, going through customs at 0.18am after midnight apparently without receiving any special attention from Turkish authorities. Turkish airport authorities acted only to prevent Jamal from being smuggled out of the country as opposed to stopping these stray Saudi operatives from leaving the country.

In fact there were four more pieces of the puzzle. Hidden among all the Turkish data was also the departure of an additional team of four conspirators propping up the operation. The consulate's secret-service chief al-Muzaini left on a commercial flight for Riyadh at 9.32pm, an hour before the 'sitting-duck' jet. Three more accredited secret-service staff at the consulate left the same evening. None would ever return to Turkey. None were prevented from leaving Turkey.

As soon as Turkey had reviewed the consulate's MoBeSe footage of thirteen cameras – how long could it have taken to review a few hours of recordings? – and had figured out that a strike team of at least fifteen men had descended on Istanbul, Turkey would also know for a fact that Jamal had never left the consulate from the footage. But such a negative was difficult to summarise in a concise piece of evidence.

The CC-TV footage from outside the consulate also captured a lot of car movements by consular vehicles. The same was true of the footage in front of the consul-general's residence. Both buildings had carports screened from the street, but the MoBeSe street-camera aimed at the consul-general's home also looked over the wall straight at his front door. The footage captured numerous large suitcases and bags being brought inside his home. All this was also known as soon as the MoBeSe footage of two of the cars led Turkish analysts to the consul-general's residence.

Ömer Çelik, a spokesman for the ruling Justice and Development Party (AKP) still said on Saturday 6 October, as if Jamal might still be alive, 'A journalist disappearing like this in a secure country like the Republic of Turkey is something that will be followed up with sensitivity.'

Yet, while he said that publicly, Turkish officials had the day before offered their version of what took place at the consulate for inter-governmental eyes only. They had met Saudi diplomats in Ankara on Friday and presented their conclusion that Jamal had been killed at the consulate. They would leak that they had this meeting to the *Wall Street Journal* three weeks later. The diplomats had promised to report this to Riyadh and the Turks were waiting for the response from their Saudi counterparts, even as Çelik still talked about the old version to the press that Erdoğan's spokesperson had put out there on 3 October.

To the consternation of Turkish authorities and Erdoğan's fury they discovered on Saturday that, instead, by way of indirect response, consul-general Mohammed al-Otaibi had invited Reuters on a televised tour of the five-storey premises at 8.17pm. 'The Saudis were making fun of us', a person close to Mr. Erdoğan said, 'It was insulting'.

But was it an act of Saudi arrogance, or was Riyadh merely convinced that their consulate's cyber umbrella was impenetrable and the operation otherwise a solid success? In the latter case, based on what Turkish officials had told them that Friday, they would have thought that Turkey was on a fishing expedition. In other words, was al-Otaibi instructed to call Turkey's bluff because the Friday version was different from what Turkey had previously told the Saudi authorities through diplomatic channels?

'We are worried about him,' al-Otaibi claimed on camera. The consul-general looked like an exceptionally well-dressed Mr Bean. He took the Reuters TV-crew on a guided walk-through, opening cupboards, the women's bathroom, small glass-doors in library cabinets and large solid doors covering shallow electrical equipment and air conditioning units, walking through the Spartan hallways in his consulate. It might have been meant to inspire the viewers' confidence, but he appeared testy instead. 'But look, he is not here', he told the camera.

He complained that 'The idea of kidnapping a Saudi citizen by a diplomatic mission is something that should not be put forward in the media.' While the consulate was equipped with security cameras, al-Otaibi said he couldn't provide images of Jamal on his way out, because the Saudi cameras only provided a 'live-stream' that wasn't backed up anywhere. He did not address the fact that all the CC-TV footage outside his consulate would have made it clear that Jamal never left the building.

He also showed the Reuters camera-crew around one of the attic offices with tall cream-coloured leather desk chairs as well as his own office, dominated by paintings of King al-Saud in the centre, King Salman to the right and Crown Prince bin Salman to the left. They looked over his shoulder when he was seated behind his desk.

The consul-general, a tall, moustachioed man dressed in a grey, slightly shiny suit with a small pin-stripe, white Windsor-collared shirt and blue discreet paisley-style silk tie, had one further observation about the man whom he knew first-hand had been assassinated by Saudi government operatives four days earlier in his consulate.

The suggestion that Jamal Khashoggi had been abducted in the building was based on 'rumours that have no proof', 'talk of his kidnapping was baseless'. Hopping between the facts like MBS, he was in a very technical sense telling the truth. He also offered that such rumours were 'disgusting'.

This Reuters visit became the trigger for Turkey to advance their new version in public. Officials leaked the first details of other facts they had established. But – in what would be the theme of Turkey's changed campaign – officials would only speak on condition of anonymity and refuse to disclose their evidence. It meant that Turkey could plausibly deny what had been leaked or tack to a different story line if that suited better.

Washington-based PhD student Selim Sazak, who had that evening tweeted the first scoop on Turkey's new version, was also given an additional scoop – that Jamal was no longer in the consulate but had been taken out of the building, based on CC-TV footage in Turkey's possession.

'They don't know that Jamal Khashoggi was murdered,' Sazak still said in an interview to the *Independent* further to his Twitter post.

'They know that he came in, didn't come out. They saw unusual personnel activity, including uncredentialled personnel, coming to the embassy almost immediately after Jamal Khashoggi's first visit so they think they were dispatched from Riyadh, and they speak of an unknown staffer, acting like he was moving out the embassy, packing stuff into his trunk, and leaving at the end of business the day Jamal Khashoggi disappeared. So they add up the pieces to infer that Jamal Khashoggi was incapacitated and spirited away.'

Other anonymous security officials then gave Reuters the world-scoop that Jamal had been killed and his death had been pre-meditated which lit up the global news wires. The Turkish officials also shared with Reuters that, 'based on their initial findings, the police believe that [there was] a team especially sent to Istanbul and who left the same day'.

This Reuters report also first mentioned that it was a team of fifteen Saudis that had arrived on 2 October and was suspected of having been sent there to seize him.

To Turan Kişlakçi, president of the Turkish-Arab Journalists' Association officials again leaked the full scope of Turkey's knowledge. 'They followed the cars, and they know what happened. We [Turkey] have all the details, and he was killed', he said.

The Middle East Eye news site was handed another inflammatory scoop on Turkey's new version of events. An anonymous Turkish official leaked to them that 'everything was videotaped to prove the mission had been accomplished and the tape was taken out of the country'. A person 'briefed on the matter' would leak on the same day to the *New York Times* that MIT had 'obtained' a copy of the video. But this additional claim, published on 9 October, that there was a video in MİT's possession was never repeated or confirmed by Turkish authorities after that date.

Fred Hiatt, editorial-page editor at the *Post* summarised the stand-off between MBS and Erdoğan succinctly: 'If the story that was told about the murder is true, the Turks must have information and videotape and other documents to back it up. If the story the Saudis are telling, that he just walked out... after half an hour, if that's true, they ought to have facts and documents and evidence and tapes to back that up.'

It was a cat-and-mouse game, with the facts about Jamal in the middle. Turkey's economy was wilting under the Turkish lira freefall. The fall itself had made moving to and buying a flat in Istanbul an easy proposition for Jamal, but it made the cost of a fight by Erdoğan with trade-partner Saudi Arabia higher. Yet the events also handed Erdoğan unexpected opportunities.

Intense diplomatic discussions continued in secret. Despite the new information Saudi Arabia continued to stonewall Turkey.

16

Pastor Brunson

On the other side of the world, the fate of pastor Andrew Brunson was like a buoy floating on the surface – tethered to the equally intense Khashoggi-related diplomacy between Erdoğan and Donald Trump. The Turkish economy, once seemingly unstoppable, was sagging with 15.9 per cent inflation and Erdoğan needed the US both as a mediator and also to resume the influx of Western money. Jamal's disappearance was shaping itself into a key that would resolve a number of hitherto intractable problems.

For the US, Brunson's 2016 incarceration had been an election rallying cry aimed at Trump's evangelical voters. For this voting block his running mate Mike Pence was the Brunson-*cause-célèbre*'s poster child. Despite persistent pressure from the US – where the Christian conservative lobby relentlessly agitated for his release and where Trump regularly tweeted about this 'great Christian' – Erdoğan had stubbornly refused to release the pastor. His release was a core 2016 election promise and when Turkey pulled back yet again from early release in August 2018, Trump had been furious. He had doubled tariffs on Turkish steel and aluminium, causing a further collapse of the Turkish lira.

The arrest was in itself curious as Brunson had had a flock of no more than twenty four congregants. But for Turkey, Brunson was connected with the cleric blamed by Erdoğan for the 15 July 2016 putsch against him. This cleric, Fethullah Gülen, lived in longstanding exile in rural Saylorsburg, Pennsylvania, protected by US law from extradition. Ironically, Gülen had been instrumental in harnessing popular Islam at the beginning of Erdoğan's rise to power in what had been secular, Kemalist Turkey operating in the image of founder Kemal Atatürk. But that was then.

Three days after Jamal's assassination, Trump excitedly tweeted on Friday 5 October, 'Working very hard on Pastor Brunson!' It was the day on which Turkey had had its meeting with the Saudi diplomats in Ankara about the affair and Erdoğan realised Riyadh wasn't going to budge as a result of their version,

In the heat of the Khashoggi stand-off with Saudi Arabia, Turkey decided to drop its refusal to hand the pastor over to the US. Erdoğan released Brunson within a week. The miraculous early release from the pastor's three-year prison sentence was officially because of 'good behaviour' and Erdoğan merely said about the release that he was 'bound by Turkish law'.

Instead of a looming public-relations disaster regarding 'a certain responsibility' of the US (in Putin's gnomic words) flaring up around the disappearance of Jamal, a US resident under the 'genius' or O-visa, there were instead jubilant headlines for Trump. Before lightning struck on Saturday, a triumphant photo opportunity for Trump with the now celebrity pastor in the White House beckoned.

On 13 October the finally-free Brunson would tearfully pray for Trump to have 'supernatural wisdom' in the Oval Office. While he kneeled before the president, Trump remained seated. Other collateral US damage of the 2016 putsch, such as a number of imprisoned US consulate workers and the holidaying NASA scientist Serkan Golge, were less fortunate than the pastor. These people remained locked up in Turkey – in the case of Golge in solitary confinement.

Four weeks later, yet more evidence of the sudden thaw in Turkish-American relations would emerge when both Turkey and the US, shortly after one another, started 'unilaterally' to roll back sanctions against black-listed government officials. Later, on 19 February 2019, the US also announced that it would withdraw troops from Kurdish Syria, which had thwarted the Turkish army. On 21 May, Turkey complied with

US oil sanctions against Iran after a 6-month reprieve given on 1 November. What had changed on Friday that brought about such a quick and unexpected resolution to the Brunson impasse, and personal sanctions against those close to Erdoğan being lifted?

Erdoğan meanwhile told Reuters on Sunday that he was closely following the Khashoggi case 'personally' and that 'entries and exits into the embassy, airport transits and all camera records are being looked at and followed. We want to swiftly get results'.

Leaks surrounding Jamal's fate by Turkish officials started to gather more pace. Now that the word 'murder' was part of the discussion, rumours started swirling around social media that Jamal had been dismembered and removed from the consulate in several parts inside body bags, fuelling further shock, embellishment and still scepticism in the absence of any real proof.

'Turkish sources insist that Jamal Khashoggi was tortured, then killed and his body cut up,' tweeted Saudi whistle-blower Mujtahidd, who had more than two million followers.

'All this was filmed and the video was sent to Mohammed bin Salman so he could enjoy the scene. If this is confirmed, then it seems like the news that he was removed from Turkey and has arrived in Saudi Arabia isn't true. Tomorrow Turkey should announce full details.'

Turkey was looking for more than that. Yasin Aktay told Qatari broadcaster al-Jazeera on Sunday 7 October: 'We demand a convincing clarification from Saudi Arabia, and what the crown prince offered is not convincing.'

Turkish daily newspaper *Hürriyet* (Liberty) another government mouthpiece owned by AKP standard-bearer Demirören group, suggested that the Saudis had taken Jamal out of the building by cutting his body into fifteen pieces – the first time this number was mentioned.

The rumour mill soon got out of control with the Iranian channel IRTV1 reporting the unfounded but sensational claim that Jamal's corpse had been found in a neighbourhood in Istanbul five days after he had disappeared.

On 8 October, Jamal's friend and Erdoğan's personal adviser, Yasin Aktay, wrote in his column in Islamist *Yeni Şafak* (New Dawn) yet another government mouthpiece, owned by the AKP billionaire Albayrak family: 'Although we are still trying to maintain optimism, we were not able to prevent the abduction or brutal killing of Khashoggi, whose ideas and stance I have followed with great appreciation and approval.... I know that all precautions have been taken.'

'We never had the opportunity to protect him, to do something when he was still alive,' he said, by way of an excuse for Turkey's impotence in preventing what had taken place. He assumed in the piece Jamal was dead. They had talked the month before about the targeting of Saudis on Turkish soil. 'He voiced his concern about possible operations against Saudi citizens.... He was confident they couldn't conduct such operations in Turkey.'

Yeni Şafak also added some conspiracy theories of its own by blaming the PLO, Israel, the UAE, the US, apart from MBS.

The non-religious, traditional Kemalist-socialist aligned *Aydinlik* (Enlightenment), a non-AKP newspaper, carried its own speculation on the affair and alleged that Jamal was a spy and had brought 'significant documents' from Saudi Arabia.

'It is known that Khashoggi had left the country with several files containing secret information. Some of them are thought to be in Istanbul while others are in Washington,' it claimed.

'The team and mentality that poisoned Yasser Arafat [the late chairman of the Palestine Liberation Organisation] to death is also behind the Khashoggi murder. Killers like Mohammed Dahlan [the former leader of Fatah in Gaza] are in the backstage. The Dahlan team studied Turkey a year before 15 July [Turkey's 2016 coup attempt] too! Although a journalist in opposition to Mohammed bin Salman has been killed, the signature belongs to Mohammed bin Zayed al-Nahyan [the crown prince of Abu Dhabi]. He is Salman's patron. And the patron of both of them is US-Israeli intelligence.'

Nearly a week after Jamal had gone missing and on a Brunson-high,

Donald Trump was ready to address the issue in public as well.

'I am concerned about it. I don't like hearing about it. And hopefully that will sort itself out. Right now nobody knows anything about it, but there are some pretty bad stories going around. I do not like it,' the US president offered.

US secretary of state Mike Pompeo asked for a thorough and open probe by authoritarian Saudi Arabia into Jamal's disappearance.

'We call on the government of Saudi Arabia to support a thorough investigation of Mr Khashoggi's disappearance and to be transparent about the results of that investigation,' he said in a statement.

Giving a coy insight into US intelligence on the matter he added the vague words that he had seen 'conflicting reports' on what had taken place at the consulate.

President Erdoğan, on a trip to Hungary, stirred the cauldron further. 'There are some people who came from Saudi Arabia,' he said, part-confirming officially what had been leaked unofficially about a team arriving in Istanbul. 'The public prosecutor's office is looking into the issue.' He added that CC-TV footage from the airport was being studied.

As for Saudi Arabia's refusal to provide CC-TV coverage of Jamal leaving he said, 'Whose duty is it to prove that he left or not? The consulate's officials should. Don't you have cameras and other things?'

Senior officials in Ankara upped the ante and leaked that a convoy of six vehicles left the consulate two hours after Jamal entered, and that this was of particular interest.

They said that security camera footage showed objects being loaded into a black van which carried diplomatic number plates. After leaving the consulate, three cars turned left on to a main road while the remaining three turned right. Investigators said one of the vehicles, a van with blacked-out windows, had become the focus of the investigation. It had already been tracked to a nearby motorway where CC-TV showed it taking the D100, the highway leading to Ataturk Airport.

'There were some vehicles,' said Yasin Aktay. 'There were fifteen Saudi personnel inside. They were carrying bags and going to the airport.

Turkish security cameras can follow up until the airport.'

Two of the vehicles were of particular interest according to the Washington-based PhD-student Selim Sazak who had been given the first confirmation that Jamal's fate was bad. He was now revealing to the *Independent* more information leaked to him.

'One, on the suspicion that it might have been used to carry Jamal Khashoggi out of the consulate. Another, on the suspicion that it might have been used to shuttle some of the people involved,' he said, citing a briefing by Turkish officials.

Though used as the opening conduit by Turkey's government, the US-based Sazak did not seem to be part of the Erdoğan inner circle. He wrote in November in the US magazine *Foreign Policy*, part of the same stable as the *Washington Post*, about civil liberty in authoritarian states, 'What is an intellectual debate in the US is a daily struggle there. It gets you sued, fired, exiled, arrested, even killed'.

Turkish newspaper *Sabah* (Morning), on the other hand, was unequivocally a government mouthpiece. Its morning edition led with speculation about the van that was involved: 'The black minibus will explain the riddle of the Saudi journalist.... [It] left the building two hours after Khashoggi entered the mission.' The paper said the police were looking for this suspicious vehicle.

The Turkish police now confirmed officially that they were examining the flight records showing that two private Saudi Gulfstream IV jets had arrived at Istanbul's Atatürk Airport on Tuesday and departed separately that same day, hours after Jamal was last seen. They already knew this on the day itself, but the Turkish government now went on the record with this information. If negotiations with Saudi Arabia had taken a different turn, it might, presumably, have never become public knowledge.

Finally there was a response. While Saudi authorities continued to insist they had played no role in Jamal's disappearance, they now acknowledged that a 'security delegation' had been sent to Istanbul. The weight of evidence from Turkish CC-TV required some response. But the Saudis did not offer a reason for the journey of this security delegation.

In Saudi Arabia, however, where MBS had an even greater control over the media and thus the story than Erdoğan in Turkey, the statements arising from the disappearance took a different turn. Jamal's media peers who now headed Saudi outlets took care to block the rumours and leaks from abroad and created a different context.

The website of Saudi-funded al-Arabiya TV said that the Khashoggi family were in contact with the Saudi authorities over his disappearance. Jamal's eldest son Salah told the station: 'The issue is that a Saudi citizen has gone missing. We are co-operating with the Saudi authorities to discover the circumstances of the incident. . . .' Obligingly he added, 'The whole thing is a personal issue and is completely unrelated to politics.' Though US citizens, both of Jamal's sons had been placed under house arrest after the murder and were barred from leaving Saudi Arabia.

After chairing a family meeting in the Saudi city of Jeddah, legal counsellor Muatassim Khashoggi also confirmed his faith in the royal family: 'We trust the government and the measures it is taking. All efforts being exerted in Jamal Khashoggi's case are being coordinated with the authorities and the embassy in Ankara.'

He accused foreign media of using his cousin's disappearance to 'attack our country for negative purposes'.

In a sidebar he added that they had never heard of Jamal's 'alleged' fiancée Hatice Cengiz.

'We don't know her and we don't know where she came from,' he said. 'She is not connected to the family in any way. Her tales and her existence could be part of her personal agenda.'

Salah, Jamal's oldest son from his first wife and a Saudi banker, agreed emphatically: 'I don't know this woman. I'd never heard of her before except from the media.'

Although Salah's brother Abdullah had told the Khashoggi family of his 10 September trip to Istanbul, when he met Hatice and his father, and of their father's marriage plans, Salah and his uncle Muatassim professed not to know anything about her to al-Arabiya. To anyone listening inside Saudi Arabia, Jamal's family were laying out the facts of the case and foreigner Hatice was lying on behalf of an enemy intent on soiling the reputation of the kingdom.

17

Horse-Trading

On the evening of Sunday 7 October, the Saudi ambassador to Washington, the crown prince's brother, Prince Khalid bin Salman or 'KBS', joined the fray to counter the rumour of Jamal's assassination.

Fred Ryan, the publisher of the *Washington Post* had sent a letter to KBS asking for clarification. It was delivered via diplomatic channels to the prince, facilitated by the Trump administration. But the administration's responsiveness to help had quickly evaporated midweek after MBS had made the call to the White House to say that Jamal was a dangerous Islamist. After Saturday's shock news of murder in the consulate by Reuters, KBS had finally responded and agreed to meet at 9pm at Ryan's Georgetown home.

'Jamal has always been honest', KBS said, 'We have never perceived him as being an asset of [a hostile country] or anyone else'.

'It's impossible that this would be covered up and we wouldn't know about it', he assured the publisher.

Asked about the rumours of the two Gulfstream jets by Ryan, KBS said this was 'baseless', the consulate's CC-TV 'weren't recording', allegations of Saudi involvement were 'ridiculous', and 'Saudi investigators' were already at the consulate. It was the same line that al-Otaibi held during his Reuters walkabout in the consulate. Ryan would later call the ambassador a liar who should be 'shunned'.

The next day KBS also sent an unprompted WhatsApp message to a news reporter in the US at a different outlet.

'I know that many people here in Washington and around the world are concerned for his fate, but I assure you that all reports saying that

Jamal Khashoggi vanished in the consulate in Istanbul, or that the kingdom's authorities detained or killed him are completely false and baseless,' the 30-year-old ambassador wrote.

He did, however, confirm both Jamal's importance to the palace and the unease of Saudi top royals about the fact that he lived outside the kingdom: 'Jamal has many friends in Saudi Arabia, and I am one of them. Despite differences on a number of issues including what he called his "self-exile", we kept in touch when he was in Washington.'

Echoing the recital by the Khashoggi family – whose members based in Saudi Arabia were under a travel ban – the prince painted a picture of 'Jamal' as someone 'who has dedicated a large part of his life to serve his country'.

KBS went a step further. He supported unreservedly the testimony of consul-general al-Otaibi and called the rumours about Jamal's fate 'malicious' and 'outrageous'.

His WhatsApp message went on to promise, 'Jamal is a Saudi citizen whose safety and security is a top priority for the kingdom, just as is the case with any other citizen. We will not spare any effort to locate him, just as we would if it were any other Saudi citizen...'

KBS flatly contradicted Hatice Cengiz's words that Jamal was nervous about his first visit to the Istanbul consulate on Friday 28 September. The ambassador claimed, 'This was not his first visit to the consulate in Istanbul, as he regularly came to the consulate (as well as the embassy in Washington) in the last few months for citizen services', though he did not provide evidence to back up this statement.

The ambassador also claimed incorrectly that 'Turkish authorities and the media were allowed to inspect the consulate building in its entirety.' All that had happened so far was that Reuters had been given a guided publicity tour by the consul-general.

There was subsequently speculation about the role of KBS in the assassination plot and that he had personally lured Jamal to either the embassy in Ankara or the consulate in Istanbul. Several friends reported that Jamal had told them he had made inquiries at the Saudi embassy in

DC, fuelling the idea that MBS's brother was a co-conspirator. If true, it would be an additional explanation of the Saudi chatter about rendition of Jamal that GCHQ and US intelligence had picked up in September, and also why Jamal was worried that consular staff in Istanbul might refuse to help him with the marriage certificates – Jamal feared he had pulled a trip wire by reaching out to diplomatic staff for marriage documentation.

But, when Jamal's fiancée Hatice Cengiz was asked about this by Turkish media, she made a point of clarifying to *Hürriyet* on 26 October that Jamal hadn't talked to her about having contacted the Washington embassy to sort out the Saudi certificates required under Turkish law. If he had, she thought, he would have told her. She herself had gone to the Fatih Marriage Office on 7 or 8 September to find out while Jamal was in the US.

It looked, however, as if Jamal wasn't always in the habit of sharing his plans with Hatice. The UN inquiry reported in June it had been given credible information 'that Jamal attempted to obtain the needed marriage documents online and within the United States but was told he needed to obtain them in Turkey' (detail 199, footnote 165). Presumably, this was an online response, logged on the computer Hatice gave to the Istanbul police. Online Jamal could apply under a pseudonym and, unless they had access to his computer, Saudi authorities would not be forewarned of his intentions.

The *Washington Post* now published the last known photograph of Jamal Khashoggi – a still from the leaked CC-TV footage showing him entering the Saudi consulate at 1.14pm. It was probably also the one Turkish authorities showed Hatice Cengiz on Tuesday at the beginning of their investigation. Turkish officials said that if Jamal left the consulate he would have come out of the same door and would have been captured on the same camera (they also had cameras aimed at the back entrance of the consulate, but didn't yet disclose this).

Meanwhile, BBC 24 published at 7.22pm off-air audio from an interview Jamal gave in London, three days before he disappeared.

Asked if he would return to Saudi Arabia, he replied: 'I don't think I will be able to go home again. When I heard of an arrest of a friend who did nothing, it makes me feel like I shouldn't go. The people being arrested aren't even dissidents, they just have an independent mind.' By way of apology for the broadcast the BBC said, 'We wouldn't normally release this conversation but we've decided to make an exception in light of the circumstances.'

The BBC was criticised on social media for airing the recordings without Jamal's consent and before there was any definitive proof of his death as opposed to mere rumours, however credible by this stage.

It was particularly upsetting to Ms Cengiz. All she had to go on was leaked media information by anonymous Turkish officials. Turkey had still not given an official account of what happened to Jamal at the consulate according to the facts in its possession. In fact, officially Turkey still treated the diplomatic impasse as if Jamal was inside the consulate.

'I no longer feel like I am really alive,' she said. 'I can't sleep. I don't eat. As his fiancée, as someone close to Jamal and in love with Jamal, I am waiting for information from my government about what has happened to him. Where is Jamal?'

While waiting for access to the premises, the Turkish police announced officially that it had formed a 'special team'. They would look for DNA belonging to Jamal inside the mission, using Luminol and infrared light to find bloodstains, as well as 'K-9' police dogs in the search, they said. It was waiting for the consulate's response to its request to search the place.

There was no official Saudi response. But it was clear that, behind the scenes, the Turkish government was still negotiating with Riyadh. Erdoğan's adviser and Jamal's friend Yasin Aktay suddenly seemed to wheel back from his earlier 'hunch' that his friend had been 'brutally' murdered and that Saudis had 'of course, disposed of the body'.

Aktay said in an interview to *Russia Today*, reported by the *Saudi Gazette*, that his friend's 'killing is not an official statement' and that 'the

Saudi state is not blamed here'. It was even reported that he 'hinted at the possibility that Jamal was abducted by a third party, or perhaps by members of what he called the "deep state",' a reference to the 2016 putsch which – according to Erdoğan when his power was secure again – had been organised by many military officers, judges, journalists, and other professionals with affiliations he didn't like. Though whether these were in actual fact Aktay's real words or ones liberally translated from Arabic by the Russian outlet and gratefully copied by Saudi-broadcaster al-Arabiya was unclear.

Turkey's willingness to compromise on the truth, however, was also flagged up by government-controlled paper *Sabah*. It said Turkish investigators were considering that Jamal had been transported in a van seen parked in front of the consulate on the last image of Jamal alive and smuggled out of the country on one of the two Saudi Gulfstream IV jets that had left in the evening of 2 October. Arab newspapers loyal to Saudi Arabia gratefully seized on *Sabah*'s new rumour.

Turkish investigators of course knew this wasn't the case from MoBeSe CC-TV coverage which they still kept a secret from everyone. At the same time, Turkish authorities told US and European officials that they were certain about the killing but that Ankara was willing to climb-down in exchange for concessions from Riyadh. It was unclear who did the leaking about concessions here, but the *Guardian* and others reported it.

Also, *Yeni Şafak* columnist Kemal Öztürk reminded everyone of the leak that 'there are claims that there is a video of the moments Jamal Khashoggi was killed. I haven't seen it' in an interview on Turkish TVNET. It was the last mention of such a video.

In Saudi Arabia, however, the press stuck to the story that Riyadh was entirely blameless in the disappearance. It hit back at its critics. It was now no longer Saudi enemies who were to blame for the brouhaha, but it was what they called an 'international media campaign that did not verify the incident but relentlessly contributed to tarnishing the image of Saudi Arabia'. Putin and China would repeat a similar argument later when complaining about double-standards in Western sanctions.

The Saudi media also reckoned the 'campaign' was 'politicised by sides that aim at settling scores with the kingdom at the expense of the truth'. Foreign media were 'spreading poison in honey' said Saudi paper *al-Yaum* (Today).

Saudi Arabia's neighbours also gave MBS full-throated support. The UAE's foreign minister tweeted that a 'fierce campaign against Riyadh is expected, as well as the coordination between its inciting parties.'

Bahrein's foreign minister added, 'The target is the kingdom of Saudi Arabia and not the search for any truth. Throw your masks away.'

Meanwhile Iran's state-run Channel One thought it could kill two birds with one stone and reported without evidence that it was likely that Israeli Mossad agents had co-operated with Saudi Arabia in Jamal's murder.

But, under pressure, Riyadh finally opened the door a crack and on Tuesday it reportedly gave permission to Turkish investigators to inspect the consulate, in an unusual deviation from immunity of diplomatic missions.

Three Turkish investigators would be given access to all parts of the Saudi consulate, but not to the residence of the consul-general. Reuters' guided tour had been a light inspection, theirs would be a more full-flavoured one. They would, however, only be allowed a 'visual' probe and not a forensic one. The Turkish trio of officials would, by *reductio ad absurdum*, be delivering the Saudi CC-TV proof that Jamal had left the consulate and that President Erdoğan had been asking for.

18

Glasgow's Dr Death

Following Riyadh's grudging concession to allow for a visual inspection only, Ankara ordered a quick, unofficial leak of new facts to the media. In its Wednesday 10 October morning edition (which was available towards midnight the night before) *Sabah* published a big front-page splash with the names of all the fifteen men of the hit squad, giving the year of their birth, and printing face pictures as they passed through passport control or checked in at their hotels. They were aged between thirty and fifty-seven. Mostly moustachioed, they were dressed in anything from a red T-shirt to a smart dark blazer and open white dress shirt. Twelve were shown guiltily looking away from the camera and three at it with insolence.

Sabah reported that the nine people arriving on the first jet HZ-SK2 checked in at 5:51am until Friday at the five-star Mövenpick Hotel, within walking distance if not eye line of the consulate. The six others, the paper catalogued, arrived in two batches on 1 and 2 October and checked in at the five-star Wyndham Grand, also within striking distance of the consulate.

Both trios of Saudis who had arrived at Atatürk Airport on commercial flights – one in the late afternoon of 1 October and the other in the early morning of 2 October – left on the last private Saudi jet out at 10:46pm. *Sabah* therefore inferred that they formed part of one and the same group and were a Saudi hit-team sent for Jamal. The thin veneer of the leak was that the piece was a result of *Sabah*'s own investigations team.

The entire fifteen crew of the hit-squad left again within twenty four hours, in a rush despite their three or even five-day reservations, *Sabah* revealed to the public in its front-page scoop. It was noted that two Saudis who had arrived on the first private jet did not leave on either jet HZ-SK1 or HZ-SK2. Instead, they mysteriously left Turkey separately at 18 minutes past midnight on a scheduled flight.

On the heels of the *Sabah* revelations, Erdoğan's government launched a second close-range shot across Riyahd's bow for the Wednesday morning news bulletins. Grainy video detail from Turkey's CC-TV footage was leaked to Turkish channel 24TV. The clip was short, damning and thrilling.

It showed one of the two Saudi Gulfstream jets that had landed in Istanbul the day Jamal vanished. Marked 'HZ-SK1' and 'HK-SK2' an info banner said, the jets were reported to have come from Riyadh. The former landed at 3:41am with nine men and the latter in the afternoon at 4:29pm, after Jamal's disappearance.

The leaked footage next showed two men in summer clothes in the dark of night, and said six of them had left their hotel in small groups between 9.40am and 9.55am on 2 October. The same morning other crew members, the clip reported, bought large suitcases in Istanbul's Grand Bazaar, a 30 minute drive from the consulate.

The footage then cut to frantic parking activity by four Mercedeses with green diplomatic license plates in front of the consulate an hour before Jamal entered at 1:14pm. One of them was a Mercedes Sprinter van with green consular number plates, though the footage was too blurry to read the license plate number (later leaks would make it clear it was 34 CC 2342).

One hour and 54 minutes later, the clip said, the Mercedes van and a sedan with license plates 34 CC 1865 and 34 CC 1248, respectively, ('34' for Istanbul and 'CC' indicating consular staff) were seen being let through the roadblock in front of the consulate.

These two were shown speeding away in different directions while the van parked a few minutes later, at 3.07pm, on leafy Meşelik Street in front of the tall cream-coloured wall of the consul-general's imposing home about a mile or so away from the consulate. While the driver chatted to the guard at the home, an Audi sedan parked as well. At least half a dozen people then entered the house while the van itself pulled into the enclosed driveway.

The clip showed short stills only at double the speed and all one could make out was that people arrived and went into the house, but not how many or what they were doing. The fast-moving images conveyed furtiveness more than what was exactly on them.

If Riyadh was unconcerned about the negative publicity, the practical consequence of Turkey's release was that the anonymity of these fifteen members of MBS's elite Tiger Team was blown. If the team's total numbered around fifty, the cover of almost a third of its highly-trained operatives had been unmasked by *Sabah*. The permission for the three Turkish investigators to do a visual inspection of the consulate was withdrawn that morning.

For the international media, Erdoğan's team had prepared its own blitz. On Tuesday, at 10.30pm Turkish time, when *Sabah* was first available, the *New York Times* published leaks by Turkish officials to its reporters that one of the fifteen men was an 'autopsy expert', Jamal had been killed during a 'quick and complex operation' and dismembered with a 'bone saw brought for the purpose'. One of the anonymous Turkish officials summarised to the paper what they had discovered in a quotable phrase: 'it is like Pulp Fiction'.

Yet, the paper also still didn't discount that the truth would never come out in favour of 'a face-saving story blaming Mr. Khashoggi's disappearance on some third party, on rogue elements of the Saudi security forces, or on an accident during an interrogation that went wrong'.

'Turkish officials have left things murky enough – speaking on condition of anonymity and refusing to publicly disclose their evidence – that such possibilities cannot be ruled out. Some pro-government news outlets have reported that the police were still investigating the possibility that Mr. Khashoggi was abducted, not killed.'

Yet, later in the day on Wednesday, President Erdoğan's personal adviser Yasin Aktay backtracked full circle and claimed that he had never said Jamal could have been 'abducted by a third party, or perhaps by members of what he called the "deep state".' He blamed trolls for misquoting him the day before.

The conflicting leaks regarding a third party were brushed aside in yet more unofficial leaks explaining that these versions of the truth were the result of a snafu between different agencies in Turkey. The fact that there were wrong-and-right leaks to the media was, so anonymous Turkish officials claimed, because of limited sharing of information between these different agencies.

'They flew away with their secrets,' *Aksam* (Evening) yet another newspaper close to the government mused in its evening edition at the end of the day.

'It seems that a period of headaches is about to begin for Saudi Arabia. A big crisis could break out between Ankara and Riyadh.' Hopefully it added, 'The horrible "extermination" of a journalist could also bring about the end of Crown Prince Salman.' *Aksam*'s owner Ethem Sancak, was in Turkey's top 50 rich list and gave his media outlets AKP-favouring editors.

By now even Hatice Cengiz's optimism was dimmed by the deafening silence from her government. Officially, Turkey's position had still not changed from the week before – Jamal was missing and they were waiting for proof that he had left the consulate.

'Although my hope slowly fades away each passing day, I remain confident that Jamal is still alive,' she said. 'Perhaps I'm simply trying to hide from the thought that I have lost a great man whose love I had earned.'

Writing in the *Washington Post*, she said her fiancé had told her that he missed his native Saudi Arabia and homesickness had taken its toll on him. He had told her: 'I miss my country very much. I miss my friends and family very much. I feel this deep pain every single moment.'

'We were in the middle of making wedding plans, life plans,' she wrote. 'After the consulate, we were going to buy appliances for our new home and set a date. All we needed was a piece of paper.'

'He had been feeling so lonely, but I could see the clouds clearing,' she added.

Despite being worried about a wave of arrests in Saudi Arabia, she said, he did not fear anything would happen to him on Turkish soil.

'I implore President Trump and first lady Melania Trump to help shed light on Jamal's disappearance,' she said. 'I also urge Saudi Arabia, especially King Salman and Crown Prince Mohammed bin Salman, to show the same level of sensitivity and release CC-TV footage from the consulate.... Jamal is a valuable person, an exemplary thinker and a courageous man who has been fighting for his principles. I don't know how I can keep living if he was abducted or killed in Turkey.'

Later she wrote in the *New York Times*: 'I keep asking the same questions to myself: Where is he? Is he alive? If he is alive, how is he?'

'Had I known it would be the last time I would see Jamal, I would have rather entered the Saudi consulate myself. The rest is history: he never walked out of that building. And with him, I also got lost there.'

According to her, he had had no idea that he was putting his safety on the line by going into the consulate. 'He didn't really think it was a vital hazard.' Even though he had 'no foreboding of what was to come... He told me to alert the Turkish authorities if I did not hear from him soon.'

Her *Washington Post* statement about her fiancé's unpreparedness twisted the knife into the US intelligence community. In a way that was never meant to happen, it now was an issue why Jamal had not been warned of the impending threat despite being a US resident.

'He was cheerful the morning we were going to the Saudi consulate,' she explained.

Sabah had already published the names of the fifteen suspects of the hit-team and their movements and airport data. The next day it revealed in another scoop more background information on two members, one of them the 'autopsy expert' teed up by the leak to the *New York Times*. Salah Tubaigy, *Sabah* revealed was a doctor on the board of the Saudi Society of Forensic Medicine and an expert in post-mortem examinations. Mohammed al-Zahrani was a royal guard.

Using the names and head shots *Sabah* had published, the global press also started filling in the CVs of the fifteen-strong hit-team. The *New York Times* noted that Tubaigy was a 'figure of such stature that he could be directed only by a high-ranking Saudi authority'. Tubaigy had learnt his trade at Glasgow University, where he took a master's in forensic medicine, and he had spent three months with the Victorian Institute of Forensic Medicine in Australia. He was now being dubbed 'Dr Death'.

Other jet passengers were also being identified by the international and Turkish media. Taken together, the background information made clear beyond doubt that these were Saudi special forces.

They found there was a lieutenant-colonel in the Saudi civil defence force; a major and lieutenant in the Saudi air force; a lieutenant in the service guarding the crown prince's palace; and Maher Mutreb was quickly identified as a member of the Saudi intelligence community and former first secretary at the Saudi embassy in London where he was a former colleague of Jamal's. They had been identified via open source internet tools by Oslo-based researcher Iyad al-Baghdadi.

On Thursday 11 October *Sabah* also published a picture of royal guard Mohammed al-Zahrani, hobnobbing with Mohammed bin Salman, while Mutreb was with the Crown Prince's entourage during his trip to the US in April 2018. The *New York Times* was to confirm their names and trace their closeness to MBS through its own research. Al-Zahrani was the first link of one degree of separation between an operative and MBS himself.

CC-TV coverage was leaked by Turkish officials on 18 October showing Mutreb checking in at his hotel, arriving at the consulate at 9.55am, outside the Saudi consul general's residence on Meşelik Street at 4.53pm and clearing airport security at 17.49pm.

And yet officially it still remained unclear what had actually happened to Jamal Khashoggi, while Turkish authorities leaked they had pulled up the X-ray images of the jets' luggage that had been scanned by airport security officials to check for body parts. The scans of the first jet were merely routine ones before the Turkish police and intelligence services had opened their investigation at 5.50pm. But they had monitored seven Saudis in the airport waiting room while they checked their luggage for the second flight. This was all leaked, but none of it was on the record.

As assassination allegations mounted, the optics of the situation were increasingly bad and the Trump administration was obliged to say something more in view of the fact that Jamal was both a US resident and part of the *Washington Post*.

US press releases started rolling in. A statement from the White House said that several members of the Trump administration – John Bolton, the national security adviser, secretary of state Mike Pompeo and Jared Kushner, Donald Trump's son-in-law and senior adviser – had spoken to the crown prince by phone and asked for more details regarding the disappearance of the missing journalist.

Asked what advice he gave to MBS, Jared Kushner said: 'To be fully transparent. The world is watching.... Take this very seriously.' According to Kushner the crown prince's response was an off-hand sounding, 'We'll see.'

'The reports that a Saudi-Arabian journalist may have been tragically murdered in Turkey should be deeply concerning to everyone who cherishes freedom of the press and human rights across the globe,' weighed in vice-president Mike Pence who could at the same time look forward to pastor Brunson's surprise release that week. He promised Washington was ready to 'assist in any way' with the investigation.

'We cannot let this happen, to reporters, to anybody.' This surprising statement was from Donald Trump and an unusual reversal from his 'fake news' approach to members of the press. 'It's a very serious situation for us and this White House. I want to see what happens and we're working very closely with Turkey and I think we'll get to the bottom of it.'

But his eye was trained on the deal that he had been negotiating with MBS all along in the background. 'We don't like it even a little bit', he said a few days later. 'But as to whether or not we should stop $110bn from being spent in this country, knowing they have four or five alternatives, two very good alternatives, that would not be acceptable to me.' The $110bn was close to the figure that the first two 'Iron Bridge' nuclear reactors would cost.

Leading Republican on the senate foreign relations committee Lindsey Graham said there would be 'hell to pay' if the Saudis had murdered Jamal. 'If this man was murdered in the Saudi consulate in Istanbul, that would cross every line of normality in the international community,' he said. 'If they're this brazen it shows contempt. Contempt for everything we stand for, contempt for the relationship.'

Senator Graham also blamed the crown prince directly, not holding his punches on Fox News: 'Nothing happens in Saudi Arabia without MBS knowing it. I've been their biggest defender on the floor of the United States Senate [but] this guy is a wrecking ball. He had this guy murdered in a consulate in Turkey, and to expect me to ignore it, I feel used and abused. The MBS figure is to me toxic. He can never be a world leader on the world stage. Saudi Arabia, if you're listening, there are a lot of good people you could choose, but MBS has tainted your country and tainted himself.'

A bipartisan group of twenty-two US senators signed a letter to Trump that triggered a US government investigation and determination of whether human rights sanctions should be imposed over the Khashoggi affair. The provisions for this mandatory investigation were in the 2012 Global Magnitsky Human Rights Accountability Act.

This Act was one of the biggest eye sores of Vladimir Putin, as its broad injunctions against foreign individuals had been passed by US Congress further to the brutal killing of a Russian lawyer, in Russian custody in 2009, who was trying to expose Russian corruption. It required the US president to determine whether a foreign individual was 'responsible for extrajudicial killing, torture, or other gross violation of internationally recognised human rights against an individual exercising freedom of expression'. If so, sanctions were to be imposed. A lot of Russian officials and oligarchs had been sanctioned under the Act.

'Our expectation is that in making your determination you will consider any relevant information, including with respect to the highest ranking officials in the Government of Saudi Arabia,' the letter said.

Asked about suggestions in Congress that arms sales to the desert kingdom be blocked, however, Donald Trump replied that such a move would hurt the US economy.

'Frankly, I think that would be a very, very tough pill to swallow for our country'.

In Istanbul, further leaks burbled up as President Erdoğan authorised the release of additional evidence to put pressure on Saudi Arabia. They were still sitting on masses of secret MoBeSe footage around Istanbul that could be released anonymously.

But his team was still careful not to cross the line and circulate evidence that was conclusive proof as to what had really happened with Jamal. It was still the case, as the New York *Observer* put it, that 'the Middle-Eastern rumour mill can't agree whether the unfortunate man was murdered or merely abducted.'

Turkish investigators turned their attention, they said, to the issue of the missing security camera footage at the Saudi consulate. Turkish authorities leaked that they believed that the hard drive was removed when Turkish staff at the consulate were abruptly told not to come back after lunch, and then taken on board one of the jets. All the leaks bolstered the notion that the Saudi government itself was involved in Jamal's disappearance act.

Under pressure now that the odds that Jamal was dead were rising, US secret-service authorities were also leaking some of their own intel that showed that something was up with Jamal and Saudi Arabia – but that they didn't know what exactly it was. The *Washington Post* cited secret American intercepts showing that the crown prince had ordered a repatriation operation targeting Jamal. The paper reported unnamed US officials saying the Saudis had been heard discussing a plan to lure the journalist from his home in Virginia and detain him.

The White House finger prints on what Vladimir Putin termed 'a certain responsibility' were quite well marked by now. In addition to the earlier chatter US intelligence had gathered, the NSA had picked up intel by 1 October that something odious was about to happen to the *Washington Post* blogger. This was the same date by which GCHQ spotted the Tiger Team flights, though the NSA's 'big ears' intercepted Saudi communications on the matter rather than flagged-up flight data.

An NSA official leaked to the New York *Observer* that this latest 'big ears' intel was relayed to the White House through the official intelligence channels, as part of the NSA's duty-to-warn procedure. 'Odious' did not seem like a non-violent arrest, but the White House didn't explain why it had not acted on the NSA's 1 October alert.

Several of Jamal's friends confirmed that, for four months, senior Saudi officials close to the crown prince had called Jamal to offer him protection, and a high-level job working for the government, if he returned to his home country, but that Jamal had refused.

'There were offers made to Jamal to return from people close to the royal family, there were quite a few from al-Qahtani,' said a friend. The friend also gave another reason why Jamal didn't think the offers were very sincere. Riyadh in general, and Saud al-Qahtani in particular, were responsible for the break-up of his third marriage in Jeddah and his difficulties in seeing his four children and two grandchildren, and thus his growing loneliness in the US.

'His divorce took place partly because his wife could not cope with the propaganda being aimed at him by the government, and al-Qahtani, of course, was running the propaganda against all who were considered enemies.' The stress on their marriage became unbearable and she divorced him soon after he had broken with the palace.

These calls from Riyadh with job offers to return home had resumed around May 2018, the month Trump tore up the Iran treaty. Khaled Saffuri, a Kuweiti-American and co-founder with Republican Grover Norquist of the Islamic Free Market Institute, spoke to Jamal minutes after one of them. 'Are you kidding? I don't trust them one bit', Jamal had said. There was also a business man close to the royal family who made a point of seeing Jamal whenever he was in Washington, DC, keen to arrange for his return. How important Jamal really was to Saudi Arabia now became clear when it turned out that the crown prince – Saudi Arabia's ruler in all but name – was thought to have made at least one of the calls to Jamal himself.

Yet, despite the growing closeness Jamal had sought to President Erdoğan after he met Hatice Cengiz, Turkey was not a very safe place for most writers either. In fact, Erdoğan's record was far worse than that of Saudi Arabia.

According to the Sweden-based advocacy group Stockholm Center for Freedom that tracks cases of prosecutions of Turkish journalists, Turkey had 245 journalists behind bars as of 24 January 2018, with another 140 journalists facing outstanding arrest warrants. 'Turkey jails more journalists than the rest of the world combined', its secretary general Levent Kenez said on 23 May 2019.

Like Vladimir Putin after his election as Russian President in 2001, Erdoğan had increasingly throttled the relatively free Turkish press since his first rise to power in 2003 through popular Islam. In contrast, Reporters without Borders said that between twenty-five and thirty professional and non-professional journalists were being detained in Saudi Arabia, a country where there had never been press freedom.

Staying in the US would by far have been the safest place to continue writing for Jamal. But in the US there wasn't the connection to the government and governance in the Arab world as in Turkey, a fiercely independent country with the same GDP as Saudi Arabia, and historically the centre of the Middle East. It offered practical advantages too, for a writer in English and Arabic. While the Turkish-language media were held in a vice by Erdoğan's government, there was greater breathing space for those writing in English or Arabic in Turkey.

Nor would you get arrested as an expat for what you said during a dinner party. In Saudi Arabia, it had come that far. Saudi friends told Jamal this had happened to a member on the Consultative Assembly of Saudi Arabia, the *Majlis ash-Shura*, an advisory council of one hundred and fifty members. They were chosen by royal appointment and their main power was the ability to propose laws to the monarch.

'This really upset, Jamal' said Maggie Salem Mitchell, his friend and the director of the Qatar Institute. 'He felt real simpatico with Erdoğan', however.

'There was some kind of bond there. In how he viewed Erdoğan, it was with an eye towards what he [Erdoğan] had been during his earlier political career. Jamal saw there was some of that still there.'

For a former Saudi quasi civil servant, there was also a fundamental difference between Erdoğan's populist Islam and Riyadh's originalist thinking about the Koran – which makes no express mention of democracy. Under MBS Saudi originalism was contracting to absolutism in a way that populist Islam never could, at least not in theory. Even Iran – whose popular revolt led by Ayatollah Khomeini against the Shah had excited him in his youth – still had popular elections.

Mainstream Saudi political debate was in any case always far more politically conservative, religion-centred and self-censoring than in socialist-Kemalist secular Turkey. For Erdoğan's team Jamal's political views were entirely non-threatening. To Turkish publication *Ak Kalemler* (White Quills) Erdoğan's advisor and former deputy chairman of AKP Yasin Aktay had observed, 'he is known as the most intellectual person in Saudi Arabia... whose opinions should be followed.'

The democratic aspect of populist Islam appealed to Jamal as an historic inevitability. 'There can be no political reform and democracy in any Arab country without accepting that political Islam is a part of it. A significant number of citizens in any given Arab country will give their vote to Islamic political parties if some form of democracy is allowed.'

Jamal made this unassailable point on 28 August 2018 in one of his last pieces for the *Washington Post* Global Opinions online.

'Jamal was always full of hope', opined Maggie Mitchell Salem, his collaborator on pieces for his *Post* blogs and whose Qatar Foundation International paid for a researcher.

19

'Tourists'

Although Riyadh had cancelled the Turkish viewing of the consulate on Wednesday morning 10 October in a pique, the rest of the day had crashed over the news wires like a hurricane. The names of the fifteen men of the hit-squad was the *coup de grace*. It was only a matter of time before it became public knowledge that the fifteen men belonged to MBS's elite Tiger Team. It was time, according to the US, for damage control.

On Thursday 11 October, after holding out for nine days that there was no case to answer and still calling the rumours of Jamal's disappearance 'baseless', Riyadh finally conceded defeat. In the evening Ibrahim Kalin, President Erdoğan's spokesperson announced, 'Upon the suggestion of the kingdom, a joint-working team between Turkey and Saudi Arabia will be formed to investigate the case of Jamal in all its aspects.'

Although Kalin's wording was respectful of King Salman's high status as 'Custodian of the Two Holy Mosques' as one would expect from a populist-Islamic government, their essence left no doubt that the kingdom had caved in and had accepted, in principle, the widest possible brief for the team. Earlier in the week, behind the scenes, Jared Kushner had spoken to MBS and applied US pressure by mentioning the need for a 'working group'.

Another official close to the negotiations now also leaked, after Saudi Arabia's 'invitation' to Turkey, that the kingdom was close to 'accepting that a major crime took place at the consulate'. The source also mooted unofficially that 'Saudis intend to blame elements within their country's "deep state",' the story line Yasin Aktay had floated earlier on and punctured the next day.

As Saudi Arabia's original 'baseless' response had changed to a question that needed investigating, MBS's brother KBS, the US ambassador, unexpectedly left Washington DC for Riyadh. The US state department's spokeswoman said, in response, 'we expect some information when he gets back', but he would not be back in the US until December.

So far, Erdoğan's team had anonymously leaked CC-TV footage as well as flight and airport data. But this was all information from outside the building. Yet already on 6 October, 'lower officials' had leaked graphic details of the manner of Jamal's death to his friend Turan Kişlakçi of the Turkish-Arab Journalists' Association.

On 12 October an anonymous 'senior' Turkish official, speaking to the Middle East Eye, lifted the shadowy lid a little further and warned that 'investigators knew in which room of the consulate Khashoggi was killed and where the body was taken to be dismembered.'

How did Turkey know all this? Now that Riyadh had officially agreed there was a case to answer, Turkey finally launched its most convincing piece of evidence, or leaked it anonymously at any rate. Presumably, this was the evidence the Saudis had chosen to ignore behind closed doors on Friday 5 October in Ankara.

Turkey's decision to go public with this secret piece of information was curious. So far Erdoğan seemed to have no principled interest in establishing the truth and sought to negotiate instead. Now that Riyadh was signalling its agreement that a 'major crime' had occurred at the consulate, what more could be achieved? 'We never had the opportunity to protect him', Yasin Aktay had told the readers of conservative-religious AKP paper *Yeni Şafak*. Regardless, it was not a sign of strength to broadcast that on AKP's watch the country was treated like a killing ground by an adversary. Erdoğan's AKP would lose two important local elections in Istanbul and Ankara further denting his invincibility over half a year later.

Turkish officials explained the decision anonymously: Turkey had been surprised by the 'unprecedented international outcry' and the wave of positive international attention for the country.

Instead of appeasement Erdoğan went for the jugular. The *Washington Post* was given the scoop that would transform everything some eight hours after the official Turkish-Saudi-Arabian announcement of a joint-team investigation. Jamal's US paper said it had new 'shocking' and 'gruesome evidence'. Turkish officials who insisted on anonymity told its journalists that their government had made contact with the Trump administration and had described to US officials that they had a 'voice recording from inside'.

'You can hear his voice and the voices of men speaking Arabic', the Turkish official said. 'You can hear how he was interrogated, tortured and then murdered'. Another official leaked to the paper that you could hear 'beating'.

Now that the Turkish government had decided to cross the Rubicon and dispel any remaining public hope that Jamal Khashoggi was alive by leaking the existence of a murder recording, the media discussion promptly changed direction. In view of confirmation of Jamal's demise, the global press now charted the risks and perils of being a Saudi national.

Prince Khaled bin Farhan, a Saudi royal living in exile in Germany, told the *Independent*: 'Over thirty times the Saudi authorities have told me to meet them in the Saudi embassy but I have refused every time. I know what can happen if I go into the embassy.'

Only two thousand out of some fifteen thousand princes control Saudi Arabia's wealth and Jamal was, due to his closeness to the royal inner sanctum, an insider. A run-of-the-mill Saudi prince, while privileged, would have even less protection than he had. Khaled bin Farhan added that there was deep anxiety among ordinary royals as to what had happened to Jamal.

'Around ten days before Jamal went missing they asked my family to bring me to Cairo to give me a cheque. I refused. Many, many princes are in jail right now in Saudi. Just five days ago a group tried to visit King Salman saying they were afraid for the future of the al-Saud family, they mentioned Mr Khashoggi's case. They were all put in jail.'

Khaled bin Farhan's story echoed the fate of another royal, prince Sultan bin Turki, grandson of Saudi Arabia's first king, ibn Saud. He had vanished on the way Egypt in 2016 after criticising the Saudi regime.

'If I disappear you know what happened to me' was the last thing Sultan said to Bel Trew, the Middle East correspondent of the *Independent*.

Another of Sultan's friends said: 'I spoke to him before he got on the flight.... He actually joked that should he not make it, it was likely he was in Riyadh and I should raise the alarm.'

The prince was lured to Cairo, travelling on a royal private jet to see his father. But he was drugged and flown to Saudi Arabia instead. He was believed to be alive but under house arrest. His friends no longer had the means of contacting him. He had previously been kidnapped and drugged in Geneva in 2003 after calling for reform. Back in Riyadh he was held under house arrest and only returned to Europe in 2015 for medical treatment.

Prince Saud bin Saif, a relatively minor prince who publicly backed calls for king Salman's removal, also went missing in 2016. Prince Khaled bin Farhan thought Saud had been tricked into getting on a Saudi-owned private jet which, instead of landing in Rome, flew on to Riyadh. Prince Turki bin Bandar, once a major in the police who took to publishing videos criticising the regime, disappeared in 2015 after applying for asylum in France. Khaled bin Farhan believed both Turki bin Bandar and Saud may be dead.

While always oppressive, it seemed that the royal regime had shifted gears under MBS. Prince Abdulaziz bin Fahd, the forty-five-year-old son of the late King Fahd, allegedly disappeared in 2017 amid rumours he had been put under house arrest. Khaled bin Farhan said that Abdulaziz's family had no idea where he was, but they knew he was unwell. Also missing was Prince Khaled bin Talal, the fifty-six-year-old brother of Jamal's sponsor Saudi billionaire al-Waleed bin Talal, who was held in November 2017 at the Ritz Carlton. Royal family members said they have no idea where he was.

And in January 2018, Prince Salman bin Abdulaziz, an expert fencer and graduate of the Sorbonne, was called to the royal palace in Riyadh with some of his relatives. Soon after they arrived, a fight broke out reportedly between them and the bodyguards of the crown prince. The thirty-six-year-old Prince Salman was beaten unconscious. He had not been heard from since. His father, who was at the scene, was arrested two days later.

Non-royal Saudis were treated even more harshly. Ghanem al-Dosari, a Saudi satirist in exile in London, said he had not set foot in a Saudi embassy for nearly a decade, even though his passport expired in 2010.

'[The authorities] have a history of trying to lure people into embassies, they asked me to go inside the embassy in 2010 and I refused,' he said after Jamal went missing. 'I haven't travelled in years for fear of entering a country where I might be picked up. I know dissidents who are now scared to leave their apartments.'

He was attacked in a London street by thought-to-be agents of MBS's regime. Dosari, who has refugee status in the UK, published footage of two men hitting him in the face in the Brompton Road on his YouTube channel that mocks the Saudi regime in August 2018. According to Dosari, they said: 'F*** London – the Queen is our slave.' He had received death threats in the past, including a threatening phone call, which he taped and published.

Major-general Ali al-Qahtani, an aide to Prince Turki bin Abdullah, the son of the previous king, King Abdullah, and a prince seen as a potential rival to MBS, died in government custody after being detained in MBS's Ritz-Carlton shake-down of leading Saudis. The *Daily Telegraph* reported that the general's 'neck was twisted unnaturally as though it had been broken' and that his body had burn marks which appeared to be the result of electric shocks. General al-Qahtani was taken to hospital, but was reportedly returned to his interrogation after being seen by doctors. The palace did not offer an official explanation for how he died.

'People are very scared,' said a senior prince about the current situation. 'MBS is the reason people in my country are no longer sleeping.'

Days after the murder of Jamal Khashoggi, reports came through that a journalist had been tortured to death in the kingdom.

The authorities said Turki bin Abdul Aziz al-Jasser secretly ran a Twitter account called Kashkool, which exposed human rights violations by officials and the royal family in Saudi Arabia. He was arrested after Saudi moles in Twitter's regional office in Dubai unmasked him.

Amnesty International also reported that three female activists in prison in Saudi Arabia were subjected to electric shocks, torture, flogging and sexual harassment by officers. One of the men accused of involvement was Saud al-Qahtani, MBS's top intelligence enforcer.

There was also concern about Salman al-Ouda, a religious scholar detained after refusing to tweet in support of the Qatar blockade and who may face the death penalty.

Middle East Eye argued that it was ever thus and MBS was no exception. It recalled the case of Nasir al-Sa'id, founder of the Arabian Peninsula People's Union (APPU). He was regarded as the first and most prominent opposition figure to the Saudi royal family. Having begun his opposition work in the 1950s, he ran an opposition radio programme. Sa'id then moved to Yemen to set up an office for the APPU before going to Beirut where he disappeared in 1979, the same year he praised the takeover of the grand mosque in Mecca by an armed group of citizens and called for the fall of the house of Saud.

Insulated by an unlimited wall of money, such unwanted attention and grisly rumours never phased Riyadh much. In August 2018, for example, Canada's foreign minister tweeted her alarm at the imprisonment of the sister of a Saudi blogger Raif Badawi, who was himself in prison for 'insulting Islam through electronic channels' and sentenced to a thousand lashes. Riyadh announced a suspension of diplomatic ties, expelled the Canadian ambassador, declared a freeze on new investment and withdrew Saudi students from Canada.

In the case of Jamal Khashoggi Saudi-funded al-Arabiya TV merely reported on Friday at 4pm that the palace 'welcomes the Turkish response to the request to form a joint team into Khashoggi's disappearance', quoting an official Saudi source. The source added, 'We trust the ability of the joint team… to carry out its mission' as well as the mantra that KBS, the Saudi US ambassador, had WhatsApped a few days before, 'Saudi Arabia is concerned about the safety of its citizens.'

MBS's position in the kingdom remained unassailable. 'The bottom line is that the king has made it clear that despite the Khashoggi affair, he is not planning on removing his son,' a western diplomat told the *Sunday Times*. 'There is no group of people who are going to revolt against the king.'

Also, MBS was popular among ordinary Saudis who backed his social reforms. Apart from his great plans for the future, the palace didn't allow anything critical to appear in the Saudi media in any case. The killing of Jamal, a member of the rarefied Saudi elite and intelligence establishment, did not have a huge impact on daily life. The diplomat said: 'In Saudi they say they're sorry it happened but my wife gets to drive and I get to go to the movies.'

There were some business consequences though. Richard Branson froze business links with Saudi Arabia following Jamal's disappearance.

'I had high hopes for the current government in the Kingdom of Saudi Arabia and its leader Crown Prince Mohammed bin Salman and it is why I was delighted to accept two directorships in the tourism projects around the Red Sea,' he said. 'I felt that I could give practical development advice and also help protect the precious environment around the coastline and islands. What has reportedly happened in Turkey around the disappearance of journalist Jamal Khashoggi, if proved true, would clearly change the ability of any of us in the West to do business with the Saudi Government.'

'We have asked for more information from the authorities in Saudi and to clarify their position in relation to Mr Khashoggi. While those investigations are ongoing and Mr Khashoggi's presence is not known, I will suspend my directorships of the two tourism projects. Virgin will also suspend its discussions with the Public Investment Fund over the proposed investment [of $400 million] in our space companies Virgin Galactic and Virgin Orbit.'

Branson also pulled out of MBS's Future Investment Initiative conference in Riyadh – known as 'Davos in the desert' – along with World Bank president Jim Yong Kim, Uber chief Dara Khosrowshahi, Viacom's Robert Bakish, Steve Case, former head of AOL and Andy Rubin, the Silicon Valley entrepreneur best known for creating the Android smartphone operating system. Patrick Soon-Shiong, the owner of the *Los Angeles Times*, and the *Economist*'s editor-in-chief, Zanny Minton Beddoes, were no longer attending, and Arianna Huffington, the entrepreneur, media mogul and Uber board member, also pulled out of the conference, having previously served on its advisory board. The *Financial Times*, the *New York Times*, Bloomberg, CNN and CNBC withdrew as media sponsors. Ford and JP Morgan also pulled out, along with government officials from the UK, US and other western nations where the media was not under state control.

In an echo of Russia's lament of 'innocent visitors' to Salisbury regarding the Russian Skripal *novichok*-poison squad, Saudi-funded al-Arabiya claimed that the fifteen-man team whose pictures appeared in the Turkish press were, in fact, 'regular tourists'. The argument was based on the fact that the last jet out had been thoroughly searched by Turkish security forces and that nothing untoward had been found on board.

Unfortunately, al-Arabiya also based it on the fact that a number of the fifteen men were photographed in the commercial arrivals hall (hence 'regular tourists') and the others in the airport's private-jet terminal, two kilometres away from the main hall. While this was true, al-Arabiya misunderstood the data. After no more than between 30 and 20 hours in Istanbul the six men al-Arabiya claimed were 'regular tourists' flew out of Turkey on the less than regular second private Gulfstream IV jet. The broadcaster was called out on its sloppy journalism.

The UN inquiry would reveal that the ground work for al-Arabiya's 'tourists' scenario had been laid well in advance by Riyadh. When booking rooms for the Tiger-Team members the Saudi secret-service team in Istanbul, for example, could be heard using a tourism company and asked for rooms with a 'sea view' (detail 199).

20

Apple Watch

With the leak to the *Washington Post* that it had a voice recording in its possession, the Turkish government had introduced a knock-out new fact into the equation. But for Turkey to have a voice recording of what goes on inside a diplomatic building would require at least some explanation about its origins to be credible to the media – quite apart from the fact that it potentially constituted a breach of the Vienna Convention, which stipulated that a designated diplomatic space must not be penetrated by the host country. Erdoğan wanted to insist on 'human conscience' but could not rely on a flagrant breach of the law at the same time.

Ironically, the unintended consequence of crossing the Rubicon was that it would make clear that Ankara's pattern of behaviour in the affair was as unreliable as Riyadh's. It gave the Khashoggi news story a continued lease of life and continued to improve Erdoğan's standing on the world stage. But from this moment leaks were increasingly manipulated by Turkish officials in the way the news was orchestrated inside the country – as an opportunistic fantasy. As will become clear, the Turkish government would contradict its own 'facts' as much as Riyadh.

Once jolted by Erdoğan's immediate instruction in the afternoon of 2 October 'that all measures be taken', the Turkish secret service MİT had retrieved the situation by following up with some urgency on Hatice Cengiz's and Turan Kişlakçi's catalytic calls to Yasin Aktay that Jamal was missing.

Yet no one could call MİT's performance stellar before 5.50pm.

Yasin Aktay had said that 'all precautions' regarding Jamal's safety were taken but, unlike the US and UK, for example, Turkey had no idea that an attack was imminent. Furthermore, once they did know, they had had at least six of the perpetrators corralled in one place, yet let them all go.

Not that there was any dishonour in this. Despite the brute global reach of Five Eyes and GCHQ, MI5 and MI6 had been blind-sided in the Salisbury-Skripal attack, too. The Russian team had flown in and out of Britain without any hindrance as if regular tourists. The same had happened in the 2006 case of Alexander Litvinenko's assassins, Andrey Lugovoy and Dmitri Kovtun, and in the case of an estimated fourteen further murders on British soil since Putin came to power in 2001.

Given the amount of CC-TV and customs data, MİT had identified the Saudi jets that were involved on the evening of 2 October, though evidently not quickly enough to be able to be able to detain the Tiger Team members in terms of Erdoğan's 'all measures available' to MİT. By their own account, they were too late for the first one, and airport authorities had also cleared the second one for take-off at 10.46pm, never mind the departure of the four Saudi secret-service staff stationed at the consulate.

Even then MİT could still intercept the last two stragglers on Turkish soil – major-general Mustafa al-Madani and Saif al-Qahtani. These two Saudis had first come through passport control at the private-jet terminal at 3.41am that day. But they only exited through passport control at 0.18am to board Turkish Airlines flight TK144 to Riyadh for scheduled take-off at 1.20am.

This gave MİT at least another two hours to detain these last two perpetrators while still on Turkish soil and prevent them from boarding or take them off the plane. Turkey did leak information their stamp-time going through the security gate in the main Atatürk terminal and it was an unarguable fact that they, too, had left Turkey unhindered that evening. But it wasn't clear whether this was because MİT failed to identify the two in time or for some other reason, or whether airport officials had at the very least thoroughly searched their luggage. Turkey's anonymous leaks were mainly dispersed through Turkish papers and that meant they were a one-way street, taken as read.

These failures were understandable in view of the evidence from outside the consulate that Turkey had so far leaked. The process of matching visual and entry data was laborious and all that MİT had at 5.50pm to start with was a CC-TV grab of Jamal at the consulate's front door. They even had to show it to Hatice Cengiz to be certain this was the man they were after. It was like looking for a needle in a haystack. At least Turkey had come within a hair's breadth of arresting the assassins – unlike Britain in the case of the 2018 Skripal attackers who flew home to Russia undetected and unbothered.

But a book, *Diplomatik Vahşet* (Diplomatic Brutality), published on 28 December 2018 by three *Sabah* journalists, transformed this simple picture in an unplanned way into one that made little sense once Turkey's facts over the space of three months were compared.

Based on the testimony of Turkish secret-service officials, the book revealed new leaked information. MİT did after all, the book said, have some advance notice that something was afoot at the Saudi consulate. This was the day before Hatice's phone call to Aktay.

The book revealed that MİT had traced the local Saudi secret service chief, al-Muzaini, when he travelled with a couple of his staff to Belgrad Forest in a consular BMW on 1 October. One of the authors, head of *Sabah* investigations Abdurrahman Şimşek, said in a book interview that 'al-Muzaini was unaware that MİT was tracking him when he went to Istanbul's Belgrad Forest on October 1 with two other Saudi intelligence officers'.

'MİT had initially thought that their visit to the forest was a part of an espionage operation but they had later understood that it was actually conducted as a reconnaissance mission before the Khashoggi murder', Şimşek continued. But, if MİT recorded audio inside the consulate, why did they not listen in to find out what was said about these espionage goals of al-Muzaini's forest visit and the trip to Yalova?

Two months earlier, in October, however, the only answer the media wanted to have was where the mystery recording came from. Erdoğan's team had prepared the answer through preceding leaks to Reuters. Turkish officials had told the press agency's reporters that MoBeSe CC-TV showed that Jamal was wearing his Apple Watch and that the watch was at the heart of their forensic investigation. They were trying to find out whether it was connected to the phones Jamal had given Hatice, and what was transmitted, the official leaked.

'We have determined that it was on him when he walked into the consulate', the anonymous official told Reuters.

'Intelligence services, the prosecutor's office and a technology team are working on this. Turkey does not have the watch so we are trying to do it through connected devices.'

This was leaked to Reuters a day before the *Washington Post* published the surprise news that Turkey had a recording of the assassination and had told the White House.

The explanation itself where the recording came from would be leaked on Saturday the 13th of October. This was a poignant day. It was the day on which Jamal would have turned 60. Hatice Cengiz tweeted in the morning, 'invited all his close friends to a restaurant on the detail TheBosporus to celebrate his birthday but detail WhereIsJamal'. She also published her oped piece in the *New York Times*.

However, in Saudi Arabia, Dr Alaa Mahmoud Nasief (@anaseif), Jamal's divorced third wife countered what Hatice said. An attractive woman with a traditional black *abaya* covering her hair who practised as a holistic life-coach trained in Myers Briggs testing, hypnotherapy, and other mediation techniques, and ran a company in Jeddah, she was interviewed on al-Arabiya.

Dr Nasief said, 'While Cengiz claims to be the fiancée of Jamal, I have not heard of that name beforehand and neither his family nor his son Abdullah, who was with him in Turkey for two weeks before his disappearance. If Cengiz was in Jamal's life, I would be the first to know, but she was never in his life.'

She was 'surprised' that Cengiz had his phones and expressed astonishment how she could have access to his personal social media, enabling 'deletions and manipulation'.

She also added, 'I did not know that Jamal moved from America to Turkey. He did not tell me that, and I do not know why'. She warned al-Arabiya's audience in Saudi Arabia that the important thing was 'that everyone has to keep silent'.

A Saudi TV pundit and writer for a Mecca newspaper, Faisal al-Shammari meanwhile tweeted on @Mr_Alshammeri pictures of Jamal's passport that showed a date of birth of 22 January 1958, as well as one of the Khashoggi family and of Jamal's divorced wife Dr Nasief with Jamal.

In a statement to the Saudi Press Agency of the same day, the Saudi interior minister still dismissed any involvement as 'outright lies' but for the first time, he acknowledged the kingdom was being accused of killing one of its subjects.

Furthermore, a senior Saudi delegation of eleven men, led with symbolism by the seventy-eight-year-old governor of Mecca, Prince Khalid bin Faisal, met Turkish delegates on that Saturday. Prince bin Faisal was to report back to his uncle, King Salman himself. Jamal's secret-service patron, Prince Turki bin Faisal, was Prince Khalid's half-brother, and according to some reports Prince Khalid himself was also a onetime patron of Jamal's. The whole Faisal family, according to Maggie Salem Mitchell, had banded together to airlift Jamal to safety at the London embassy when he ran into trouble with Saudi's Wahhabi clerics in 2003.

It was AKP paper *Sabah* that led with the scoop on the morning of Jamal's birthday. Abdurrahman Şimşek, the head of its investigative team, explained the provenance of recording in his piece.

'Reliable sources' had leaked that Jamal had 'paired the smart watch on his arm with his iPhone' that he had left with Hatice. From Jamal's wrist, the Apple Watch had recorded how he 'was interrogated, tortured, and then killed', and transmitted the recording to the iPhone and his i-Cloud. The Saudis realised all this, Turkish officials leaked to the paper, and they had tried to log into the i-Cloud account with a password and the Apple Watch by PIN but failed and instead had used Jamal's fingers, or at any rate 'fingerprints to log in and try to erase some files'.

'Saudi intelligence... managed to erase some files. However, it could not delete all of the files', *Sabah* dutifully reported on the leaked information it had been given.

It was sensational, like a scene from From Russia with Love. But it was also entirely untrue. Reuters had done its due diligence on the Apple Watch in its piece of 10 October and reported that such a watch can 'provide data such as location and heart rate'. But, even so, that would depend 'on the model of watch, whether it was connected to the internet, and whether it is near enough an iPhone to synchronise.'

However, neither the Turkish investigators nor, indeed, *Sabah*'s investigative journalists had checked the Apple Watch facts with equal care.

Apple stated fingerprint access was not an Apple Watch feature (Saudi trolls jeered sarcastically that there must have been a 'Turkish update'). As for the connection, the third-generation phone visible on Jamal's wrist couldn't directly connect through Turkish cellular networks to an iPhone or its iCloud. Hatice herself was out of range for a bluetooth transfer of the audio file to the iPhone. This left the consulate's wifi as the only alternative for the transmission, and the idea that Jamal, in self-imposed exile, would have logged in on the consular network before entering was unbelievable. He knew that he would have to hand his phones over to consulate security anyway if he brought them inside.

Not only had Turkey been caught out in a lie, MİT had shown itself to be less technologically savvy than the news reporters of Reuters. With the shoe now on the other foot, Saudi-sponsored al-Arabiya howled 'Another blatant inaccuracy.'

Sabah had badly relied on the expertise of its government sources (as had the Middle East Eye's Turkey correspondent, who had tweeted the story on without critical comment). Abdurrahman Şimşek, 'got angry' and complained 'directly to government officials that Turkish newspapers were not getting information on the case' though he didn't complain about the Apple Watch story as such – for which he bore joint-responsibility. Instead, he was angry about the fact that Cengiz had been writing pieces for the US papers, whereas Turkish readers also wanted to hear from her. Next day, Sunday 14 October, *Sabah* published the first-exclusive interview in Turkey with her.

The international media, however, was giving MİT and *Sabah* a pass. It appreciated the fact that the Apple Watch story proved to be bogus. In a case of reverse psychology, it was seen as an acceptable ruse to cover up how Erdoğan's team had come in possession of a recording in breach of diplomatic law – even though it was doubtful Western papers would have let their own spooks get away with such a clumsy fantasy about the facts. How an intelligence organisation that mistakes basic technology could make sophisticated recordings was a question left for what it was.

In a rare exception to their keenness to leak information about the Khashoggi case, Turkish officials decided less was more and did not leak more on the Apple Watch.

21

Crucial Hours

Where, then, did the recording come from was now the big question and the subject of fevered guess work. International speculation ranged from bugs placed in the consulate itself to a directional microphone focused on the building from outside – both technically within the realms of Turkey's capabilities, it was thought by pundits. Another possibility, being discussed in Turkey and elsewhere, was that some operatives of the hit squad recorded the abduction on their own phones for trophy purposes and that those recordings were either intercepted in real time or retrieved from at least one of the killers' phones – though why would MİT come up with the bungling Apple Watch tale in that case?

Now that the watch explanation had been shot down, what did Turkish officials say on the record about the provenance of the recording in their possession?

One senior official who would answer that question directly was Turkish defence minister Hulusi Akar on 19 November at the Halifax International Security Forum. His words were not widely reported, except in a number of Turkish media. In a tenacious interview in English on the Khashoggi affair, Afghani-Australian BBC correspondent Yalda Hakim asked the minister point-blank, 'There are a lot of questions about the consulate being bugged. Is this common practise for Turkey?'

'There is no such thing as us bugging within the consulate. We do not disclose the origin of the audio recordings', Akar replied with a wan smile.

Akar's concession that Turkey wasn't the author of the recording was also consistent with the words of Ibrahim Kalin, Erdoğan's personal spokesman. He said on 3 October, 'according to the information that we have, this Saudi citizen is still in the Saudi Arabian consulate in Istanbul. We don't have any information to the contrary.' If MİT had already heard everything there was to know, Kalin's words were just another Turkish Apple Watch story with hindsight – and the same, for that matter, Akar's words. The ponderous watch lie had exposed that the words of two of Turkey's highest officials could not be trusted.

Nine days after telling the Apple Watch tale to *Sabah*, Turkish security officials volunteered to reporters of the *Wall Street Journal* a new story about the recording in their possession. 'The recording was available as early as the evening of 2 October', the journal reported. This date leaked by Turkish security officers was at least consistent with the time-line given to Şimşek for his 13 October Apple-Watch news article. He had reported that the recording 'was found by the security forces after his fiancée handed over the phone' on 2 October (setting aside the fact that Hatice said in a Turkish interview that she did this the next day).

Yet it was this claim that made the *Wall Street Journal* story also problematic in view of what the Turkish officials later said in *Diplomatik Vahşet*.

On the Monday before Jamal's second visit to the consulate, MİT thought al-Muzaini and two intelligence staff were on a spying mission in Belgrad Forest, as leaked to Abdurrahman Şimşek *et al.* in December for their book. In the same book, however, the officials also leaked that there were recordings from before the moment Jamal entered the consulate.

MİT now claimed to the *Journal* it had pulled up the audio for that day inside the consulate after 5.50pm when the consulate was closed. The senior official leaked to the paper that these were 'passive' recordings.

The al-Muzaini intel would have been a red flag more than 24 hours before Erdoğan's three-line whip to MİT came through. Had they listened to consular audio, it would likely also have led them to Khashoggi-related chatter from Friday onwards, maybe even before that day, as phone calls to Riyadh were made the moment Jamal visited the consulate for the first time on Friday. The *Wall Street Journal* didn't know about al-Muzaini and so couldn't ask why MİT hadn't pulled up 'passive' audio when their suspicion was first raised the day before. The *Sabah* journalists didn't address this question.

Turkish officials also leaked to the *Wall Street Journal* that 'within hours they reached a sobering conclusion: Mr. Khashoggi never left the consulate'. This created yet a further mystery with what they leaked two months later.

If MİT had the recordings on the evening of 2 October – as they would tell the writers of *Diplomatik Vahşet* in December – this would have removed any doubt as to what had happened. It would have been evident that a serious crime had been committed on Jamal's person and that this was not merely a hostage situation in the consulate or a case of abduction. Certainly, what was on it was so gruesome that its violent nature spoke volumes when CIA Director Gina Haspel and select other top-level investigators were later given, or allowed to listen to, an edited clip of the recording. It again exposed Kalin's words spoken on behalf of President Erdoğan, 'we don't have any information', and Hulusi Akar's as entirely made up.

The time-and-date information also raised a more practical conundrum. The recording, available according to MİT officials on 2 October, made anyone inside the consulate at the time a murder suspect, not least the seven of the Tiger Team MİT tracked down via MoBeSe etc waiting in the Atatürk Airport's private-jet lounge for the second jet to leave.

At the end of December, Turkish officials would give another precise time detail about the audio to the journalists who wrote *Diplomatik Vahşet*. They said 'sound analysts... solved MİT's question within two hours' (*Ses analistleri geriye doğru analizlerini yapti ve iki saat içinde MİT olayi çözdü*).

Thus, according to the *Wall Street Journal–Diplomatik Vahşet* leaks, MİT knew all they needed to know from about 7.50pm on 2 October. This was around the time that MoBeSe CC-TV captured three Tiger Team men – Tubaigy, al-Hawsawi, and Khalid al-Otaibi – leaving the consul-general's residence in consular Mercedes Vito Van with plates 34 CC 1865 for the private-jet terminal where the 'sitting duck' Gulfstream IV was waiting for them on the tarmac. It would be another full two hours before the final four of the seven Saudis on this jet – brigadier-general Abahussein, major al-Arifi, al-Zahrani, and al-Bostani – had their passports scanned between 9.44 and 9:46pm and their luggage X-rayed.

That meant there were up to two hours (three if one included the time the jet took off at 10.46pm) to brief Erdoğan on the gravity of the situation and to threaten Riyadh with exposure, even before a decision to detain the Saudi crew or delay their jet's departure was made. Turkish authorities had already leaked that calls to Saudi authorities remained unanswered on the evening of 2 October, which told its own tale: Riyadh knew.

Yet, despite solving the problem 'within two hours' according to MİT, not 'all measures' were taken, as Erdoğan had instructed. All that happened was that the 'sitting duck' jet, the luggage, and passengers were thoroughly searched for Jamal before the Gulfstream IV was cleared for 10.46pm take-off.

If Turkey knew murder had been committed, why did it not act? It could have detained at the very least four of these seven Saudis on suspicion of a serious crime. The Vienna Convention only prohibits entry to a designated diplomatic space without the mission head's permission. But by 9.45pm all remaining nine members of the Tiger Team had left the consul-general's residence anyway and seven were grouped together at Atatürk's Genel Havacilik lounge for private jets.

Four of the private jet passengers – al-Bostani, al-Hawsawi, al-Zahrani and Khalid al-Otaibi – were travelling on regular passports. Only major al-Arifi travelled on a diplomatic passport, while professor Tubaigy, the forensic expert, and brigadier-general Abahussein travelled on government passports, which also afford a certain diplomatic protection. Not all diplomatic immunity is the same, though. Only the highest-ranking diplomats have absolute immunity under the Vienna Convention.

In addition, Turkish authorities could have tracked down and detained another two team members – al-Madani and Saif al-Qahtani – who left on the commercial flights well after midnight. These two, who brought up the rear of the Saudi operation, also flew on regular passports. Up to a total of six, or more than a third of the Tiger Team, could have been detained without a Vienna Convention conflict.

While the recording would have removed any doubt that a criminal foul had been committed, the MoBeSe evidence itself showed that Jamal never left the building and that, apart from kidnapping, there were suspicious movements and large pieces of luggage being shunted around. With their president's *carte blanche*, did the Turks need anything more to delay the departure of the jet under the broad sweep of Turkish law, if not some of the operatives, pending further investigation?

From Tuesday to Saturday evening, Ankara accused Riyadh of holding Jamal hostage. During those days, Turkey's bargaining power would with two, let alone up to six or nine operatives, have been a sharp incentive for a rapid solution. Doubtless, Saudi Arabia's fobbing off of Ankara would have been different if Turkey held, for example, the man with the bone saw, professor lieutenant-colonel Tubaigy.

Why would any nation let a hostile 'Skripal team' slip through their fingers? Two months later, on 30 November, the Istanbul Crime Court would indeed issue warrants for the arrests of all fifteen members of the Tiger Team *in absentia*, and demand that Saudi Arabia extradite them. But on 2 October Turkey had most of them, right there and most of the evidence it was going to get, based on what officials had leaked.

Did Turkey really know as much on that day as it said it did in December? What was the point of searching a plane and luggage for incriminating evidence if Turkish authorities were investigating a complaint of kidnapping and already knew the seven passengers were murder suspects? It seemed a good question to ask.

Abdurrahman Şimşek, head of *Sabah* investigations, in fact, was the one who had also reported on 10 October on Turkey's search of the second jet for *Sabah.* He wrote in that piece that it had been be done 'by eye' with the seven team members waiting in the lounge, and that the Gulfstream jet was cleared for take-off after 'it was seen [Khashoggi] was not among the passengers.' Either that October story was yet another Apple Watch story, or the December one, while the person who had reported on both seemed uninterested in finding out which was which.

In October, Turkish officials segued over the complication the audio story was creating. The *Wall Street Journal* reported, 'it took security agencies time to identify Arabic voices on the recording, but noted its content and a detailed analysis were shared among investigators within two days.' Folded inside this time lag was the explanation why Turkey did nothing on 2 October. The 'two days' suggested that by Thursday or Friday Turkey was in a position to act but not before. This was congruent with the moment when Turkish officials leaked the bombshell on Saturday that 'Mr Khashoggi has been killed at the consulate' and his death was 'premeditated' and also with the leaked secret meeting on Friday with Saudi diplomats in Ankara in the same piece.

While the *Wall Street Journal* leaks corresponded to the facts, then, they deepened the mystery surrounding the recording once MİT claimed through *Diplomatik Vahşet* to have grasped the crux of the audio on the same evening. MİT would hardly have merely 'noted' what was on the tape and done nothing for two days.

Did Turkey's MİT obtain the recording 'as early as the evening of 2 October', or later? It didn't seem that Turkey's officials kept track of their own leaks. A few days later would explain why Turkey didn't act against the perpetrators within arm's reach. But a date of 2 October less so. The former would also mean that two senior Turkish authorities – Hulusi Akar and Ibrahim Kalin – didn't tell stories that they knew to be untrue and which implicated President Erdoğan himself in misrepresentations. Yet the 'evening of 2 October' is the date MİT claims for itself, like the Apple Watch story.

While host nations try to listen in clandestinely to diplomatic missions, guest nations, particularly rich and technologically sophisticated ones, typically do everything they can to keep unwanted ears out of their buildings, and safe, sound-proof rooms.

Nor was Saudi Arabia a notably unsophisticated country. There were reports in December 2019 that Jamal's WhatsApp messages were intercepted and, on 31 March 2019, that even the messages of Amazon's billionaire owner Jeff Bezos, the richest man in the world, had been hacked by Saudi Arabia to expose his marital infidelity which led to his divorce. The kingdom had a skilled edge in digital warfare. On the other hand, Turkey's handling of technology during the first waters of the Khashoggi case seemed as muddled as Ankara's later publicity strategy was nimble.

The Riyadh mastermind behind the operation, Saud al-Qahtani, MBS's right-hand man, was a long-standing specialist in new technology. A lawyer and Saudi air-force captain, he had been hand-picked by King Abdullah's most powerful civil servant to lead an electronic intelligence army as early as 2012, acquiring sophisticated tools and spyware – money being no object.

With permission of the new Crown Prince (then) bin Nayef, al-Qahtani had started managing 'lawful intercepts' of even ultimately bin Nayef himself after al-Qahtani caught the eye of King Salman's upwardly-mobile son MBS for whom he was to become the go-to image protector. In 2015, the year of King Salman's accession to the throne and two years away from MBS's appointment to crown prince, al-Qahtani was promoted from 'advisor to the royal court' (the same rank that Jamal reportedly had under King Abdullah) to the rank of 'minister'.

In 2017, the year that MBS became crown prince and al-Qahtani formed the Centre for Studies and Media Affairs, he created a black list of twenty people of which Jamal, who had just gone into self-exile, was one. When the fifty-strong Tiger Team was formed in deep secrecy at the same time, al-Qahtani also became a pivotal part of this operation, with his centre providing the cyber, digital and technological expertise – the centre had trained up warriors which such skills before the formation of the Tiger Team.

Brigadier-general Maher Mutreb was also an early Saudi cyber expert and fluent in English. Wikileaks revealed on 19 October that Mutreb's had taken part in an advanced two-week spyware course in Riyadh in 2011, organised by Hacking Team, an Italian specialist firm. Speaking rarely and nicknamed 'glum face' by the training team because of his gloomy Lurch-like presence, he would 'come and go' and was in the group that received training in 'physical intelligence… so cameras, microphones'.

Both men first met when al-Qahtani invited Mutreb to become member of another organisation he chaired, the Saudi Federation of Cyber Security, Programming, and Drones. US intelligence said that, thereafter, Mutreb was tapped in 2017 as assistant secretary-general for security at al-Qahtani's new Centre for Studies and Media Affairs.

The Tiger Team brought at least one scrambler, apart from other comms. Undoubtedly the Saudi consulate itself also relied on more expensive and sophisticated technology than most nations to maintain secrecy – certainly more than merely dismissing or sequestering Turkish staff at key moments. Although the consulate was otherwise plain, it did have two large and one enormous white parabolic satellite dishes pointing to the sky on terrace-level at the back of the building. They were not visible from the street. Due to the sloping of Istanbul's hills, the terrace itself was the roof of a one-level basement extension at the back that opened up to a court with its own carport and the exit through which the six consular cars left without being seen by Hatice Cengiz waiting at the front of the building.

Nor was it very likely that the Tiger Team had opted for recklessness or a gamble on the occasion of their covert rendition on 2 October. Whichever organisation pierced the electronic cloaking devices of the

Saudi consulate and made clear recordings must have been skilled in such intercepts.

There is one country that can undoubtedly match the Five Eyes Alliance's technological capability and manpower, or indeed that of Saudi Arabia's. If British and US intelligence knew about the attack beforehand, that country may well have known, too.

If one looks at the 2016 US elections, the UK Brexit Referendum, and democratic elections elsewhere in Europe, Russia's deployment of digital technology may, in fact, be superior in some ways to the Five Eyes. US Special Counsel Robert Mueller said Russia's US electoral interference was 'sweeping and systematic' in his report of 10 April 2019. Once unified behind one holistic communist ideology ('electrification and Soviets' according to Lenin), under Putin it was gigabytes and cronies. Given Istanbul's abiding importance to Russia from Catherine the Great's expansion to the Black Sea, it would not be a surprise if there were almost as much Russian-spyware cabling underneath its pavements as in Moscow.

In December, *Sabah* would proudly report in Turkish that Gina Haspel, director of the CIA (a Turkish speaker and one-time chief of station in Ankara), praised MİT chief Hakan Fidan for a success achieved only 'once or twice in the history of intelligence', as leaked to the authors of *Diplomatik Vahşet*. One of the points of the leaks for that book seemed to be a hagiographic one – how quickly MİT had 'solved' the Khashoggi case – transmogrifying MİT's middling performance to one that the Turkish population could be proud of.

But even if the recording was a lucky break by Turkey all along from 2 October 5.50pm – when Erdoğan said the investigation started – it was also a brick through the window. Once again the Trump administration was in trouble abroad and at home, now as a result of the ramifications of the Khashoggi affair.

One of *Sabah*'s columnists observed on 18 October, Vladimir Putin 'patiently waits for Trump to make mistakes and employs diplomacy to exploit them. As a leader who knows the Western alliance's weaknesses, he never misses an opportunity... Washington has been withdrawing from its former sphere of influence, and the Russians replaced the US at a low cost.'

22

'Rogue' Operators

On Monday evening, thirteen days after Jamal disappeared, Turkish criminal investigators were finally allowed to enter the Saudi consulate to collect evidence. The joint-group of Saudi and Turkish officials had at last signed off on the rules of engagement under a diplomatic protocol of temporary access to both the consulate and the consular residence. Turkish investigators would be given access for six hours to the consulate and thirteen hours to the consul general's residence, and the consular fleet of cars had to be inspected in this time as well. Strictly speaking, the cars and residence were not covered by diplomatic immunity and did not require Riyadh's permission, but Turkey was afraid of Saudi 'retribution' the UN rapporteur would write later. The palace only gave permission for 'swabbing'.

The night before, King Salman had called President Erdoğan. The governor of Mecca Prince bin Faisal who headed the king's Khashoggi delegation had reported back to him from Turkey and allegedly said 'It is really difficult to get out of this one'. While in Ankara, the prince had 'begged the president to save them', a Turkish source leaked to the media. In return, the source further leaked, Erdoğan had demanded 'complete cooperation' from Riyadh. Turkey wanted to 'search the consulate and the consul-general's house, and interview the consul-general... and that the Saudis tell them where Khashoggi's body is buried', the news site Middle East Eye reported. They also wanted to inspect the twenty-two cars that had driven in and out of the consulate on 2 October.

Erdoğan had been direct to the king on the call. In return the king had thanked the president for not using the murder as an opportunity for exploitation.

That evening King Salman would instruct the Saudi prosecutor general Sheikh Saud al-Mojeb to start an internal investigation, issuing royal decree 5709. To CNN Turk, Riyadh leaked no more than twenty-four hours later through two sources that the prosecutor would discover that 'Khashoggi's death was the result of an interrogation that went wrong, one that was intended to lead to his abduction from Turkey.'

Hours before the Turks entered the consulate, a Saudi team of 'investigators' had done their preparatory job at the consulate on Monday. They were really a cleaning crew who had arrived to set about their work defiantly under the full glare of the TV cameras outside the consulate. Eight large bottles of floor-cleaning fluid along with other chemicals and six hundred bin liners were wheeled through the big silver-riveted gate with a large gold relief of two swords and a palm tree – Saudi Arabia's national emblem.

Prince bin Faisal's delegation four days earlier had also included a chemist and a toxicologist – Ahmed al-Janobi and Khaled al-Zahrani. They hadn't returned to Riyadh with the prince, but stayed on to work secretly on removing all traces from the two buildings. The two highly-trained forensics experts would remain in Istanbul until the 20th, repairing every night to an elegant five-star hotel 20 minutes or so away from the consulate.

The Turkish forensic investigators, including specialists from the Istanbul anti-terror branch and crime-scene investigation, arrived in a motorcade of six cars at night. The Turkish prosecutor had entered the yellow-cream building earlier in the day with a policeman and the joint-team had gathered at a police station for a meeting that lasted almost two hours. The Saudi investigators entered the consulate an hour before the prosecutor arrived and remained inside until the Turkish search was concluded on Wednesday morning.

The chiaroscuro of night time increased the dramatic impact of press photos from outside, with long shadows cast from blindingly-bright halogen lights. The dark window frames with their finely crafted Islamic-patterned grills captured the Turkish forensic team executing certain tasks that required crouching on all fours and who were lit up like reality TV. Clad in white dust-free overalls, gasmasks, which some investigators even kept on outside, blue-and-white shoe protectors, blue gloves, vests that looked bullet proof, they went into the consulate under more stark halogen lighting. Meanwhile policemen in riot gear brandishing automatic rifles stood on either side of the consulate to protect and escort the team moving like a pageantry of science.

The Turkish investigators were carrying limited equipment after the Saudis had banned the use of Luminol, a forensic chemical that reveals bloodstains even if they have been washed clean. Nonetheless, their kit consisting of large, dark, heavy-duty, professional-looking plastic cases that the team carried into the building looked impressive. After a night-time search of up to nine hours, the Turks left with numerous uniform brown-paper bags and brown cardboard boxes and samples, including soil from outside the consulate.

President Erdoğan suggested in a press conference that his team found evidence of fresh coats of paint and 'toxic materials', but did not elaborate. One senior Turkish official leaked anonymously to the *Washington Post* that there had been apparent attempts to scrub the scene and repaint areas, commenting: 'People who have nothing to hide don't behave like this.' Another official said to Associated Press they had 'found evidence' that Jamal had been killed there, but didn't expand on those words.

The two Saudi specialists had, in fact, done a meticulous job in scrubbing the building clean over more than a week while Riyadh had stalled the Turks. The forensic evidence Turkish investigators found that could support their murder case was modest. Turkish officials would leak three small forensic details of their investigation over the next half year. But Turkey never officially released the full findings of its inspection, nor would actual measurements or other scientific details ever be leaked or published.

Meanwhile the US continued to mediate. President Trump said that he had spoken to the infirm King Salman himself, who professed to having no knowledge about the missing journalist. Trump then speculated that 'rogue killers' may have been responsible for the murder, a repetition of the story Aktay had first introduced and then withdrawn. By now there had already been several Saudi leaks in the press that the palace was preparing to make a statement along those lines.

'Been hearing the ridiculous "rogue killers" theory was where the Saudis would go with this. Absolutely extraordinary they were able to enlist the president as their PR agent to float it,' retorted Chris Murphy, a Democrat senator.

The *New York Times* took up President Trump's theme. Information had been leaked by Saudi officials that the crown prince had indeed approved the questioning of Jamal, or his rendition back to Saudi Arabia. But a member of its intelligence services, who merely happened to be a friend of the crown prince, had been 'tragically incompetent'. He had been trying to prove himself during the operation, which led to the journalist's death. The shift in the Saudi position had come after the US finally threatened sanctions against the kingdom.

On Tuesday, Secretary of State Mike Pompeo flew out to meet with King Salman and have dinner with the crown prince, ostensibly to have talks over Jamal Khashoggi's disappearance. He said, 'They made a commitment they would show the entire world the result of their investigation. They also indicated they would get this done quickly'. On the same day, $100 million would be transferred from the palace's coffers to the US treasury.

President Trump also spoke to MBS on the phone. He tweeted: 'Just spoke with the crown prince of Saudi Arabia who totally denied any knowledge of what took place in their Turkish consulate.' Trump defended Saudi Arabia from further criticism over the case, telling Associated Press that it was a case of 'you're guilty until proven innocent, I don't like that'.

Then, on Tuesday afternoon, as Turkish police started putting up barricades around his elegant residence, consul-general Mohammed al-Otaibi left for Riyadh after the UN asked for his immunity to be lifted. He had not left his home for days and all his appointments had been cancelled.

In the early hours of Wednesday 16 October, Jamal's younger son Abdullah tweeted a typed Arabic statement posted 'for immediate release', which the *Washington Post* picked up and published. It said: 'We, the children of journalist Jamal Khashoggi are following with growing concern the conflicting reports on his fate after we lost contact with him two weeks ago following his entry into the Saudi consulate in Istanbul.'

'The family is now trying to overcome the shock of the developments and gather all his children. Out of our moral and legal responsibility, we demand the immediate formation of an independent and neutral international committee to gather the facts into his disappearance and conflicting reports on his death.'

But the message also reaffirmed the family's belief in the Saudi government and the Khashoggi family name.

'Ultimately, the family calls on all sides to respect our privacy, particularly at this difficult time, and refrain from politicising his case and undermining his good reputation, which all people attest to.'

Inside the kingdom those who only received Saudi media and didn't have access to foreign media were now thoroughly confused by Riyadh's investigation whether Jamal Khashoggi had been killed at the Istanbul consulate. His disappearance no longer seemed like false-news agitation by foreigners.

President Erdoğan was to meet Mike Pompeo the same day and Turkish authorities released a barrage of lurid leaks from the recording ahead of his arrival from Riyadh in Ankara. The Turkish publicity team first circulated that they had edited a 3-minute clip from the audio recording at their disposal – not unlike the first clip of CC-TV coverage – and given it to *Sabah*. At, least that is what was rumoured.

'Jamal Khashoggi's killing took 7 minutes', the Middle East Eye revealed at 7pm at night, before the first news leak appeared in a morning newspaper. Its source, who provided the scoop, the news site said, was an official who had listened to the 'whole recording' rather than the short 3-minute clip that was edited for *Sabah*.

'Horrendous screams were heard', the site revealed. 'Khashoggi was dragged from the consul-general's office at the Saudi consulate in Istanbul and onto the table of his study next door.'

'The consul[-general] himself was taken out of the room. There was no attempt to interrogate [Khashoggi]. They had come to kill him', the source leaked.

Jamal was then injected with a substance and the screaming stopped. While he was still breathing, it was suggested, professor Salah Tubaigy, the forensic expert on the team, started dismembering him in a third room set up for this purpose.

Tubaigy – the President of the Saudi Fellowship of Forensic Pathology – had perfected the seven-minute autopsy and invented a mobile autopsy unit for use during the Hajj, when millions of pilgrims visit the city of Mecca for six days and as many as thousands have died as a result of a stampede.

'When I do this job, I listen to music. You should do [that] too', he advised the team members in the consulate, the source had leaked to the website.

'Tubaigy began to cut Khashoggi's body up on a table in the study while he was still alive. The killing took 7 minutes,' the source also claimed.

To be complete the Middle East Eye heralded what it had been told, 'A three-minute version of the audio tape has been given to Turkish newspaper *Sabah*, but they have yet to release it.'

But – if *Sabah* had indeed been given a clip – the paper never published it or released it on its website, and nor did any other paper. The reason was, likely, not so much that the false Apple-Watch story had compromised *Sabah*'s reputation for telling the truth, but rather that Ankara had no intention of releasing any part of the recording directly to the public. It wanted to dangle the threat of full exposure over the palace in Riyadh. Certainly the subsequent theatrical smoke-and-mirror release of the audio into other hands confirmed this stratagem.

The rumour that *Sabah* had a (non-existing as yet) three-minute audio clip had, meanwhile, done its job. *Sabah* itself would merely report that day what other papers disclosed on the audio. It would take *Sabah*'s head of investigations Abdurrahman Şimşek, until December, when his book *Diplomatik Vahşet* came out, to publish anonymous new leaks on the audio recording at the consulate in *Sabah*.

In the morning, more gruesome scoops tumbled across the media on Pompeo's arrival. 'Recordings reveal Khashoggi tortured then dismembered while still alive', ran *Yeni Şafak*'s headline on Wednesday morning, ahead of the world press, saying there were 'several recordings'.

'If you want to live, be quiet!' consul-general al-Otaibi had snarled at the US resident he had invited up for tea.

Jamal Khashoggi was 'tortured', the paper claimed. His fingers were 'cut off during the interrogation process before he was decapitated.'

'Shut up if you want to live when you return to (Saudi) Arabia', the team had shouted at the consul-general himself when he pleaded, 'Do this outside. You're going to get me into trouble'.

Later that day the Saudi press would report that consul-general al-Otaibi had been sacked by Riyadh. President Erdoğan would claim credit for this modest victory. In a landmark speech to the Turkish parliament he referred to the consul-general's dismissal and said that he had complained to both Prince bin Faisal and King Salman about the consul-general's refusal to allow entry to the consulate and consular residence to Turkish investigators.

To Qatar-based al-Jazeera Turkish officials leaked that 'the journalist was assaulted immediately after he entered the consulate.' This was based on an '11-minute recording' with three Arabic voices, in addition to Khashoggi's own voice, shortly after he entered the consulate.

Turkish investigators now leaked that they had tracked down a consular BMW (possibly carrying plates 34 CC 2665) to Belgrad Forest on the city's northern outskirts captured on CC-TV at 6.28pm. 'The widening of the investigation came only a few hours after Turkish crime scene investigators finished a nine-hour overnight search of both the consul general's residence and a second search of the consulate itself', *Sabah* reported. This was the story *Diplomatik Vahşet* would revisit in December.

Turkey has taken 'open and transparent actions' in the Khashoggi case, interior minister Süleyman Soylu told Anadolu press agency. The press agency was under tight AKP control and took the minister's word for it.

Turkish prosecutors also focused their attention on farmlands in Yalova Province about fifty miles from Istanbul on the other side of the Marmara Sea. A woman who lived there said that there had been more traffic than usual on the night of 2 October.

At the same time, Turkish authorities fed rumours about the additional complimentary question – where were the victim's body parts? The rumour from 'sources' circulated that Jamal's body had been dissolved in acid after he had been murdered. An anonymous source close to the investigation told Sky News that the assumption was that a 'very fast-acting chemical' had been used.

Meanwhile, in the afternoon, Turkish investigators were allowed access to consul-general al-Otaibi's residence. They had so far been refused entry because the consul-general's family was still in residence. Floodlights and a drone were deployed in a search of the garden because Turkish authorities were not given access as Turkey's diplomatic delegates hadn't thought that far ahead and had not listed the outside of the property on the diplomatic search protocol they had thrashed out with Riyadh.

23

Last Words

Jamal Khashoggi then found a voice from beyond the grave. His last column, ostensibly submitted on the day he went missing, was finally published in the *Washington Post* on 18 October.

In a note with the column, Karen Attiah, the *Post*'s global-opinions editor, said the piece perfectly captured Jamal's commitment to freedom in the Arab world, 'a freedom he apparently gave his life for.'

The *Washington Post* had held off publishing it in the hope that Jamal was still alive and would return, but with talk of rogue Saudi operators and bone saws intelligence services on all sides seemed to have confirmed Jamal's death.

'Now I have to accept: That is not going to happen,' she wrote. 'This is the last piece of his I will edit for the *Post*.'

In the article, headed 'What the Arab world needs most is free expression', Jamal described how the optimism of the Arab Spring in 2011 was quickly dashed and replaced by the Middle East's version of an Iron Curtain, imposed by domestic forces as they grappled for power. The rest of the world had done little as journalists were arrested and newspapers silenced, he observed.

'Instead, these actions may trigger condemnation quickly followed by silence', the column continued. 'As a result, Arab governments have been given free rein to continue silencing the media at an increasing rate….'

'The Arab world is facing its own version of an Iron Curtain, imposed not by external actors but through domestic forces vying for power. The Arab world needs a modern version of the old transnational media so citizens can be informed about global events. More important, we need to provide a platform for Arab voices....'

'We suffer from poverty, mismanagement and poor education,' he wrote. 'Through the creation of an independent international forum, isolated from the influence of nationalist governments spreading hate through propaganda, ordinary people in the Arab world would be able to address the structural problems their societies face.'

Before the weekend more background data started circulating in the press on the hitherto unidentified members of the fifteen-strong assassination squad.

The leaks provided visual proof that connected the squad directly to MBS. Turkish officials leaked high-resolution pictures of the identity cards of the seven men on the second jet, saying the cards of the other eight members might be released another time. The *Washington Post* published all seven pictures with the faces pixilated in a piece by Kareem Fahim, who had written the first piece on Jamal's disappearance for the paper. Next day NBC, given the same IDs, published its follow-up scoop: the cards without pixilation.

The *Post* said it reviewed 'posts on social media, and emails, previous reports in local media and other material' of the men which showed links with Saudi security forces. Using Menom3ay, a caller-ID app popular in the Middle East, it found the telephone numbers of twelve of the fifteen men and called one of them, royal guard Mohammed al-Zahrani, whom *Sabah* had first identified together with professor Tubaigy. He denied being in Turkey at the time and calls to the other eleven members remained unanswered. The *Post* also, somehow, was given access to US travel records by US authorities and was able to establish that five of the fifteen Tiger Team members had travelled to the US at similar times as MBS, together with press photographs of the trips.

It became embarrassingly clear that almost all members were intimately connected with MBS's personal security and intelligence team. Among the operatives was Abdulaziz al-Hawsawi. A French colleague of his who had worked with the Saudi royal family told the *New York Times* that al-Hawsawi was a member of the security team that travelled with the crown prince.

Thaar al-Harbi was mentioned in Saudi media in 2017, when he was promoted to lieutenant in the Saudi royal guard, apparently for his bravery defending the crown prince's palace al-Salam in Jeddah during an attack by a Saudi man called Mansour al-Amri.

Then there was Mohammed al-Zahrani, who had answered his phone. A 2017 video by the Saudi-owned TV channel al-Ekhbariya published on YouTube showed a man wearing a royal-guard uniform and name tag standing next to the Crown Prince. At one, time he had also been on the embassy staff in London according to a list given to the *Daily Telegraph*.

Middle East Eye also identified Badr al-Otaibi as an officer in the crown prince's entourage. He had helped with the preparations for the Ritz Carlton imprisonment and travelled with MBS to France in 2018, along with major Nayif al-Arifi, also a security and protection officer for the crown prince. On Saudi number-sharing app Menom3ay he identified himself as an 'employee of the crown prince's office'. A document seen by Middle East Eye also listed Mansour Abahussein as an officer for the crown prince. He was one of the oldest of the soldiers, and a big heavy set man who was a brigadier-general – in November he would be identified indirectly as the leader of the Tiger Team rendition by the Saudi prosecutor.

Fahad al-Balawi was listed as a member of the royal guard by two users on Menom3ay, while seven Menom3ay users identified Saif al-Qahtani as an employee of the crown prince. Khalid al-Otaibi also identified himself as a member of the royal guard. He travelled to the United States at the same time as official visits by members of the Saudi royal family. Hit-squad member sergeant-major al-Sehri was identified as an air force officer from an online video, while the Facebook profile of Meshal al-Bostani said he was an air force lieutenant who lived in Jeddah and had studied at the University of Louisville, Kentucky. He died in a traffic accident at about this time and it immediately raised suspicions that he had been silenced by the Saudi regime in the crackdown on the team that had loyally executed the rendition. Born in 1961 Mustafa al-Madani was by some way the oldest of the group. The UN team would first reveal his high-rank as major general as late as 19 June 2019. No public information had been unearthed regarding Turki al-Sehri but he was thought to have links to the crown prince, too. The UN confirmed seven months later that the media research was correct – the latter was an intelligence officer. It also found that Badr al-Otaibi may have been Jamal's intelligence colleague under Prince Turki.

At least three of the suspects – lieutenant Thaar al-Harbi, major Waleed al-Sehri and Abdul al-Hawsawi – had been part of MBS's entourage when he made a three-day visit to London in March 2018, where he met the Queen and Prime Minister Theresa May. Al-Qahtani's subordinate, brigadier-general Maher Mutreb, was also seen emerging from a car in Downing Street during the visit. In total the UN report would link at least eight operatives directly to MBS and find that there were at least seven commissioned officers on the team ranging from a rank of lieutenant to two-star general.

Despite the mounting weight of circumstantial evidence, MBS still denied ordering the killing or involvement with it. If it wasn't MBS, who, then, was going to be the fall guy for him? The prime suspect emerged as a two-star general 'new' to intelligence work. According to the *Washington Post*, this was major-general Ahmed al-Asiri, the boss of the Saudi-Istanbul secret-service chief al-Muzaini. The general was deputy head of the Saudi general intelligence directorate and one of the crown prince's right-hand men after MBS was made defence minister when his father came to power as king in January 2015. A graduate of Sandhurst, West Point in the US, and St Cyr Academy in France, al-Asiri was a career air-force officer who came to prominence as spokesman for the Saudi-led coalition fighting in Yemen that had been unleashed by the crown prince as one of his first acts as Saudi defence minister.

In March 2017, al-Asiri was filmed sticking his middle finger up at protesters in London. This did not seem to damage his standing with the crown prince.

He had no formal training in intelligence it was leaked by way of explanation, yet he won the Crown Prince's permission to interrogate Jamal on the suspicion that he had become part of the Muslim Brotherhood, the Islamist political faction whose rise during the Arab Spring worried the Saudis and their allies in the UAE. Riyadh also wanted to intimidate Jamal as they reckoned he had taken money from Qatar, an assumption no doubt fed by his closeness to Maggie Salem Mitchell of the Qatar Foundation International, who had certainly paid for translation and research help with his *Post* pieces. According to the *Daily Beast*, 'the over-eager general exceeded bin Salman's intentions. He improvised a rendition to send Khashoggi from Turkey back to Saudi Arabia – and botched it, killing him. Then he lied to his Saudi superiors about what happened.'

How plausible were these new rumours leaked by anonymous Saudi 'sources'? 'It's not going to wash,' said Bruce Riedel, a former CIA official and the Gulf expert at the Brookings Institution. 'It's ludicrous in the extreme. Saudi Arabia doesn't work that way. They don't do freelance operations.'

'If this is a rogue operation, the rogue is MBS,' said Barbara Bodine, a retired US ambassador to Yemen.

24

Uncomfortable Truths

Saudi Arabia officially admitted that Jamal was dead at 12pm on Friday 19 October. Jamal had, Riyadh claimed, died in a fight in the Istanbul consulate. But it had been an accident. In a statement on state TV the country's prosecutor said that the fifteen-man squad confronted Jamal when he entered the consulate and a brawl broke out. In another evening call with Erdoğan, King Salman had already given the president advance warning of this announcement.

The Saudi statement read: 'In implementation to the directives of the leadership of the need to clearly know the truth and declare it transparently whatever, the preliminary investigations conducted by the Public Prosecution showed that the suspects had travelled to Istanbul to meet with the citizen Jamal Khashoggi as there were indications of the possibility of his returning back to the country.'

What the phrase 'indications of the possibility of his returning' meant according to the palace was not easy to understand, as Jamal had been vocal, when asked by al-Qahtani on many occasions over two years, that he had no intention of moving back to Saudi Arabia and instead intended to get married in Turkey that week and had applied for US citizenship.

In a reference to Jamal's first 11 minutes at the consulate, the prosecutor's statement said: 'The results of the preliminary investigations also revealed that the discussions that took place with the citizen Jamal Khashoggi during his presence in the consulate of the kingdom in Istanbul by the suspects did not go as required and developed in a negative way, this led to a fight and a quarrel between some of them and the citizen Jamal Khashoggi, yet the brawl aggravated to lead to his death and their attempt to conceal and cover what happened.'

The prosecutor said that eighteen people had been arrested in connection with his death: all fifteen men in the hit squad along with two consular staff and a driver, pending investigations. Saudi Arabia said the eighteen would be tried in Saudi courts. Saudi Arabia now conceded they were Saudi soldiers and intelligence operatives. Nonetheless, no individual names were given. And since the kingdom is hermetically sealed to the free press, there was no way of checking whether anyone had actually been arrested.

Showing that they were taking Pompeo's words 'get this done quickly' at face value, it was also revealed that the death penalty would be sought by the Saudi prosecutor general against five of the eighteen in an exceptionally rapid development of the criminal case. Saudi Arabia had still not been given Turkey's recordings, but Sheikh al-Mojeb presumably had the visual and audio evidence that the Tiger Team had made during their mission.

Furthermore, four other intelligence officials were also sacked from their high-level jobs, including major-general Ahmed al-Asiri, the deputy intelligence chief, and Saud al-Qahtani. Al-Qahtani, viewed as Prince Mohammed's enforcer, had been considered untouchable by many Saudis. During the Ritz-Carlton shake-down, his secret files containing years of wiretaps of the high-flying Saudi guests were no doubt useful in convincing them to part with their money rather than face disgrace at the hands of Sheikh al-Mojab in court.

When the message came through on Twitter, Hatice Cengiz dropped the phone she was holding while talking to one of Jamal's friends. She had woken up to morning prayer at 5.30am and stayed inside all day to follow the news. She had relied heavily on her father during this lonely and confusing time for her. But for the first time the truth hit home. 'That's when I felt he was dead', she said.

Information was now leaked by Turkish sources that a Skype call from Saudi Arabia to the consulate in Istanbul was made on 2 October after Khashoggi entered the building. During that call MBS adviser Saud al-Qahtani had begun to hurl insults and profanities at Jamal. According to the Turkish official, Jamal answered al-Qahtani's insults with his own. 'Bring me the head of the dog,' al-Qahtani thereupon told his men – suggesting that the Turkish leak was meant to incriminate al-Qahtani as the one who gave the assassination order. No audio was released to make the leak 'open and transparent'.

Critics of Saudi Arabia completed the link back to MBS. They pointed to several tweets by al-Qahtani as evidence that the crown prince was fully aware of the orders his aide was executing. In one 2017 tweet, al-Qahtani said: 'Do you think I make decisions without guidance? I am an employee and a faithful executor of the orders of my lord the king and my lord the faithful crown prince.'

On the same day he apparently warned a Saudi dissident living in London that his 'assassination file has been reopened'. Even after being sacked, al-Qahtani tweeted: 'I express my gratitude to the king and the crown prince for the great confidence they have given me and for providing me with the great opportunity to serve my nation over the past years.' He added: 'I will always be a loyal servant of my country.'

King Salman now ordered MBS to head a committee to restructure the intelligence services within thirty days, suggesting that the crown prince was not to blame as far as the king was concerned.

'The kingdom has taken the necessary procedures to find out the truth,' the state news agency said, adding that the country's leadership had stressed 'the importance of knowing the truth clearly and announcing it transparently, whatever it is'.

However, from exile in Germany, Prince Khalid bin Farhan insisted on German TV that King Salman instead should abdicate in favour of his Sudairi brother in London-exile, Prince Ahmed. He accused the king of wanting to hog the royal succession with his bloodline and deplored a future where 'your offspring monopolises the throne'. Prince Ahmed, he told the Saudi king via DW TV is 'highly ethical, and you are aware of this'.

Prince Ahmed himself avoided the media spotlight. But there was one chance piece of Youtube footage. Noisily heckled on the Yemen war outside his £50 million London home on 5 September 2018, Prince Ahmed had engaged with the protestors and politely asked his Pakistani interlocutors not to lump the whole al-Saud family with those who ran it.

King Salman was the opposite of his brother, in the opinion of Prince bin Farhan, and indistinguishable from MBS. He is a 'tyrant ruler who uses violence because he lacks political experience... When he became king, he applied a similar method to the one he used to follow when he was the governor of Riyadh Province.'

There was no doubt in bin Farhan's mind that 'the killers would have received a direct authorisation from the head of state'. But as Salman was merely a 'facade' 'the order must have been executed by crown prince Mohammed bin Salman.'

Former MI6 mandarin Sir John Sawers told the BBC more nebulously: 'All the evidence points to it being ordered and carried out by people close to Mohammed bin Salman.'

But, pointing a finger at the US, Sir John believed that MBS thought he had a 'licence' from Donald Trump, who frequently condemned journalists as the 'enemy of the people', even praising Republican Congressman Greg Gianforte for body-slamming *Guardian* reporter Ben Jacobs, saying 'he's my kind of guy'.

'I don't think [MBS] would have done this if he hadn't thought he had licence from the US administration to frankly behave as he wished to do so,' said Sir John. 'I think President Trump and his ministerial team are waking up to just how dangerous it is to have people acting with a sense that they have impunity in their relationship with the United States.'

The former spy chief also judged that 'there has been such tension between Turkey and Saudi Arabia over the last ten years or so they would have been monitoring very carefully what goes on inside Saudi offices.'

He went on to speculate that Turkey was listening in to the assassination as it unfolded. 'They could well have had the consulate general bugged in some way or there may have been other devices carried by the squad which carried out the assassination which they were able to intercept.'

It was not easy to see how, even in October, Sir John's words were congruent with the known facts. On his own watch at MI6 from 2009 to 2014, British intelligence had not been able to prevent six Russian assassinations on British soil and Sir John's words flattered the capability of Turkish intelligence with being far greater than that of Great Britain. Yet there was a categorical difference between Britain's secret-service, which did know in advance of attack on Jamal, and MİT, which didn't – even by their own admission – nor had they arrested team members when they could.

Another 'senior' British security source's speculation sought anonymously to impute even greater powers of foresight to MİT: 'Turkey launched a large-scale surveillance operation. Many in the intelligence community believe the consul was bugged, and this Saudi team was followed.' Turkey, the 'source' suggested, had been taken by surprise.

'Turkey was expecting a rendition attempt, which they could interdict, rescuing Khashoggi. Instead, they witnessed a murder,' the source said. 'The uncomfortable truth may emerge one day that the hit team was listened to live as they killed Khashoggi, but [Turkey] was powerless to do anything about it.'

Leaving aside that no one had ever claimed there was audio inside the consul's residence, it is not easy to see how this claim could be true either. It assumed that MİT officials knew everything there was to know even before 1.13pm – after all, they 'witnessed' the murder – when Jamal entered the consulate and, therefore, that they had already decided not to do anything. Somehow it was Hatice Cengiz's calls, inconveniently standing outside, that forced MİT to change that decision not to intervene.

If Turkey had already decided not to do anything about Jamal while they heard the assassination taking place, the official investigation would have started the next day. The Turks could have played exactly the same game of hide and seek with the evidence and force Riyadh's hand. In addition, Turkey wouldn't look inept in having caught some of the perpetrators and yet setting them free anyway.

If it was an MİT internal decision not to act that had been overruled by Erdoğan at 5.50pm, initiated by Hatice's-Turan's-Yasin Aktay's calls, the facts merely indicated temporary indecisiveness. The people who set MİT policies in Ankara evidently reached the same decision a few hours later to stay out of it by allowing the final Gulfstream IV to take-off, confirming the decision their Istanbul inferiors had already reached while executing Ankara's policies before the president got in touch. Ordinary criminal investigators in Istanbul did get the audio recording only two days later, as leaked to the *Wall Street Journal*. But in a diplomatic case with the president involved, Istanbul officials would unlikely call the shots.

Saudi officials now leaked anonymously that the kingdom had an automatic general order on its books – presumably issued by MBS himself as crown prince – for Saudi dissidents to return home. The overly-keen major-general al-Asiri, as the leaked unofficial story went, had wanted to impress MBS and acted on his own to plan an operation to capture Jamal in Turkey.

'There were no orders for them to kill him or even specifically kidnap him,' a Saudi official. 'Crown Prince Mohammed had no knowledge of this specific operation and certainly did not order a kidnapping or murder of anybody. He will have been aware of the general instruction to tell people to come back.'

Yet on the record during his Bloomberg interview on 3 October when asked whether Jamal was 'facing charges' the crown prince had not mentioned this 'order' and that it applied to his friend Jamal. Presumably this was because – if indeed such a palace directive existed – the six Bloomberg journalists might well have understood the word 'order to return' to mean that there was a royal charge against the exile after all. In the first few days, the palace wanted to present Jamal and MBS as friends to avoid any suggestion that they were instead after him.

25

Bone Saw

As Erdoğan's demand to the king for interviewing consul-general al-Otaibi and for Jamal's remains had not been met, there were renewed calls by Turkey for the Saudis to hand over the body. Turkey refused to hand over its recordings and evidence to the kingdom until such time. Meanwhile, the official Saudi investigators found that Jamal's remains had been carried out of the building by the team of fifteen 'rogue' operatives. They had been handed over to a Turkish 'local collaborator' to dispose of. Riyadh didn't know where it was, so the story ran. But when pressed to disclose the name of the Turkish 'collaborator', Saudi prosecutor general Sheikh al-Mojeb declined to provide details to his Turkish counterparts.

After the admission of Jamal's death on Saturday, official Saudi sources started anonymously leaking further details to the media. Among other things, it was explained that the government had wanted to convince Jamal to return to the kingdom from voluntary exile in America as part of a campaign to prevent Saudi dissidents from being recruited by the country's enemies. This did sound close to the truth.

Major-general Ahmed al-Asiri, had put together the fifteen-member team from the intelligence and security forces to go to Istanbul, meet Jamal at the consulate and try to convince him to return to Saudi Arabia.

The anonymous 'sources' also came up with an explanation how the *deus-ex-machina* regulation on dissidents worked under the Saudi rule of law. 'There is a standing order to negotiate the return of dissidents peacefully, which gives [the Saudi secret service] the authority to act without going back to the leadership' the official said. 'Al-Asiri is the one who formed the team and asked for an employee who worked with al-Qahtani and who knew Jamal from the time they both worked at the embassy in London.' This employee was brigadier-general Maher Mutreb.

The official said al-Qahtani had sent one of his subordinates to conduct the negotiations. According to the plan, the team would hold Jamal for some time in a safe house outside Istanbul, but would release him if he ultimately refused to return to Saudi Arabia.

Things went wrong from the start as the team overstepped al-Asiri's and al-Qahtani's orders and quickly employed violence, the anonymous Saudi official said while leaking Riyadh's new story. Jamal was ushered into the consul general's office where Maher Mutreb, consul-general al-Otaibi and another man were waiting for him. Mutreb spoke to Jamal about returning to Saudi Arabia. Jamal refused and told Mutreb that someone was waiting outside for him and would contact the Turkish authorities if he did not reappear within an hour.

According to the Saudi official, Jamal told Mutreb he was violating diplomatic law and said, 'What are you going to do with me? Do you intend to kidnap me?'

Mutreb replied, 'Yes, we will drug you and kidnap you.'

The official also observed that Mutreb's words were an attempt at intimidation that, regrettably, violated the mission's peaceful objective.

When Jamal raised his voice, the team of Saudi officers panicked. They tried to restrain him, placing him in a chokehold and covering his mouth, the official said.

'They tried to prevent him from shouting but he died,' the government account went on. 'The intention was not to kill him.'

Asked if the team had smothered Jamal, the anonymous official subtly shifted the cause of death away from the team: 'If you put someone of Jamal's age in this position, he would probably die.' It was accidental suffocation as a result of age and ill health according to the Saudi investigation.

Saudi investigators also did not think that the special-ops Tiger-Team had dismembered Jamal, nor had they tortured him in their opinion, they leaked. After Riyadh's public admission on 19 October that Jamal had been killed at the consulate, Turkish authorities would, in tandem, both stop deploying the words 'torture' and 'interrogation' in their leaks and deny the existence of facts that indicated a slow and painful death. This watershed moment was remarkable. Before this date Turkish-government contacts at newspapers had painted a garish Pulp Fiction murder story on the basis of official leaks. After this date, the new leaks that characterised the Saudi operation in the Turkish press – and therefore the rest of the world as only Turkey and possessed evidence of events at the Turkish consulate – became less twisted and more business-like. By the time of the UN inquiry into Jamal started in January 2019 the two words had disappeared entirely from the news narrative. In line with this new picture, nine months later to the day, the June UN report into Jamal's killing would label it as an 'execution' and dig no deeper. That word was an accurate description of the sum total of leaks after the watershed (though not before). Estimates of how quickly Jamal was killed after entering the consulate concurred – between 7 and 11 minutes – and previous story lines were sanitised. It is not easy to escape the conclusion that through bare-knuckle mediation Trump administration officials got Ankara to remove the most stinging facts from its assault on Riyadh in exchange for a public admission of responsibility that was palatable to the palace and usable for Saudi home-media consumption.

In an attempt to cover up what they had done in a panic, so the Saudi leaks went, the Tiger-Team team had rolled up the whole of

Jamal's body – intact and Agatha-Christie-style – in a consular rug. When questioned, the anonymous Saudi officer could not give the nationality of the local man. After the rug-rolling and disposal, forensic expert Salah Tubaigy tried to remove any trace of the incidents inside the consulate. Here, the Saudi story was very different from the Turkish version. And it was one red line over which Saudi Arabia would continue to publically rebuff Turkey.

The mutilation of the body, even of non-Muslim enemies, is repulsive to the orthodoxy of Wahhabi Islam. However, the strict Wahhabist interpretation of sharia law prevalent in Saudi Arabia does not label legal punishments – such as beheading or the cutting off of extremities – as mutilation. Instead such penalties are thought to be sacrificial and therefore not abhorrent to religious practise. It is not for nothing that the Tiger Team's secret code-name for Jamal was 'sacrificial animal', a term used by Maher Mutreb while waiting for Jamal and by pathologist Tubaigy when talking to other team members (UN report detail 91). The story of the Tiger-Team operation could either be 'rogue' yet respectful of Jamal's body, or legally ordered under Saudi law by the palace, 'sacrificial' with permissible mutilation by a pathologist brought along for this reason, say, but not be both at the same time. For obvious reasons of consistency, Riyadh's narrative was the former.

The team-gone-rogue subsequently wrote a false report for their superiors, saying they had allowed Jamal to leave once he warned them that Turkish authorities might get involved, and he had promptly left the country before they were discovered. This false report was cited as the reason for the dramatic changes in the official Saudi version. The team and three other local employees had been arrested and were under investigation.

Saudi foreign minister Adel al-Jubeir expressed his condolences to the Khashoggi family, saying his death was a 'huge and grave mistake' and promised 'to punish those who are responsible for this murder'.

He told Fox News: 'This operation was a rogue operation, this was an operation where individuals ended up exceeding the authorities and responsibilities they had. They made a mistake when they killed Jamal Khashoggi in the consulate and they have tried to cover up for it. That is unacceptable in any government. We are determined to uncover every stone. We are determined to find out all the facts. And we are determined to punish those who are responsible for this murder. Even the senior leadership of the intelligence service was not aware of this.'

He described the media outcry over the death of Jamal as 'hysterical', which flagged that Riyadh had moved dropped the word 'disgusting' used by consul-general al-Otaibi and KBS.

The crown prince himself called Jamal's oldest son Salah to express his condolences as a sign of respect. Together King Salman and MBS later received Salah and Jamal's brother Sahel at his palace.

Hatice Cengiz, Jamal's fiancée, meanwhile complained that the crown prince never sent his condolences to her.

'This incident, this assassination, took place inside a Saudi diplomatic mission,' she said. 'In such circumstances, the Saudi Arabian authorities are responsible.' There were fears for her safety – although it was not clear from whom – and the Turkish authorities gave her twenty-four-hour police protection.

Only Egypt's president Abdel el-Sisi backed the new Saudi story. With the aid of Saudi Arabia, the el-Sisi regime had overthrown the rule of Mohamed Morsi, the Muslim Brotherhood president elected after the Arab Spring. The Brotherhood was once again illegal in Egypt after Morsi's failed attempt to replace the Mubarak regime with his Islamist-style regime like Iran. El-Sisi was in effect the new Mubarak.

Few other nations found the new Saudi version of events credible, however. Even Donald Trump said he struggled with the Saudis' account, while the UK, France and Germany issued a joint statement saying there was 'an urgent need for clarification' on what happened inside the Istanbul consulate that day.

It was the image of the bone saw that militated against the Saudi story. 'You don't bring a bone saw to an accidental fist fight,' said Ben Sasse, a Republican congressman from Nebraska. 'The Saudis have said a whole bunch of crap that's not right, accurate, or true.'

Democrat Senator Jack Reed agreed across the aisles. 'This appears to have been a deliberate, planned act followed by a cover-up,' he said. 'You don't bring fifteen men and a bone saw to a fistfight with a sixty-year-old.'

Unsurprisingly, Turkish prosecutors did not accept the Saudi story either. 'We have clear evidence that what happened in the consulate was planned in advance,' they said. But they didn't disclose that 'clear evidence'.

The Saudis had given the Turkish government details of the eighteen suspects, and they had also interviewed twenty-five employees of the consulate in Istanbul. It was speculated that the hit-squad would simply be beheaded by the Saudis to prevent them from talking. Turkey was seeking the extradition of the men, but Saudi Arabia's justice minister and chairman of its higher judicial council, Waleed al-Samaani, said that those responsible for Jamal's death would be tried inside the kingdom.

Agnes Callamard, UN special rapporteur on extrajudicial, summary or arbitrary executions, agreed with Turkey and said the Saudi explanation was 'not plausible'. 'No government should accept it, or the pretence at investigation,' she said.

Protesting outside the Saudi consulate, Turan Kişlakçi, the head of the Turkish-Arab Journalists' Association summarised all questions that remained unanswered with regards to the 'rogue' operation.

'Did they kidnap him? Where did they take him? How did they do this? These questions don't matter,' he said. 'There's only one thing that matters right now. Give Jamal back to us. Give him back so that we can raise his funeral. Let the whole world watch Jamal

Khashoggi's farewell.'

Erdoğan and Trump spoke comprehensively about the case on Sunday, and President Erdoğan promised 'to enlighten all aspects.'

Next Monday morning at 8am, 22 October, Turkish state broadcaster TRT aired a new leaked surveillance video showing what Turkish security officials described as suspicious movement in a car park in Istanbul's Sultangazi neighbourhood. This included the image of a man moving a bag from one vehicle to another. It suggested that Saudi consular workers were still trying to get rid of evidence of the crime on the orders of Riyadh.

Turkish crime-scene investigators went to the car park and found a black 2011 Mercedes E-series sedan with plates 34 CC 1736 covered in dust belonging to the Saudi consulate. The man had parked a grey BMW with consular license plates 34 CC 2665 in front. This appeared to be the same car the consulate's secret-service chief al-Muzaini had driven to Belgrad Forest on 1 October. The man was seen moving three bags, two quite large, between them and leaving the car park on 18 October. He was a regular user, identified as attaché Mohammed O. Another consular Mercedes was also parked in the parking garage.

'We know him as he has been using our parking lot sometimes. However, normally it's his Turkish driver. But on October 7, the attaché was driving it himself', one of the employees told *Hürriyet.*

He said he helped him and had joked 'Khashoggi's body is not inside the suitcases, is it?' and 'He laughed and answered no'.

A mask had fallen out of one of the bags and 'The attaché took it and put it in a trash bin' and 'I took the mask and showed it to a doctor. He told me that it was a mask that is used by those who work with heavy chemicals'. Scared the employee had thrown it away.

After investigators got a waiver to inspect the car they found two suitcases that contained clothes. A kettle and an iPhone box were visible on the backseat. Much media speculation surrounded the pictures and whether any or all belonged to Jamal, although it was unlikely he had brought a kettle into the consulate and 18 October was more than two weeks after the fact.

Earlier investigators had examined a Mercedes Vito minivan with plates 34 CC 1865 belonging to the consulate, and featured in the very first CC-TV clip leaked to the media. Turkey's team claimed that 'after being loaded with several pieces of luggage, a minibus with the license plate 34 CC 1865 parked within the consulate grounds left the building around 3pm… for the consul's residence and believed that the bags held the remains of Khashoggi's dismembered corpse.' The forensics team spent three hours on the minivan with special chemicals and Luminol and found various DNA samples. It also wanted to inspect the Mercedes Sprinter with plates 34 CC 2342, as it could be seen in the last photo of Jamal's stepping into the consulate, and several others used during the day.

These investigations didn't lead to forensic discoveries either. But they, too, at least had the result of being covered widely in media around the world.

26

'Crap'

Then CNN Turk reported on a new leak whose visuals became iconic and further dented the new Saudi story as told by the Saudi prosecutor. On Monday 22 October, the broadcaster revealed new details about the oldest member of the Tiger Team, the fifty-seven-year-old Mustafa al-Madani, an employee of Saudi's central intelligence agency.

The short, evocative, leaked clip showed al-Madani entering the consulate two hours before Jamal at 11.03am with two equally casually-clad team members, one of whom – Saif al Qahtani – shook the hands of the official in a dark-suit who is ushering them inside. The fifty-seven-year-old al-Madani was of a similar height and build as Jamal. The leak made the point he had been carefully picked and brought along as a body double as act of premeditation by the Riyadh organisers of the rendition, though – unlike Jamal – al-Madani did not have a beard or glasses coming into the building.

The CC-TV footage leaked by the Turkish authorities showed al-Madani wearing a fake beard when he left the consulate by its back door at 2.52pm, while Hatice Cengiz was waiting out front near the roadblock. He was then also wearing Jamal's black jacket and glasses and had swapped his loud blue-and-white checked shirt and dark blue trousers for Jamal's light-grey shirt and grey trousers.

'Khashoggi's clothes were probably still warm when al-Madani put them on,' a senior Turkish official speculated.

However, when al-Madani emerged from the consulate he was still wearing the same pair of dark trainers, with a white stripe around the sole, he had on when he entered the building. Jamal, instead, had been wearing dark brogues. And while al-Madani had a full head of hair, Khashoggi was balding. CC-TV showed al-Madani was accompanied by a man wearing a hoodie and a hooped shirt, and was carrying a plastic bag believed to contain the clothes al-Madani had worn when he entered the consulate. They hailed a taxi.

Half-an-hour later al-Madani was captured at 4.06pm on CC-TV six miles away at Istanbul's famous Blue Mosque in the Sultanahmet district. About half-an-hour after that, al-Madani and his accomplice entered a public toilet, emerging again at 4.22pm. Al-Madani was now once-again dressed in the clothes he wore when he entered the consulate, while the plastic bag his accomplice was carrying was thought to contain Jamal's outfit.

The two then had dinner in the Mesale restaurant near the Blue Mosque, seemingly unperturbed by the events of the day. Then they took a taxi towards their hotel at 4.29pm and threw the bag into a large bin nearby. They were later seen back at the hotel laughing and smiling at 6.09pm, checking out four hours later at 10.25pm from the Mövenpick Hotel, which was the end of the short news clip. They could have flown back on either jet, but

Al-Madani and associate were to leave Turkey unhindered on a commercial flight to Riyadh, going through customs at 18 minutes past midnight to catch their flight to Riyadh taking off at 1.25am (likely Turkish Airline flight TK 144). They had arrived on the first private jet 24 hours earlier, and were the last two operatives to leave Istanbul after midnight unhindered despite MİT's investigations that evening.

Turkish officials leaked to the *Wall Street Journal* that it hadn't taken them long to identify Jamal's imposter and his route through Istanbul. The impersonation was so self-evidently fake. Yet investigators moderated this boast by telling the *Journal* they had also concluded they had 'missed chances' to detain members of the hit-squad – including al-Madani.

This humble pie would be replaced with self-congratulation two months later in *Diplomatik Vahşet.* In this book MIT claimed to have understood everything within 'two hours'. But the news about al-Madani's early detection as a key part in the Saudi operation again begged the question whether Turkey had the audio on 2 October and whether they had made it in the first place, or whether that was yet another variation of the Apple Watch story to sound plausible.

If al-Madani had been quickly unmasked from MoBeSe footage alone, and they also had the audio, why hadn't they detained him in the 6 or 7 hours at their disposal. They had 2 extra hours after they had let the 'sitting duck' jet go and all they had to do was wait until he checked in. That seemed like more than a 'missed chance' with the audio in hand.

'It does give us a better understanding... why exactly the Saudis were sort of brazenly peddling this lie for the first several days if not the first week that Khashoggi had left the consulate unharmed. It may have been that they were waiting for the Turks to reveal surveillance footage', a CNN commentator in the US speculated.

More footage was leaked from the MoBeSe footage bank. Two men in suits standing around a burning oil drum in the consulate's back yard were throwing in sheaves of papers. 'This is how the Saudis destroyed the evidence in the consular garden one day later', Turkish TV station Haber TV headlined. The footage had been gathered by a drone on 3 October by Turkish security forces. The fire continued that day until night time, another clip given to Sabah TV showed. It didn't add much without knowing what they were burning, but it made Riyadh seem shifty.

Jamal had written a number of articles critical of Saudi Arabia for the Middle East Eye news site, but not under his own name as he feared for Saudi retribution. The kingdom suspected the London-based website of being a Qatari-funded organisation supportive of the Muslim Brotherhood. The Middle East Eye now revealed the news that Jamal's assassins were by and large members of the *Firqat el-Nemr*, or Tiger Squad, the Saudi team of around fifty highly-skilled intelligence and military operatives formed under the supervision of MBS upon becoming crown prince.

This volley of new Turkish MoBeSe footage broke the day that Jamal's brother Sahel and oldest son Salah met King Salman and the crown prince at the royal palace. In a tweet, the Saudi foreign ministry shared a photograph of the four men shaking hands with the caption: 'King Salman receives Sahel bin Ahmed Khashoggi and Salah bin Jamal Khashoggi in the presence of the crown prince and share their deepest condolences and sympathy to the family of Jamal Khashoggi, may God rest his soul.'

However, according to the *Guardian* the meeting of the sons was electric: 'They stared straight at each other, seemingly locked in the moment: the bereaved, Salah Khashoggi, had eyes of cold sorrow while the man offering condolences, Mohammed bin Salman, gazed back at him with steely focus.'

Earlier, King Salman had shaken Jamal's brother Jahel's hand, pointed and stabbed his index finger at him while talking. The royals and Jamal's Salah were wearing the patriotic Saudi red-blocked *ghutra* held by a black *igal* on their heads while Jamal's brother Jahel had a white one, indicating purity. All wore white long-sleeved *thaub* robes, but the two royals also wore magnificent flowing black royal *bishts* of transparent wool with an elaborate gold-threaded *zari* trim. The elderly king barely looked at Salah, who respectfully listened and edged aside as the most powerful royal in the kingdom moved away leaning on his cane.

The meeting took place in the gilded and salmon-marbled offices of the crown prince. Salah Khashoggi did not speak as MBS clutched his hands. But clearly relations, though stiff, had been satisfactory for both sides. The ban on Salah, who holds joint US-Saudi citizenship, against leaving Saudi Arabia was lifted. He flew to Washington two days later with his family.

On the same day, a rumour was released by two sources talking to Sky News that the victim's body parts had been found in a twelve-metre well in the garden of the Saudi consul general's residence. Not only had the body been dismembered, but Jamal Khashoggi's face had been disfigured and the fingers were missing. As Turkish investigators had complained about the fact that Saudi Arabia would not change the diplomatic protocol and permit investigators to search the garden or its two wells, it was not clear how Sky News thought Turkish authorities could have made such a discovery for which physical access was a requirement.

Another source leaked to the Middle East Eye news site that the victim's fingers had been flown back to Saudi Arabia to be presented to the crown prince as proof of the mission's success. The story about the fingers had been mooted very early on as well. What was new was that the source also leaked that Jamal had been injected with morphine.

Meanwhile President Erdoğan stoked the fire once again personally in a keynote address to the Turkish parliament on Tuesday 23 October, three weeks after the assassination. It was Turkey's first public account given by a named, top official directly in charge of Turkey's murder investigations and significant for that reason alone. His entire narrative, however, was either based on Saudi Arabia's concession of 19 October that Jamal was killed at the consulate or merely confirmed what could be deduced from evidence outside the consulate or the access given by Turkey's investigators to the diplomatic buildings.

Erdoğan reiterated that the hard drive of the consulate's CC-TV system had been removed. Turkish officials had already anonymously leaked this information, but Erdoğan confirmed it officially and revealed that it had been done just before the murder, showing Saudi premeditation.

'We have strong signs that the murder was the product of a planned operation,' he told Turkish MPs. 'This is a political killing.'

Erdoğan also insisted that the eighteen suspects be tried in Turkish courts. However, that would not be enough.

'Leaving some security and intelligence forces holding the bag will not satisfy us or the international community,' Erdoğan said in his speech, claiming to speak for the world. The Turkish leader had not given support in the case of nerve-agent poisoning in Salisbury that had led to the death of Dawn Sturgess and incapacitation of Sergei Skripal by *novichok*, Russia's top-secret chemical weapon.

'Saudi Arabia has taken an important step by admitting the murder. As of now we expect of them to openly bring to light those responsible – from the person who gave the order to those who carried it out – and to bring them to justice.'

He also promised that Turkey would reveal the 'naked truth' about Jamal Khashoggi's death.

'All evidence gathered shows that Jamal Khashoggi was the victim of a savage murder,' he said. 'To cover up such brutality would hurt human conscience.'

President Erdoğan was again careful not to mention MBS by name or rank in his speech. But, Abdulkadir Selvi, whose *Hürriyet* (another newspaper beholden to the Turkish government, owned by the Demirören conglomerate) columns were studied for indications of Erdoğan's thinking, had no such qualms. He wrote, 'We cannot close this file until the crown prince is brought to account and removed from his post.'

Selvi also offered a new salacious leak of information – the victim had not only been cut into fifteen pieces, he had been strangled slowly.

As Erdoğan said the body had not been found, speculation continued with leaks saying that it had been dissolved in acid, possibly in the consul-general's garage. Family and friends in Saudi Arabia were still asking for its return so Jamal could be buried properly and they could mourn.

Sources leaked to the Middle East Eye that Crown Prince Mohammed's intelligence officer Maher Mutreb, was thought to have taken part of the journalist's body out of Turkey in a large bag. When he left on the private jet the day of the murder, it was suggested, his bags were not checked before the plane left Atatürk Airport. It was also revealed that Mutreb placed seven calls to the mobile phone of Bader al-Asaker, manager of the crown prince's private office on the day of the murder, four times after the murder itself. There was no tabulation of data however, as when the names and airport entry times of the fifteen operatives were first revealed. That was, in fact, the first and last time such factual information had been released by Turkey alongside a leak in order to back it up. Hungry for new things to say, the media no longer insisted on such evidence.

Donald Trump called the Saudi story 'the worst cover-up ever' and his administration put penalties on the conspirators. Among those sanctioned were Maher Mutreb and his team, but also Saud al-Qahtani, and consul-general al-Otaibi. MBS, however, was not named. Congress did not agree.

'We are putting all our weight behind the Global Magnitsky request,' said a senior Senate aide. 'We do not want to sanction the low-hanging fruit, we want to go as high as possible.'

Prime Minister Theresa May followed President Trump's lead and announced that the Saudi officials suspected of being part of the plot to murder Jamal would be barred from entering Britain. Again there was no mention of the crown prince whom she had recently met as an honoured guest.

It was, in any case, not a very daring move by the US or the UK as the men had all been arrested in Saudi Arabia and, if not, would unlikely be allowed to leave the kingdom anytime soon.

It seemed that, privately, Saudi media personnel were not buying the government's account of Jamal's death either – though they couldn't cross red lines and make any of their reservations public within the kingdom, or go on the record by name.

'People around me are feeling frustrated by this justification of it. They understand and know that everything, no matter how small, is ordered by the government. They don't buy it,' said one television journalist who worked for a pro-government station. He had worked alongside Jamal when he was a prominent media figure in Riyadh and still in favour with the regime.

Although the journalist had to peddle the official line on air, he said, from his knowledge of the crown prince, 'there is no way he would not have known'.

27

'Pre-meditated'

When the poorly attended Future Investment Initiative conference – Davos in the desert – kicked off on 23 October in Riyadh with many of the key participants missing, even MBS was absent from the opening session that Tuesday morning.

He did turn up in the afternoon though. Bankers, corporate executives and Saudis stood as one to applaud in the ornate conference room when he finally arrived. But the applause was subdued compared to the thunderous ovation he had received at the Future Investment Initiative a year ago. Crown Prince bin Salman spent only 15 minutes at the event and left without giving his planned speech.

On the second day, he spoke to a packed auditorium, smoothly calling the murder of Jamal Khashoggi a 'heinous crime which cannot be justified' and vowing to bring the perpetrators to justice. Crown Prince Mohammed called the death of the *Washington Post* blogger 'very painful for both the Saudi people and the world'. In an echo of the Bloomberg interview he gave the day after Jamal Khashoggi had been dismembered, he claimed that the barbaric assassination was being exploited with malice by some to drive a wedge between Saudi Arabia and Turkey.

'I want to send them a message: They will not be able to do that as long as there is a king called King Salman bin Abdulaziz and a crown prince called Mohammed bin Salman in Saudi Arabia, and a president in Turkey called Erdoğan,' he said. 'Justice will be seen in the end.'

He could invoke the president's name because earlier on MBS had had his first telephone call with Erdoğan since the Khashoggi affair erupted. Tight-lipped, press agencies of both countries merely said the two leaders had agreed on 'joint efforts'.

While MBS said the two countries would work together to bring all the perpetrators to court, he did not address accusations that he ordered the assassination.

'He's not going to address the humongous elephant in the room, I bet,' one conference attendee, *Financial Times* Middle East correspondent Heba Saleh, had speculated before the crown prince gave his speech. Stunned silence met the first mention of Jamal's name, and a palpable relief followed. MBS's remarks received a short burst of applause, though the atmosphere remained strained.

Alongside MBS on the stage was the Lebanese prime minister. A year before, Saud al-Qahtani had led the Saudi interrogation of visiting then-prime minister Saad al-Hariri during a longer stay than planned about the growing Iranian influence in Lebanon. The upshot was al-Hariri's announcement on TV from Riyadh that he intended to resign. The man now seated next to MBS was – Saad al-Hariri

The crown prince joked that al-Hariri would only be staying in the kingdom for two days this time – 'so I hope you don't spread rumours that he was kidnapped,' he told the audience.

Al-Hariri laughed nervously and applauded. He had come back in favour after a leading Lebanese talk-show host was summoned to appear before al-Hariri in Beirut. The comedian had made a joke at the expense of the crown prince. Associated Press reported that 'reacting to a clip on a rival network advising bin Salman to swear off fast food for his health, [the talk-show host] suggested he should swear off fast arrests, fast politics ... fast military strikes, instead.'

Some delegates did not join the *folie à deux* and did little to hide their disdain for both the crime and the subsequent attempts to cover it up.

'These idiots have taken us back to the Stone Age,' said one. 'How do I defend this country to anyone anymore? The stupidity here is unparalleled.'

Others said the attempt to distance bin Salman from the slaying and blame it on his closest personal staff was doomed, but that they were forced to go along with it.

'It suits many of us to believe this, because the alternative is just too impossible,' said a Saudi businessman. 'But anyone who has lived here understands the fiction. And his friends outside cannot be expected to look away like us.'

Another said: 'This is very complicated. It is painful for the family and for the people. It is best to live in denial here.'

Abroad the crown prince's condemnation of the murder of Jamal was also seen as disingenuous.

It was now leaked by a US official that, in the days following the assassination, MBS had told top White House officials that Jamal was a member of the banned (in Saudi Arabia) Muslim Brotherhood and a dangerous Islamist. The top officials he spoke to were Jared Kushner and US national security advisor John Bolton. Unlike Tillerson, Bolton subscribed to the Trump – el-Sisi – MBS triangle that the Brotherhood was a terrorist rather than a political organisation.

'It will be harder under MBS to have the same degree of confidence we can work with Saudi Arabia in light of the brutal murder of Khashoggi,' said a former top western intelligence official. The cryptic comment almost seemed to suggest there had been a level of cooperation or, at any rate, sharing of information between the US and their close Saudi ally under Donald Trump on Jamal Khashoggi's rendition; and that cooperation on another rendition would be less likely because Saudi Arabia couldn't keep the lid on things.

On 25 October, Saudi Arabia changed its explanation of Jamal's death yet again. Now, the killing had no longer happened accidentally during a fistfight with rogue operatives.

Officials finally confirmed, that, yes, the fatal rendition had been planned all along. The Saudi prosecutor general Sheikh Saud al-Mojeb issued a statement on state television, saying: 'Information from the Turkish side affirms that the suspects in Khashoggi's case pre-meditated their crime.'

The Saudi announcement came hours after CIA director Gina Haspel, while on a fact-finding trip to Turkey, had listened to excerpts from the audio recording. While Riyadh might be sanguine ('we'll see'), the US seemed to worry that the domino stones would fall once the audio was in the public domain in the West. Riyadh blinked first.

'The public prosecution continues its investigations with the accused in the light of what it has received and the results of its investigations,' the sheikh said.

Turkey kept up the pressure on Saudi Arabia by making public instead the information it had possessed for weeks on the two members of the Saudi delegation led by Prince bin Faisal who had been sent to clean up the crime scene. Unlike the consulate, again it didn't make the sheikh's investigation look squeaky clean.

'We believe that the two individuals came to Turkey for the sole purpose of covering up evidence of Jamal Khashoggi's murder before the Turkish police were allowed to search the premises,' an anonymous senior Turkish official leaked the *Independent*. 'The fact that a clean-up team was dispatched from Saudi Arabia nine days after the murder suggests that Khashoggi's slaying was within the knowledge of top Saudi officials.'

After assiduously staying out of the media on Riyadh's orders, Jamal's two sons now suddenly took the spotlight on CNN to talk about their father in Washington DC. Jamal's oldest son Salah would later return to his family in Jeddah.

Seated next to each other they described their father as 'courageous, generous and very brave'. Thirty-five-year-old Salah told CNN: 'We just need to make sure that he rests in peace. Until now, I still can't believe that he's dead. It's not sinking in with me emotionally. It's not a normal situation, it's not a normal death at all. All what we want right now is to bury him in Al-Baqi [cemetery] in Medina with the rest of his family. I talked about that with the Saudi authorities and I just hope that it happens soon. It's an Islamic tradition. It's a basic humanitarian issue.'

Thirty-three-old Abdullah added: 'I really hope that whatever happened wasn't painful for him, or it was quick. Or he had a peaceful death.'

Asked how his father should be remembered, Salah said: 'As a moderate man who has common values with everyone… a man who loved his country, who believed so much in it and its potential. Jamal was never a dissident. He believed in the monarchy, that it is the thing that is keeping the country together. And he believed in the transformation that it is going through.'

The brothers also said their father was 'like a rock-'n'-roll star' when they were out with him in Saudi Arabia because of his career as a celebrated writer.

Their affection for their father showed the private and emotional side behind the news tragedy. Salah's words on his father's belief in the monarchy and its direction at the same time propped up the Saudi royal palace's latest version of events that deep-state secret-service officials had gone rogue.

The most significant new information was that Abdullah, Jamal's younger son now confirmed he knew Hatice Cengiz, contradicting the words of his older brother in the first week to al-Arabiya he had never heard of her. In fact, he knew her well. Abdullah said his father's Turkish fiancée was making Jamal happy. He was the last of Jamal's four children to see him alive on 10 September. He said: 'We hung out in Istanbul. We had fun. I was really lucky to have a last moment with him. I feel very grateful.'

Despite the allegations that the crown prince had ordered the assassination, older brother and Jeddah-banker Salah again reaffirmed his loyalty to the Saudi regime.

'The king has stressed that everybody involved will be brought to justice. And I have faith in that. This will happen. Otherwise Saudi Arabia wouldn't have started an internal investigation,' he said.

Jamal's two daughters, Noha and Razan, paid tribute to their father in the *Washington Post*, vowing that 'his light will never fade'. They called him 'Baba – a loving man with a big heart' and chimed in with their brothers.

'In truth, Dad was no dissident. If being a writer was ingrained in his identity, being a Saudi was part of that same grain,' they wrote, emphasising his passionate love of his homeland. 'It was vitally important to him to speak up, to share his opinions, to have candid discussions. And writing was not just a job; it was a compulsion. It was ingrained into the core of his identity, and it truly kept him alive.'

They recalled their childhood, when he would allow them to rifle through his paper-stuffed office.

'We loved it when he took us every weekend to the bookstore,' they wrote. 'We loved looking through his passport, deciphering new locations from pages covered with exit and entry stamps.... As children, we also knew our father as a traveller. His work took him everywhere, but he always returned to us with gifts and fascinating stories. We would stay up nights wondering where he was and what he was doing, trusting that no matter how long he was gone, we would see him again, wide-armed, waiting for a hug. As bittersweet as it was, we knew from a young age that Dad's work meant that his reach extended far beyond our family, that he was an important man whose words had an effect on people over a great distance.'

They recalled visiting him in Virginia during Ramadan (15 May – 14 June) in 2018. 'Dad... told us about the day he left Saudi Arabia, standing outside his doorstep, wondering if he would ever return. For while Dad had created a new life for himself in the United States, he grieved for the home he had left. Throughout all his trials and travels, he never abandoned hope for his country.'

They returned to his home in Virginia after his death. 'The hardest part was seeing his empty chair,' they said. 'His absence was deafening. We could see him sitting there, glasses on his forehead, reading or typing away. As we looked at his belongings, we knew he had chosen to write so tirelessly in the hopes that when he did return to the kingdom, it might be a better place for him and all Saudis. This is no eulogy, for that would confer a state of closure. Rather, this is a promise that his light will never fade.'

28

Theatre

Anonymous Turkish investigators leaked to *Yeni Şafak* on Sunday 26 October they believed Jamal's remains were still in Istanbul and had stopped searching elsewhere.

The anonymous officials speculated that Hatice Cengiz's call to the consulate, sometime after public hours had ended at 3.30pm, had panicked the Tiger Team and forced a change of plan and a decision to hide the remains of the body in garden well of the consul-general's residence. The original plan, Turkish investigators thought, had been to bury the body in Belgrad Forest.

The team had by now gone through 3,500 hours of MoBeSe footage from one hundred and thirty seven cameras placed in seventy two locations. After finally receiving Saudi permission to enter, they had searched the consulate, the twenty two cars going in and out, and the consul-general's residence. They had meanwhile been allowed to take water samples only of the residence's twelve-metre-deep garden well covered with a slab of marble. Prosecutors demanded that it would be drained for inspection, but Saudi Arabia refused to give any further access citing the fact Turkey had not included the garden in the protocol for access to the kingdom's diplomatic property in Istanbul.

The reason for this public summary moment in Turkey's leaks became clear on the Sunday night of 28 October. Arriving for a three day fact-finding tour, clad in flowing white robes, a black *bisht* of transparent wool with ornate gold-threaded *zari* trim, and driven around in a top-of-the-range black Mercedes, looking from underneath the same style white *ghutra* head-covering as Jamal's brother indicating purity, the

Saudi prosecutor general, Sheikh al-Mojeb, met with his counterpart in Istanbul Irfan Fidan and visited the consulate and the offices of MİT. He requested the handover of all evidence, audio, images as well as testimony in the possession of Turkey. He was also very interested in a virtual copy of all the data on Jamal's iPhones even though Turkey had not been able to crack their encryption.

To *Hürriyet* Turkish prosecutors leaked testily, 'We did not get the impression that they were keen on genuinely cooperating with the investigation'. To Middle East Eye, it was furthermore leaked that public prosecutor Fidan had felt 'humiliated' by the sheikh. It was noted that the Saudi prosecutor general was seen laughing and joking publically on camera in front of his hotel, the Swisshotel. This hotel – once, but no longer, Istanbul's top hotel since the arrival of a slew of more exclusive hotels in the economic upsurge following Erdoğan's rise to power in 2003 – had famously been stormed by Chechen Islamist terrorists in 2001 who rained bullets through its yawning marbled lobby and vast window overlooking the Bosphorus and took some 600 guests and staff hostage – though on that occasion no one had actually died.

Since al-Mojab did not provide the location of the body or the name of the collaborator, the Turkish team leaked that they declined to cooperate with his requests. Nonetheless, Erdoğan would confirm later that some audio from the consulate was played to the Saudi prosecutors, including the Skype calls by Saud al-Qahtani. One of the Saudis present said it was 'truly atrocious' and had speculated more randomly that one operative had taken 'heroin'.

The day after the Saudi prosecutor general left Istanbul, Erdoğan wrote in a *Washington Post* oped piece that Sheikh al-Mojeb 'refused to answer simple questions' until his third day when he extended an invitation *in lieu* of answers to Turkish investigators to come to Riyadh. They could then interview suspects themselves. Erdoğan said it felt like a 'desperate and deliberate stalling tactic'. He added, 'We know that the order to kill Khashoggi came from the highest levels of the Saudi government'. Now that it was clear that the audio recording was real,

Erdoğan threw down the gauntlet once more by implying their voices, or at least names, were on the recordings in Turkey's possession.

Istanbul chief prosecutor Irfan Fidan now issued his own statement, presenting for the first time his conclusions about the investigation into the assassination in a very brief statement.

'Jamal Khashoggi was strangled to death immediately after entering the consulate... The victim's body was dismembered and destroyed... in line with advance plans.' This statement nailed Turkey's colours to the mast and circumscribed the crime. It was now the official version based on forensics from which Turkey couldn't really shift position without looking unreliable. Fidan also noted that al-Mojeb had again refrained from saying anything about the supposed Turkish 'local collaborator'.

Less officially, Yasin Aktay commented in *Hürriyet* for the first time the detail that the point of the dismemberment of the victim was to make dissolving the body 'easier'. He didn't offer any evidence of this new hunch, however.

The official Saudi response to Turkey's anger was finely parsed. It simply made the point that the trial would proceed without Turkish evidence being taken into consideration. When criminal proceedings started against eleven of the accused on Thursday 3 January, the Saudi Press Agency would note that the prosecutors had sent four letters to their Turkish counterparts (two on 12 December, one on 17 October, another on 31 October). These letters had requested 'any evidence connected to this case'. The release stated, Sheikh al-Mojeb was 'still waiting [for] their response'.

Riyadh was implying that fair justice was being done and that Turkey should put up or shut up. Arguably this suited Turkey. While it had issued an arrest warrant *in absentia* for twenty one Saudis, handing over to someone else the criminal evidence they had gathered against the twenty one would also mean losing control of moulding the facts.

Amnesty International called Turkey's bluff. 'What we have are two so-called investigations', commented its UN delegation's head Sherine Tadros drily to *Business Insider* on 2 November.

Turkey's conduct had been 'highly suspect' and 'highly politicised'. While Erdoğan would claim a few days later on 2 November in his *Washington Post* oped that 'Turkey has moved heaven and earth to shed light on all aspects of this case', Amnesty International's UN delegate instead noted the opposite in that Turkey's leaks to papers at times contradicted Turkish official statements. It was polite of her not to reference that Erdoğan was the world's leading jailer of journalists by a long chalk.

On 15 November Turkish foreign minister Mevlüt Çavuşoğlu would call an international investigation 'a must'. The UN had, in fact, expressed interest in this on a number of occasions, but its officials could not act without a formal request from the Turkish government itself. When Çavuşoğlu met UN Secretary-General Antonio Guterres on 20 November, no request was made.

Such a probe would 'set a precedent for future inquiries' into its own journalists, which explained Turkey's procrastination, said Amnesty International's Tadros. What was really needed now was not Turkey's dubious and opportunistic approach but a 'credible' and 'transparent' investigation into Jamal Khashoggi's death.

Nor – in a rare moment of diplomatic dissonance – was the French foreign minister, Jean-Yves le Drian, very impressed with Erdoğan. Like Amnesty International he accused the Turkish president on France 2 of playing 'a political game'. His ministry later wheeled his words back a notch, noting more diplomatically that their minister had meant there was 'an absence of the 'full truth'.

Borzou Daraghi, international correspondent of the *Independent*, published probably the most disturbing piece of news in the middle of a 4000-word panoramic article in the news site's Long Read section on 30 October.

It had been passed on to him by sources who 'in the past provided accurate information about the Khashoggi case'. Separate from one another they had been informed respectively by a Saudi and a Turkish expert with first-hand knowledge of their country's forensic evidence that Jamal had been brutally tortured and beaten and interrogated.

This was in addition to what had already been leaked respectively publicly conceded by Turkey and Saudi Arabia. The Tiger Team had questioned Jamal violently about notes he had kept on the time he had worked with Prince Turki in the aftermath of 9/11, what he had been planning for the future, and about Saudi and Arab activists he knew.

The Turkish source said the ordeal had lasted for an hour whereas the Arab source had been given to understand it went on for two hours. Neither the details of the interrogation nor its duration was picked up by other media, even though the words 'tortured' and 'interrogated' had been regularly used in the leaks by Turkish officials since 7 October. Notably, in Turkish officials first-ever anonymous leak (to Middle East Eye) of what had been recorded they said, 'you can hear how he was interrogated, tortured... beaten'.

Daraghi's news filled in for the first time what had happened from the moment Jamal arrived at 1.15pm to the moment the consular cars left at 3.08pm. So far, Turkish leaks had covered at most 11 minutes.

No further Turkish leaks that corroborated Daraghi's account would appear thereafter. Turkish officials had already stopped using 'interrogated', 'torture' and 'beating' in their leaks. Irfan Fidan, the Istanbul lead prosecutor, had also just stated officially that Jamal had been 'strangled to death immediately after entering the consulate' and anything contradictory would undermine the credit Turkey had built up in salving 'hurt human conscience', in the words of Erdoğan to his parliament on 22 October.

Despite leaked protestations of being 'humiliated', the Istanbul prosecutor Fidan's statement concurred exactly on this point with the conclusions of Saudi prosecutor general Sheikh al-Mojeb. With the benefit of hindsight, the highpoint of entropy had certainly been reached. The interrogation/torture question never returned to the news cycle after this date.

Back in Saudi Arabia, the crown prince was shoring up his support among the ruling al-Saud family by finally releasing from custody Prince Khaled bin Talal, a nephew of King Salman, leading to speculation that other high-profile detainees would also be freed. Prince Khaled, the brother of billionaire investor Prince Alwaleed bin Talal, Jamal's sponsor who had been detained at the Ritz-Carlton anti-corruption shakedown, had criticised MBS's reforms and the mass Ritz-Carlton detentions. Prince Alwaleed himself had joked uneasily in an interview after his release that he had used his time as market research for the Four Seasons hotel chain in which he owned a substantial share.

Khaled and Alwaleed's father was the king's half-brother Prince Talal, or the 'red prince', nick-named after his liberal beliefs, whose mother was founder-King ibn Saud's sixteenth wife Munaiyir. After Jamal's assassination, the talkative financier Prince Alwaleed dispensed effusive praise for Saudi Arabia's crown prince during a television interview, though he looked 'visibly uncomfortable', the *Financial Times* said. His brother, Prince Khaled, had by then been held for some eleven months with dissidents and activists in al-Hayer prison, south of the capital, without charge and without his family knowing where he was held.

Prince Khaled's belated release on 3 November came days after the return from self-imposed exile in London of seventy-three-year-old Prince Ahmed, the king's younger brother of their mother Sudairi, ibn Saud's fourteenth wife.

The release of Prince Alwaleed's brother was thought to have been a condition for Ahmed's return. Another condition was the guarantee for Prince Ahmed's own safety by the US and the UK. Though removed from succession in 2012, he was rumoured to be still *papabile* and being lined up as possible replacement for MBS as crown prince. Whether true or not, his return also marked a subtle end to the high-tide of MBS's power grab against the old guard of royal princes.

In a further attempt to limit the fallout from Jamal's murder, King Salman embarked on a week-long tour of Saudi Arabia, his first domestic tour since taking the throne in 2015.

The crown prince claimed that only eight people were still being detained from the Ritz-Carlton shake-down, but the *Washington Post* put the figure closer to forty five. Despite MBS's claim, oppression was not easing. New regulations were introduced to control the media. They were, it was decreed by the government, intended to protect public order, strengthen national unity, preserve the social fabric, and preserve values and virtues. Women working in media also had to comply with strict Islamic dress codes.

MBS wants just 'one voice', said Yahya Assiri, a former Saudi airforce officer and UK-based activist. 'In the past there could be some criticism with red lines for the media, but now there's just one line, one voice, repeating MBS and that's it,' he said.

Notwithstanding the rumour of government torture of some of MBS's 2017–2018 non-royal guests at the Riyadh Ritz-Carlton, its hotel staff was named 'Hotel Team of the Year' and its general manager 'Highly Commended' at the 2018 Hotelier Middle East Awards held in Dubai.

The royal palace itself was seeking to recruit yet more London- and US-based public relations agencies to rehabilitate its shattered international image with huge fees.

Prince Khaled would be rearrested on unspecified charges days after his influential father died on 22 December.

29

The Recording

Turkey still wanted Saudi Arabia to admit Jamal's death had been an assassination planned in Riyadh and not an operational accident. On 10 November President Erdoğan officially acknowledged the existence of the audio inside the consulate by confirming a clip had been released to the secret services of the US, UK, Germany, France and Saudi Arabia. France hadn't received its copy yet when Erdoğan made the announcement, which had prompted the comment by the French foreign minister that the president was playing 'political games'.

Like a cluster-bomb, it renewed global coverage with a vengeance. By handing over the recordings (or rather, the edited excerpts) to spooks, Turkey ensured that the recording retained its mystique while creating further news headlines. At the same time, the recipients would now be expected to give an official response to what they had been given.

President Erdoğan said: 'We played them to all who wanted them including the Saudis, the US, France, Canada, Germany, Britain. The recordings are really appalling. Indeed when the Saudi intelligence officer listened to the recordings he was so shocked he said: "This one must have taken heroin, only someone who takes heroin would do this".' The Saudi's implication that Tubaigy ('this one') had taken heroin clarified that the Tiger Team had gone off-*piste* in a Manson-style murder, which underlined the 'gone rogue' story on which the governments involved seemed to have settled finally.

He also called on Saudi Arabia to identify the actual killer from among the fifteen-man team who had arrived in Istanbul before the murder.

'There's no need to distort this issue, they know for certain that the killer, or the killers, is among these fifteen people,' he said.

President Erdoğan, furthermore, suggested, 'Saudi Arabia's government can disclose this by making these fifteen people talk.'

Inevitably more detail of the assassination was leaked. Turkish newspaper of government record, *Sabah*, said on 12 November that Jamal's words at the beginning of his death were: 'I'm suffocating... Take this bag off my head, I have asthma.'

Donald Trump confirmed that the US had the tape, but expressed little interest in listening to it.

'We have the tape, I don't want to hear the tape. There's no reason for me to hear the tape,' he said. 'Because it's a suffering tape, it's a terrible tape. I've been fully briefed on it, there's no reason for me to hear it. I was told I really shouldn't. It was very violent, very vicious and terrible.'

Others did listen to the recording and once again its contents began to leak. It was said that, soon after Jamal entered the consulate, he could be heard saying at the beginning of the altercation: 'Let go of my arm. Who do you think you are? Why are you doing this?'

'It was premeditated murder,' Turkey's foreign minister Mevlüt Çavuşoğlu told Germany's *Sueddeutsche Zeitung* newspaper. Germany, was the first country to sanction Saudi Arabia over Jamal, suspending arms sales to the kingdom on 22 October (only The Netherlands, Finland and Denmark would follow suit).

'It can be heard how the forensics expert instructs the others they should listen to music while he cuts up the body. One notices how he enjoys it. He likes to cut up people. It is disgusting.'

He added that the Saudi crown prince 'said he wanted the journalist silenced' and confirmed that Jamal was dead within 7 minutes. Though he did not mention the three-hundred-and-eighty-four Turkish journalists in gaol or under criminal investigation his government sought to silence. Nor was he asked about them.

While the Saudis had conceded there were 'advance plans' for Jamal's dismemberment given the bone-saw, President Erdoğan impressed again on everyone that the order had come from the top level of Saudi authorities.

But he also added he could not think such a thing of King Salman, for whom he has 'limitless respect'. On the day of the Jamal's sons' conciliation meeting with King Salman in October, the Turkish head of state had also gone out of his way not to embarrass the head of state of Saudi Arabia, his peer, and instead lauded King Salman's 'sincerity' in his address to Turkish parliamentarians. This was despite the fact that he had billed his speech on the day as the moment he would reveal 'the naked truth'. Erdoğan's speech hadn't even acknowledged the recordings, despite the leaks by Turkish officials.

Then, on 13 November, Erdoğan for the first time criticised MBS directly: 'The crown prince says "I will clarify the matter, I will do what is necessary". We are waiting patiently', and, 'It must be revealed who gave them the order to murder.'

Foreign minister Çavuşoğlu made public that the crown prince had asked to meet President Erdoğan at the forthcoming G20 meeting in Buenos Aires. 'At the moment there is no reason not to meet with the crown prince,' Çavuşoğlu said tortuously.

He added incredulously that Riyadh had offered to send identikit photos of the putative local 'collaborators' who had taken away Jamal's body in a rug. 'Why identikit pictures? The Saudis know the names,' he told the *Sueddeutsche Zeitung*.

Other countries kept the pressure up, too, for more to give. Secretary of State Mike Pompeo phoned MBS to tell him that the US would 'hold all of those involved in the killing of Jamal Khashoggi accountable, and that Saudi Arabia must do the same', while British Foreign Secretary Jeremy Hunt brought the matter up with King Salman during a visit to Saudi Arabia.

Turkey's game of leaks to the media continued. The *New York Times* reported on 12 November that shortly after the assassination a member of the kill team said, in a hacked phone call – leaked to the *New York*

Times – to his superior: 'The deed is done, tell your boss.' The words were uttered by brigadier-general Maher Mutreb. The source added that American intelligence officials believed 'your boss' ('yours' transliterated from the Arabic) was Crown Prince Mohammed bin Salman. At least three outside calls were placed by Mutreb and during the last one he had said this, speaking calmly.

Sabah published on 13 November four X-ray scans of some of the Tiger Team's luggage. Turkish officials had the scans for more than month but the images now told their own stark story in a fresh jacket. Visible in the grainy orange pictures were the outlines in blue of walkie-talkies, a signal jammer, scalpel blades, staple guns, long scissors and syringes. Also visible were, the paper said, electro-shock devices, though *Sabah* didn't speculate why they had been brought along. The bags themselves were not opened due to diplomatic immunity, the paper said.

As was increasingly the case with the Turkish leaks of visual material, it was not exactly stated whether it was luggage loaded on the first or the second jet. One paper even showed a leaked CC-TV grab of major-general Abahussein in his white *thaub* with a red-white blocked *ghutra* arriving at Atatürk Airport on the afternoon of 1 October in tow with al-Hawsawi in a blue T-shirt and baseball cap pushing two large rolling suitcases. The four X-rays pictures were linked by arrows to the four pieces of luggage they were rolling in total, suggesting that the scans may not have dated to 2 October but to the day before when they arrived and were made at the commercial terminal, where they entered, rather than at the Genel Havacilik private-jet lounge.

Most papers, including *Sabah*, implied, however, that the four suitcases belonged to Jamal's former colleague Maher Mutreb – who went through Genel Havacilik's airport security 5 minutes before MİT opened its investigation. Yet this in itself contradicted what an anonymous official had leaked weeks before to Middle East Eye that Mutreb's bags had not been checked, and that he might have taken body parts back to Riyadh. That leak, then, precluded news-cycle questions why MİT had not arrested the operatives on the second jet after it had identified the tools used for the assassination which they supposedly knew about along.

In Riyadh, Saudi deputy prosecutor Shalaan al-Shalaan revealed on 15 November that by now twenty one 'conspirators' were in custody – although it was not possible to verify what this meant, given the prohibition of a free press in Saudi Arabia. Eleven of the people in custody were indicted, with the death penalty being asked for five of them, while investigations continued into the remaining ten. The death-penalty five were negotiation-team leader Mutreb, Tubaigy, al-Balawi, Waleed and Turki al-Sehri. Four others were indicted under lesser criminal charges and included al-Madani, Saif al-Qahtani, and al-Zahrani. The operatives who had gone to the consulate were not charged, except for major-general Abahussein, who was in over-all command of the operation. Of the Istanbul consulate staff only attaché al-Musleh was indicted, but not al-Muzaini. From Riyadh, only major-general Asiri was charged (UN detail 192, Table D).

The prosecutor gave a rare press statement to set out in person in seventeen bullet points what Saudi Arabia agreed had happened. Although, al-Shalaan didn't mention names, he did mention the official functions of the perpetrators.

Saudi Arabia conceded that the killers had set their plans in motion on 29 September, three days before Jamal was murdered and the day after he had first visited the kingdom's consulate in Istanbul. The deputy chief of Saudi Arabia's intelligence, major-general Ahmed al-Asiri, issued the order to repatriate Jamal. But the head of 'the negotiating team', brigadier-general Mutreb, was in fact the one who had issued the order for his killing while in Istanbul.

The team had consisted of 'three groups (negotiations/ intelligence/ logistics) to persuade and return the victim' and Mutreb had been assigned as leader of the negotiation team, 'because of his previous relationship with the victim' when they were both working at the London embassy. As to the body, the leader of the three groups major-general Abahussein, 'contacted a collaborator in Turkey to secure a safe location in case force had to be used [to] return the victim'.

'After surveying the consulate, the head of the negotiation team [Maher Mutreb] concluded that it would not be possible to transfer the victim by force to the safe location in case the negotiations with him to return failed', the prosecutor told the press. 'The head of the negotiation team decided to murder the victim if the negotiations failed.'

'The crime was carried out after a physical altercation with the victim where he was forcibly restrained and injected with a large amount of a drug resulting in an overdose that led to his death'.

Riyadh accepted that Jamal Khashoggi had been assassinated by royal officials. The conditional decision, they now said, had been made by Mutreb on the day to kill him with an overdose.

'Those who ordered and carried out the murder, totalling (five) individuals', the Saudi press statement added, 'have confessed to the murder.'

Unfortunately, the whereabouts of the body were unknown, because there was the mystery 'local collaborator' who received the body from one of the team. That team member, however, did give a description which was the basis for a 'composite sketch.'

Prosecutor al-Shalaan went on to insulate MBS from criticism by providing other reasons to show it was an operational cockup that led to the victim's death. MBS's top advisor al-Qahtani had stressed at the beginning of the rendition that returning Jamal to Riyadh would be a 'significant achievement.'

Moreover, major-general al-Asiri had been lied to, the Saudi prosecutors claimed. The negotiation team headed by brigadier-general Mutreb and the leader of the operation major-general Abahussein confessed to filing a false report with their superior major-general al-Asiri that said 'the victim had left the consulate building after the failure of negotiating or forcing his return.'

It was a compelling story, except for the fact that, ostensibly, al-Asiri 'The Beast' had accepted that a fifty-nine-year old suffering from a severe cold and asthma seemed to have single-handedly outmanoeuvred the Tiger Team to walk away from the consulate, unharmed, by wielding words.

Mevlüt Çavuşoğlu, Turkey's foreign minister, claimed he was not satisfied and said in response to al-Shalaan's statements, 'those who gave the orders, the real perpetrators need to be' caught. His Saudi counterpart foreign minister Adel al-Jubeir responded curtly, 'we refuse any attempt to criticise' the independence of the Saudi judiciary. King Salman duly praised the Saudi magistrates for exonerating his son.

On 16 November, however, the *Washington Post* reported as a riposte that the CIA had concluded that Crown Prince bin Salman ordered the assassination of journalist Jamal Khashoggi. It was later leaked that MBS sent at least eleven messages to Saud al-Qahtani, who was overseeing the operation, in the hours surrounding the murder. Al-Qahtani was one of the officials who was sacked as part of the investigation by the Saudi prosecutor general and one of seventeen people sanctioned under the Magnitsky Act by the US treasury department for being linked to the killing. Al-Qahtani's last public tweet was on 22 October, twenty days after Jamal's last tweet.

Again Saudi officials repeatedly denied that MBS had any involvement. Unofficially, a CIA official, however, told the *Post*: 'The accepted position is there is no way this happened without his being aware or involved.'

The agency had reached its conclusions after examining multiple sources of intelligence, including a phone call that the prince's brother, Khalid bin Salman, the Saudi ambassador to the United States, had with Jamal. The CIA officer's implication was that Jamal and KBS had spoken about where to have the two marriage documents certified, and that KBS had said, not in DC but only in Istanbul or Ankara.

Khalid tweeted back furiously: 'I never talked to him by phone and certainly never suggested he go to Turkey for any reason. I ask the US government to release any information regarding this claim.'

KBS also tweeted that a text on 26 October 2017 was his last contact with Jamal, nearly a year before the journalist's death. The CIA did not release the information it claimed it had in its possession.

On the same day, the *Washington Post* had another bombshell. A strikingly beautiful fifty-year-old Egyptian woman living in the Persian Gulf region going by the *nom de plume* of Hanan Atr said that she was the fourth wife of Jamal's. She and Jamal had met at a conference a decade ago but became romantically involved in 2018 and they were married under Sharia law in June by Anwar Hajjaj, an imam and professor at American Open University in Virginia (he didn't return the *Post*'s call). She had pictures of the ceremony and text messages and a 'long-time associate' of Jamal's confirmed he was at the ceremony. She did not have civil marriage papers however as neither she nor Jamal had made the arrangement legal when their marriage fervour didn't last. Despite the religious marriage their relationship had fizzled out, and she last saw him in early September – presumably before the 10th when Jamal travelled to Istanbul to introduce his youngest son Abdullah to his new, fifth wife – when Ms Atr was in the US on business.

Ms Atr confirmed that she had contacted Saudi officials at her local Gulf-area consulate with the pictures. Under Sharia law, the legal wife with no issue is entitled to up to one-fourth of the estate (more than if there are children). She 'explained that as a Muslim wife, I want my full right and to be recognised'.

The pictures of her as fourth wife and Jamal as husband soon emerged on a Twitter feed loyal to Riyadh and showed a beaming Jamal kissing Ms Atr dressed in what looked like a white marriage gown with an expensive-looking necklace of ruby-red jewels surrounded by what looked like diamonds and matching long earrings dripping with matching stones – one photograph was a selfie of the necklace and part of their faces. Jamal himself was dressed in a casual light-blue blazer and oxford-striped shirt, grey trousers and black leather shoes. In another picture he kissed Ms Atr tenderly on her cheek. The time of year of the marriage seemed to be warm and rainy, but not yet hot. In a further picture taken earlier in the season they were both smiling full-size to the camera while she was dressed in a heavy sabre-style fur coat and Jamal wore a shearling sheepskin jacket with his arm around her while holding a debonair grey trilby in his right hand on her waist and an elegant gift bag in his left hand.

Hatice Cengiz, who had been told about the previous three marriages, said she had 'never heard of the woman'. Was this the kingdom publicity machine striking back she wondered? Later, in February 2019, when she gave an interview to *Sabah* in order to publicise the release of her book *Jamal Khashoggi,* she tempered her judgement and said 'I do not know the life Jamal had before me. I only know the part about me'. Although she did think it was wrong to claim money or to seek publicity with photographs. 'It is not moral', she rebuked Jamal's fourth wife in the paper.

The news of the fourth marriage that the Saudis had fed into the news cycle blotted Jamal's memory and Istanbul responded with a barrage of newly leaked facts taking aim at the Saudi narrative that the murder decision was taken in Istanbul by Mutreb alone.

'Khashoggi's body injected with clotting agent,' shouted a *Yeni Şafak* headline on 17 November. Officials leaked to the paper that, after he was strangled, the drug the Saudi prosecutor had mentioned was meant 'to leave no blood trace' rather than cause his death by overdose. Like the bone-saw, bringing blood-clotting agent showed the degree to which his death had been anticipated during the Tiger Team's operational preparations in Riyadh – it was not a decision on the hoof in Istanbul, it implied.

The paper also said Turkish investigators claimed that 'hydrofluoric acid and other chemicals' were found in the water samples of the well of the consulate-general's garden, indicating that the body was dissolved. Again, the implication was that these chemicals had been brought in anticipation of Jamal's assassination. But no measurements that at least *prima facie* in a forensic way supported these anonymous leaks was provided.

There was also a new lugubrious audio snippet 'It is creepy to wear the clothes of a man whom we killed 20 minutes ago,' Jamal's body-double al-Madani said on the consulate audio. It was leaked on 19

November to *Haberturk*, part of the same media conglomerate as Bloomberg Turkey – one-time owner of then independently-minded *Sabah* before the Turkish government seized it on a technicality and sold it at a knock down price to Erdoğan's AKP friend at the Demirören group with a state loan.

Al-Madani also complained that Jamal's shoes were too small and his feet got stuck. He asked the team leader for permission to wear his own sneakers, which led to the exterior CC-TV debacle. Before al-Madani left the consulate's backdoor at 2.52pm, he and Saif al-Qahtani were given instructions to 'first walk for four streets, take a taxi, go to Sultanahmet, get rid of clothes, and meet us at the consulate-general's residence'. They didn't execute the last instruction, perhaps an indication that Tiger-Team leader brigadier-general Abahussein gave the men new orders when Turkish authorities showed up at the private-jet terminal looking for Jamal and he therefore didn't want the look-alike on the jet, or an indication that they were disturbed by Hatice's call to the consulate at 4pm, an hour after al-Madani and Saif al-Qahtani had left.

To *Haberturk*'s Çetiner Çetin a story about the locations of the microphones in the consulate was leaked, including statements by Turkish investigators that some of the signal jamming by the Saudis had been successful.

Writing in *Hürriyet* – whose owner had wept in 2014, calling Erdoğan 'boss', when rebuked over a negative piece on the president – Khashoggi-conduit Abdulkadir Selvi also reported leaked information that the CIA had a recording of MBS giving instructions to 'silence Jamal Khashoggi as soon as possible'. The recording had been made as the result of a US wiretap. The crown prince and his brother KBS were reportedly heard discussing the 'discomfort' created by Jamal's public criticism of the kingdom's administration.

How a Turkish paper would obtain privileged CIA information was not clear, unless perhaps the CIA had leaked this as a gesture of the new *détente* to the Turkish government and as an answer to KBS's furious tweet to show their evidence.

Selvi also introduced a new character, injecting more family drama into the affair.

'The hit squad, which was composed of close aides of Crown Prince Mohammed, told Khashoggi to send a message to his son, otherwise he "would be brought to Saudi Arabia"... [whom they] had earlier contacted.'

Magnifying the mystery, *Hürriyet* did not spell out what that message might have been. Instead Selvi merely stated Jamal rejected the demand in order to protect his son, which in turn 'led to the quarrel that ended with his killing by strangulation with a rope or plastic bag.' Spelling out the finishing touch to the tragedy, Selvi wrote: 'The subsequent murder is the ultimate confirmation of this instruction [by MBS].'

President Trump still refused to accept that the crown prince knew anything about the murder, because had himself talked to the man.

'He told me he had nothing to do with it,' Trump argued. 'He told me that, I would say, maybe five times. He did certainly have people that were reasonably close to him and close to him that were probably involved.... But at the same time we do have an ally and I want to stick with an ally that in many ways has been very good.' This was presumably a reference to the $350bn and counting deal he was keen to bring in.

It was now argued that – as Riyadh had conceded a potentially fatal rendition had in principle been sanctioned by high Saudi officials close to the crown prince – MBS must have known about it. A Western diplomat in Riyadh told the *Sunday Times*: 'He is the only real centre of power in the kingdom. There's no one that is seriously challenging him. And that also means there is no one else that could have ordered the murder.'

Mourners gathered in mosques in Mecca and Istanbul though still no body had been produced and there was nothing to bury.

The mystery concerning the body's whereabouts deepened when this time one of Turkey's most senior politicians, defence minister Hulusi Akar, went officially on the record as one of the few Turkish senior authorities apart from Erdoğan.

He once again speculated that the killers might have taken the body parts out of Turkey, even though this conflicted with statements from the criminal investigators working for the Istanbul chief prosecutor who seemed to have abandoned this idea days before Sheikh al-Mojeb's fact-finding tour in Istanbul, and also with statements that the luggage on both private jets had gone through airport X-ray. Was he saying that the leaked X-rays were of the second jet, and that Turkey had no X-ray records of Mutreb's team's luggage going through security to the first plane due to lax security at Atatürk private-jet terminal as reported by the Middle East Eye? Either way, his comments created a talking point that tied in with the news – this time the virtual burial ceremony in Istanbul's Fatih Mosque.

'One probability is that they left the country three to four hours [on the 'getaway' Gulfstream IV] after committing the murder. They may have taken out Khashoggi's dismembered corpse inside luggage without facing problems due to their diplomatic immunity,' he said in Halifax, Canada.

While the CIA said that MBS was behind the murder of Jamal, President Trump maintained this didn't mean that the jury wasn't still out on 20 November.

'Our intelligence agencies continue to assess all information, but it could very well be that the crown prince had knowledge of this tragic event,' he said. In a sideways move he equivocated not on the facts known to the CIA, but rather on their sum total. He doubted whether these facts merited the CIA's conclusion beyond reasonable doubt: 'Maybe he did and maybe he didn't!... We may never know all of the facts.'

Trump agreed to meet MBS at the upcoming G20 meeting in Buenos Aires, a city overlooked by a Trump hotel in Punta del Este. He was after the nuclear arms deal and was duly praised by MBS's friends in the Gulf States for his stead-fast loyalty to the crown prince.

However, two senior senators again wielded the 2012 Global Magnitsky Act in an attempt to order the president to determine whether the crown prince was responsible for Jamal's death.

'In light of recent developments, including the Saudi government's acknowledgement that Saudi officials killed Mr Khashoggi in its Istanbul consulate, we request that your determination specifically address whether Crown Prince Mohammed bin Salman is responsible,' they wrote.

'I disagree with the president's assessment. It's inconsistent... with the intelligence I've seen... The intelligence I've seen suggests that this was ordered by the crown prince,' Republican senator Mike Lee said on NBC's Meet the Press. Plainly he felt President Trump's assertion was at odds with the evidence.

'It is not in our national security interests to look the other way when it comes to the brutal murder of Mr Jamal Khashoggi,' Republican senator and former presidential rival Lindsey Graham concurred. 'Mr Trump has betrayed American values in service to what already was a bad bet on the thirty-three-year-old prince.'

Writing on Twitter, Bob Corker, chairman of the Senate foreign relations committee added witheringly: 'I never thought I'd see the day a White House would moonlight as a public relations firm for the crown prince of Saudi Arabia.'

While Donald Trump continued to insist that the CIA had not found MBS responsible and had come to no conclusion, Jack Reed, the senior Democrat on the senate armed services committee, put it more bluntly and said yes that the President was 'lying', foregoing the usual media euphemisms of 'false statements' or misspeaking.

'The CIA concluded that the crown prince of Saudi Arabia was directly involved in the assassination of Khashoggi,' he said. Not only that, Reed added the CIA had 'high confidence' in its assessment.

'It's based on facts, it's based on analysis,' he said. 'The notion that they didn't reach a conclusion is just unsubstantiated. The CIA has made that clear.'

The considerable pressure that was building up on Saudi Arabia to do something, and Trump's defence of his friend in the desert kingdom, did have one further result though.

In December 2016, with Trump a month away from moving into the White House, MBS as minister of defence had started discussing the purchase by the palace of the US THAAD air defence system designed to shoot down all types of hostile missiles. Lockheed had developed the system after the experience with Scud missiles in the first Iraq War.

On 28 November 2018 the kingdom signed a letter of offer and acceptance for a 'massive sale' of forty four THAAD launchers, missiles and related equipment. The deal was worth $15bn. On 1 April 2019 the Pentagon would announce the first step in rolling out the system to Saudi Arabia.

30

High-five!

Before travelling to the G20 in Argentina on 30 November, MBS visited the United Arab Emirates, where he met his closest ally, Sheikh Mohammed bin Zayed crown prince of Abu Dhabi, the federation's *de facto* ruler. He would go on to Gulf state Bahrain, Egypt and Tunisia – all thought to be friendly allies sponsored by the kingdom – on his way to Buenos Aires. The tour sent a message to the world that MBS's position remained unassailable in the kingdom. It was the diplomatic equivalent of saying there will be no change and it is safe for the crown prince to be out of the country.

Nonetheless, when MBS landed in Tunisia, the birthplace of the Arab Spring, there were demonstrations and popular protests. A large banner hanging from the headquarters of the Tunisian journalists' union showed the crown prince wielding a chain saw – a reference to the dismemberment of Jamal's corpse. Demonstrators carried placards saying, 'The murderer is not welcome' and 'Go away assassin', while some held up hacksaws.

'It's inhuman to see an Arab leader killing his brothers in Yemen, and the murder of a journalist is the icing on the cake,' said Basma Rezgui, a teacher brandishing a red-stained bone saw.

'He's a very dangerous person because he doesn't seem to understand politics or respect his own people or other people,' said Radwan Masmoudi, president of Tunisia's Centre for the Study of Islam and Democracy, who was among those protesting MBS's visit. 'There's no way he'll bring stability. His actions speak louder than his words.'

On the same day that MBS started his trip, the Istanbul chief prosecutor revisited defence minister Akar's words and decided to restart the search for Jamal's body in a new location. This was even though his officials had said before Sheikh al-Mojeb's Istanbul visit they considered the well in the consul-general's garden Jamal's last resting place. Turkish police now, trailed by the media like MBS on his trip, publicly searched a palatial villa near the town of Termal in the Yalova province near Istanbul. This was the area where MİT had accidentally traced the consulate's secret service staff in the evening before the murder.

The villa belonged to Mohammed al-Fawzan, a Saudi businessman close to MBS. On 26 November, Istanbul's chief prosecutor duly added this name to the roster of the Saudi hit squad.

Al-Fawzan, codenamed 'Ghozan', had been called by brigadier-general Abahussein, the leader of the hit squad, when he arrived in Istanbul on the day before Jamal's assassination.

'The chief prosecutor's office believes that this phone call was about disappearing or hiding the body parts of the murdered journalist Jamal Khashoggi,' the official press statement said. Al-Fawzan was not in Turkey when Jamal Khashoggi was killed, but Turkish investigators believed he may have let the hit squad use his property – though there was no suggestion that al-Fawzan personally knew of the assassination or that that the hit squad would try to hide Jamal at his property. Large photographs of King Salman and the crown prince adorned the walls inside the villa.

Investigators clad in white suits with blue gloves and show covers took a particular interest in a well on the grounds of the villa, which they drained and in which they said they found traces of chemicals – though not which ones and what it signified. They used drones and dogs in the ten-hour search, which covered the grounds of a neighbouring property. The TV footage of their progress matched the progress of MBS's tour through the Middle East.

'Jamal Khashoggi's body was cut into pieces and dissolved after his murder in the Saudi consulate in Istanbul,' said the prosecutor's press release. 'As a part of the ongoing investigation, it has been detected that the day before suspect Mansour [Abahussein] got in touch with Saudi citizen Mohammed Ahmed [al-Fawzan] in Yalova. It is assumed that their conversation is connected to the Khashoggi murder, and the dissolving and hiding of his body.'

The prosecutor also noted that a man named Mohammed Ahmed al-Fawzan had been appointed head of a Saudi company shortly after the crown prince seized control of it from one of the rich Saudis he had imprisoned on corruption charges at the 2017 Riyadh Ritz Carlton shakedown.

In Buenos Aires, Human Rights Watch submitted papers calling on Argentina to use a clause in its constitution to prosecute MBS for the murder of Jamal Khashoggi and war crimes in Yemen if he attended the G20. A file containing details of Jamal's slaying and other cases of torture was sent to the Argentinian prosecutor's office. Argentina's constitution recognises universal jurisdiction for war crimes and torture. This meant the authorities can investigate and prosecute those crimes no matter where they were committed. The Argentine prosecutor did accept the request to prosecute Mohammed bin Salman, but when MBS arrived in Argentina, he was warmly received by government officials nonetheless.

When the G20 summit opened in Buenos Aires on 30 November, Prime Minister Theresa May said she would confront the crown prince about the killing of Jamal Khashoggi. They shook hands, at any rate. A Downing Street spokesman said: 'The Prime Minister stressed the importance of ensuring that those responsible for the appalling murder of Jamal Khashoggi are held to account, and that Saudi Arabia takes action to build confidence that such a deplorable incident could not happen again.'

French President Emmanuel Macron also had a word. MBS told him not to worry about Jamal's murder.

'I am worried,' Macron had replied. 'You never listen to me.'

'I will listen, of course,' MBS replied. 'It's OK. I can deal with it.'

But the most significant meeting was between President Putin and

MBS.

Putin had grown up in Soviet Russia at the height of its power and had been stationed as Komissariat-5 KGB officer in East Germany where the Stasi, the German equivalent of the KGB, held files on over one third of the total population. MBS, unlike most Saudi royals, had never lived abroad or outside a Saudi palace. Both authoritarians (together with Erdoğan and, arguably, Trump) instinctively treated their national media as a power tool.

Putin was well-seasoned in flouting international opinion since his rule began in 2001 – it didn't penetrate the Russian media carapace. Like MBS he had started out being the darling of the Western media, hailed in his case as a breath of fresh air after dipsomaniac Boris Yeltsin. It had lasted until the excruciating death by poisoning on 23 November 2006 of his former colleague, FSB colonel Alexander Litvinenko, in London, with rare isotope Polonium 210 exclusively produced in a high-security Russian-government facility.

He had countered what was levelled at Russia with his own 'facts' and 'conclusions' in a precursor to what other governments called 'false news' and 'alternative facts'. Since then he had invaded and incorporated Crimea as part of Russia, fired on Ukrainian boats in the Kerch Strait, and violated the air space of other nations among other more insidious interference in local politics often through its superior understanding of cyber warfare.

Apart from Litvinenko, Putin had got away with the assassination of many inconvenient people outside of Russia. There were mysterious deaths, fifteen notable ones in Britain alone. Dr Matthew Puncher, the scientist who identified Polonium 210 committed suicide after a visit to Russia, as did Putin's arch-opponent Boris Berezovsky, seemingly choosing a shower-curtain rail and a tie to hang himself. There were even some unexplained deaths of Russians once close to Putin in supposedly safe America, such as Putin aide Mikhael Lesin in 2015. Russia's latest casualties was Dawn Sturgess, who had tragically died on 8 July 2018 of the poison intended for fellow Salisbury-resident, the former GRU colonel Sergei Skripal. Little deterred Russia.

When Putin launched his surprise attack on 'traitor' Sergei Skripal at the energy conference on 3 October, it was the day after Jamal Khashoggi had been assassinated. His disappearance was feverishly being debated on Middle-Eastern social media, and Putin had summarised his own experience with the fall-out of international opinion for his listeners – including MBS's right-hand man, energy minister Khalid al-Falih.

Dismissing it as 'hubbub', he advised his audience that opinions would always die down eventually. The brouhaha was not a real problem. The real challenge for a government, Putin observed, was that 'espionage, like prostitution, is one of the most important professions in the world. Nobody has managed to stop them and nobody is still able to do it.' When dealing with a traitor, as a government you ignore the talk and focus on what is really important – you lance the boil.

Two days before the G20, the Kremlin had promised a face-to-face meeting between MBS and Putin where they 'would discuss the killing last month of Saudi journalist Jamal Khashoggi… oil markets and the conflict in Syria'. Russia was the third largest oil producer in the world. Saudi Arabia was at the fulcrum of global chatter due to the assassination recordings. MBS, head of Aramco, was also the world's largest oil producer after the US.

Like school boys MBS and Putin high-fived and it was all smiles.

There was no publicity value in being seen with either and President Donald Trump appeared to snub them both. President Erdoğan didn't meet MBS after all. As Erdoğan had just started including MBS's name in his public calls for 'justice' it would create a mixed message.

In Washington, DC, protestors renamed the street outside the Royal Embassy of Saudi Arabia 'Khashoggi Way'. Their fake street sign was accompanied by an inflatable rat made to mimic Donald Trump.

Also shortly after the summit, a trove of private text messages between Jamal and Montreal-based activist Omar Abdulaziz surfaced. They revealed yet another part of Jamal's secretive side.

One read: 'Like Pac-Man... the more victims he [MBS] eats, the more he wants. I will not be surprised if the oppression will reach even those who are cheering him on.' Another called the ruler who had never lived outside the kingdom a 'beast' – also the nickname of the sacked major-general al-Asiri.

It was claimed that Jamal was preparing a social media protest against the regime before he was murdered. He and Abdulaziz outlined plans to post documents detailing human rights abuses carried out by Saudi Arabia and to spread the information via the tweets of young Saudi dissidents, CNN reported. Jamal had pledged $30,000 towards the plan, which included sending untraceable foreign Sim cards to activists in Saudi Arabia.

Jamal was also at the heart of an 'online army' of Saudi activists fighting a misinformation cyberwar. He had recently given $5,000 to '*Geish al-Nahla*', or the Bee Army, an opposition movement offering cyber protection to Saudi activists needing a safe platform to speak out inside the oppressive kingdom. This was also the brainchild of twenty-seven-year-old Omar Abdulaziz.

According to the *Independent*, Jamal's texts may have been accessed by Saudi security officials, contributing to the execution. Abdulaziz sued NSO Group, an Israeli software company that provided a spyware package called Pegasus to the Saudis. The Israeli company was benefiting from the fact that selling such spy-technology to Israel's authoritarian neighbours was considered the avenue to neighbourly peace by the Israeli government. NSO conceded that both Saud al-Qahtani and major-general al-Asiri had been clients. On 1 October Canada-based Citizen Lab had reported Abdulaziz's phone had been infected by an infiltrator linked to Saudi Arabia. It allowed the kingdom's government to hack his messages which were conveyed via the normally securely-encrypted WhatsApp. The software also gave spy-access to his contacts, photos, text messages, online chat logs, emails, other personal files, camera as well as microphone to listen in on his conversations. On 1 August, Amnesty International had reported the same about the phone of UK-based former Saudi air-force officer Yahya Assiri.

This news mattered more than what might come of Abdulaziz's law suit. As did the surprise news that the kingdom Tiger Team members had been trained in intelligence work in the US by companies owned by Cerberus Capital Management, NY, whose co-CEO was on Trump's Intelligence Advisory Board.

In the US, government-to-government deals, 'foreign military sales' or 'direct commercial sales' require a government arms license reviewed by the senate. Furthermore, under 'Leahy vetting' the US state department has a federal duty to ensure no 'gross violations of human rights' (GVHRs) are committed by foreign entities, such as 'torture, extrajudicial killing, enforced disappearance, and rape under colour of law' its website clarifies.

Following the news of Jamal's assassination all licensing to Saudi Arabia had swiftly dried up. Weary of the unwanted attention, on 14 February 2019 the controversial NSO Group was sold by its owners for $1bn to the group's founders funded by 'ethical' London private equity firm Novalpina Capital. This firm with at least $1bn in investor money had been co-founded in 2014 by Stephen Peel, a visiting fellow at the Blavatnik School in Oxford and an advisory board member at Yale's Jackson Institute. How invasive NSO's products were became clear on 14 May 2019 when it was reported that all 1.5bn WhatsApp users were at risk from NSO's spyware after a security breach.

On 6 December an Istanbul court issued further arrest warrants for former deputy head of Saudi intelligence major-general Ahmad al-Asiri and Saudi royal minister Saud al-Qahtani for 'wilful murder with monstrous sentiment'. This raised the total number to twenty – the two new ones, plus the fifteen Tiger Team members and the three secret-service staff at the consulate. Istanbul prosecutor Fidan would add another staff member later, bringing the number up to twenty one, the same as the Saudi prosecutor general.

'The prosecution's move to issue arrest warrants for Asiri and Qahtani reflects the view that the Saudi authorities won't take formal action against those individuals,' a Turkish official said. It also conceded in as many words that the arrest warrants were being used for political purposes.

Damagingly to the White House, it was reported in the *New York Times* that Jared Kushner had enquired during the first months of Trump's move into the White House, and before MBS took over crown prince on 21 June 2017, whether the US government could 'influence' the royal succession in MBS's favour. Kushner certainly did his best. In March 2017, when Trump and Saudi minister of defence MBS first met impromptu when Angela Merkel cancelled because of a snow storm, it was an unusual meeting. MBS was merely deputy crown prince then. Yet he received full head-of-state honours. The White House denied the first story as 'false'.

The US senate had finally had enough. It reached for a new measure to overrule President Trump's foreign policy regarding Saudi Arabia's war in Yemen and his response to the murder of Jamal Khashoggi. The move, significantly, was not partisan and had the support of both Republicans and Democrats. Following a briefing by CIA director Gina Haspel, leading senators also said relatively plainly that the Saudi crown prince was 'complicit' in the killing of Jamal Khashoggi.

Senator Lindsey Graham (R) told reporters: 'There's not a smoking gun, there's a smoking saw. You have to be wilfully blind not to come to the conclusion that this was orchestrated and organised by people under the command of MBS and that he was intricately involved in the demise of Mr Khashoggi. I think he is complicit in the murder of Mr Khashoggi to the highest level possible. I cannot support arm sales to Saudi Arabia as long as he's in charge.'

Senate foreign relations committee chairperson Bob Corker (R) told reporters: 'I have zero questions in my mind that the crown prince directed the murder… If he was in front of a jury he would be convicted in 30 minutes. Guilty. So, the question is what do we do about that.'

On 13 December, the US senate passed a unanimous resolution stating that Saudi Crown Prince Mohammed bin Salman was responsible for Jamal Khashoggi's murder and in a separate resolution it formally voted to withdraw US support for the Saudi war in Yemen that MBS had started.

The Saudi foreign ministry released a statement saying: 'The recent position of the United States, which has been built on baseless allegations and accusations, includes blatant interference in its internal affairs and the role of the kingdom at the regional and international level. The kingdom has previously asserted that the murder of Saudi citizen Jamal Khashoggi is a deplorable crime that does not reflect the kingdom's policy, nor its institutions, and reaffirms its rejection of any attempts to take the case out of the path of justice in the kingdom.'

'The kingdom hopes that it is not drawn into domestic political debates in the United States to avoid any ramifications on the ties between the two countries that could have significant negative impacts on this important strategic relationship.'

Vladimir Putin couldn't have wished for greater volatility in the Saudi-American relationship. Mevlüt Çavuşoğlu, the Turkish foreign minister, raked it over by saying that Trump was turning a blind eye to the murder. He then lashed out at the EU's response, which he complained was no more than 'cosmetic'. It was a change from having to defend Turkey's own record on free speech. Three weeks earlier, Australian BBC correspondent Yalda Hakim had observed to foreign minister Hulusi Akar that Turkey had more journalists in prison than China. He had curtly fielded semantics that could have come from Donald Trump, 'They are not journalists. They may have the title of journalist.'

Emboldened by the senate's accusation of MBS as the responsible king pin, Erdoğan said, 'We have learned this from the audio recordings: of those who arrive, those closest to the crown prince played the most active role,' said President. 'The perpetrators are clear to me.'

Citing Nikki Haley, outgoing US envoy to the United Nations, who took the same line as the US Senate, President Erdoğan said hopefully, 'She openly named people', and, 'This shows something. Now, the whole incident is fully resurfacing.' He added: 'It's clear where this business will end up.' Though it wasn't entirely clear where 'where' was.

Sean Penn, meanwhile, turned up in Istanbul to make a documentary on Jamal Khashoggi and *Time* magazine named Jamal and three persecuted journalists as its 'Person of the Year'. The three were Maria Ressa who was the co-founder of Filipino news site *Rappler* and who had criticised President Duterte's anti-drug crackdown which had killed nearly five thousand people since 2016, and Reuters reporters Kyaw Soe Oo and Wa Lone who were arrested in Myanmar on 12 December 2017 while investigating the execution of ten Rohingya men. They had been sentenced to seven years in prison.

The day before the Senate vote, *Haberturk* published new grisly information on cue. 'They opened Khashoggi's veins and drained his blood into the sink!' its headline shouted.

The consulate had also allegedly used three times as much water over the nine days leading up to the access of Turkish forensic investigators in order to dilute any forensic traces, according to its Khashoggi-insider Çetiner Çetin. High-pitched spinning noise of an autopsy saw and chopping and cleaving sounds could be heard on the audio, he also revealed.

'Eleven times that sound goes on for quite a long time', officials leaked in the article. The number of body parts may have been lower than fifteen, the paper speculated.

The *Washington Post* pieced together on 22 December in an in-depth investigation what Jamal's real plans had been while in exile. The journalists had spoken to friends and colleagues, and gone through text messages and papers, including a 200-page trove left behind by Jamal. His four children themselves, however, declined to be interviewed.

It was a mixed bag. The papers made clear that Jamal Khashoggi was deeply torn between wanting to be both close to his children and crafting a new identity for himself in exile.

He had sought funding for a variety of projects while travelling to dozens of conferences every year. In August 2017, before his first

Washington Post blog, Saudi information minister Awwad al-Awwad had called him in Virginia to say his writing ban had been lifted, would he be interested in setting up a pro-Saudi think tank, and meet with MBS? Jamal had duly submitted a proposal for a 'Saudi Research Council' with a funding of $1-2 million, something akin to the Qatar Foundation International run by his friend Maggie Salem Mitchell.

In effect, Jamal's 'research council' would act like a US advance post of al-Qahtani's cyber-war department, the Centre for Studies and Media Affairs. 'Irresponsible media' connect the kingdom to terrorism, and the idea, Jamal wrote in his proposal, was to monitor 'potential negative news... that might explode against the kingdom', 'notify the ministry' and allow the country to 'regain its positive role and image'. The think tank would be an amalgam of his previous semi-government roles in Saudi intelligence, and as newspaper editor, spy and diplomat.

Salah, his eldest son, and other members of his close family who lived in Saudi Arabia were urging him to go down this route. They had suffered enough from harassment and travel bans, as a result of Jamal's independent stance.

Meanwhile, Jamal was flatteringly approached to write a piece for the *Washington Post*'s new online section in September. Jamal published this first piece for the *Washington Post* on 18 September – 'Saudi Arabia Wasn't always This Repressive. Now It Is Unbearable'. Attiah told her colleagues she hadn't realised it would be his 'coming out' declaration.

Yet knowing that these subtle negotiations were being handled in the background, the piece also looked like Jamal's litmus test of the renewed permission to write MBS had given him. The previous king had also banned him from writing. Riyadh had laid down red lines around certain topics such as the Arab Spring and el-Sisi's Saudi-funded putsch in Egypt. Jamal was submitting his full allegiance to work for the Saudi government as intelligence spy and taking orders under the protocol written into the Saudi Research Council's funding statutes. But, the *Post* piece was a *caveat*. Now based in DC, he also claimed his previous independence to skirt around fine lines in the margins that weren't touched by whatever red lines he agreed to with Riyadh.

Riyadh passed the *Washington Post* test with flying colours. Although MBS was spitting with rage and told Jamal's colleague Aldakhil, al-Arabiya's CEO, privately he wanted to go after Jamal 'with a bullet', MBS's royal intelligence minister al-Qahtani let nothing on. In a follow-up call, al-Qahtani continued to pass on friendly messages from MBS and urged him to keep 'writing and boasting'. It was also on 26 October 2017 that Jamal had his last text exchange with the Saudi ambassador, MBS's brother KBS. And it was around this time that KBS had called Jamal up for a chat in his office while he was in the embassy.

Jamal finally accepted Karen Attiah's proposal to write more online pieces for the *Post* and did so in a crescendo of five quick blasts, almost a quarter of the number of pieces he would write for her Global Opinions section: 'Saudi Arabia's Crown Prince Wants to Crush Extremists. But He's Punishing the Wrong People', 31 October, 'Saudi Arabia's Crown Prince Is Acting Like Putin', 6 November, 'Saudi Arabia Is Creating a Total Mess in Lebanon', 13 November, 'Saudi Arabia Has Devastated Yemen – But a Lesson from 1965 Can Help Fix the Mess', 22 November, 'Saudi Arabia Is Paying the Price for Betraying the Arab Spring', 5 December.

Jamal reached out to MBS one more time to offer his allegiance and assistance to the crown. A leading businessman told the *Washington Post* writers anonymously that Jamal asked him in the Autumn of 2017 to give the crown prince a personal message, that MBS needed an advisor like Jamal – presumably as advocate of the devil, writing policy reports like the rapid-fire of *Post* pieces. MBS, however, told the businessman it would never happen given Jamal's ties with Qatar and the Muslim Brotherhood. Riyadh's response to the *Post* pieces was equally decisive. Salah cut off contact for months and Jamal's third wife divorced him.

Jamal's think pieces were a great success, however, at the *Post*, which appointed him in December as a regular commentator. He wasn't a staff member, but they did give him a masthead on the Global Opinions website. It was a great moment for him, and he was very proud of his new title.

'When is the press release? When is the press release?', he kept pushing his *Washington Post* editor Attiah.

Yet increasingly Jamal was lonely and depressed during this time as a result of severing his ties with the palace. He WhatsApped his *Post* editor Attiah, 'I'm really sad and depressed. They put travel bans on my family. They're trying to get to me. It's making me sad.' He started the relationship with Hanan Atr, who regularly visited Washington on business.

Yet such moments alternated with enthusiasm for new ideas and meeting new people in DC. Jamal was anything but high-handed. Sigurd Neubauer, a researcher, got to know him during this period and met the Tysons Corner Pain Quotidien. 'Everybody who was interested in Saudi Arabia or in the region, he would make himself available to', Neubauer said. Jamal gave guest lectures and met people on Washington DC's foreign-policy circuit. He even met regularly with Saudis who towed MBS's line and debated issues with them without acrimony.

It was in 2018 that he met Turkish PhD student Selim Sazak of Brown University half a dozen time in DC. Sazak told the *Independent* news site he thought Jamal was 'sharp, quick-witted' and a 'contrarian' who was not 'guided by any particular ideology'.

Jamal's visit to the *Post* news room with Attiah brought out his Mr Jekyll to Mr Hyde. The *Washington Post* could be al-Arab 2.0, the TV station in Bahrein that closed down in a day in 2015.

'His eyes lit up' Attiah recalls, 'I wish we could build this in the Middle East' he said. As he had been told the blog was a success, he mooted in September to Attiah that the *Post* would create an Arabic Section of Global Opinions, a sort of *International Herald Tribune* – which the *Washington Post* used to co-own with the *New York Times* – for the Middle East.

Jamal bombarded her with WhatsApps and email, using many thumbs-up emojis. In his last messages to her he repeated his dream of creating a broader platform [of] honest news and commentary in Arabic with the *Post*. 'He was pushy – not in a bad way, but very', Attiah said.

He asked 'When are we meeting about this?'.

Another completely different plan for which he sought secret financial backing was to be called Democracy for the Arab World Now (DAWN), which would rank countries, and he asked Nihad Awad, the head of the Council on American-Islamic Relations for support. They had known each other for twenty five years and met at a DC Panera for breakfast, 'And we were just working on details' said Awad.

This initiative would not have pleased Riyadh in the least either as Awad was also the leader of the US Muslim Brotherhood. The 'bombshell' of this secret cooperation was dropped by Kurdish media network Rudaw in Iraq on 17 October 2018. MBS seemed to have been well-informed when he spoke to the business man.

The *Post* also found an exchange between Maggie Mitchell Salem of the Qatar International Foundation of August 2018 in which she prodded him to write about Saudi alliances from the US to the European far right. When he sent her draft, it had become an article about Canada, and she castigated him: 'you veered off topic... ITS HIGHLY PROBLEMATIC'. When he submitted the piece for his *Post* blog on 6 August – in which the monarchist seemed to have turned democrat in some of its lines – he WhatsApped his friend the Qatari lobbyist, 'They're going to hang me when it comes out'.

Although he had had a column for seven years in *al-Hayat*, the London-based Saudi newspaper for the Arab diaspora, it is clear Jamal was more interested in the shaping of ideas on the large canvas of the Middle East than in the handiwork of his youth, writing single pieces of journalism.

Also, billionaire Jeff Bezos's *Washington Post* paid him $500 per blog entry, which meant that, setting to one side the prestige of having an online masthead and the love of writing, there was no more than pocket money in the association with the *Post*.

In his posthumous piece of 17 October, Jamal Khashoggi thanked the *Washington Post* for taking 'the initiative to translate many of my pieces into Arabic'. This gratitude was no doubt genuine, but it told only part of the financial picture behind Jamal's freelance fee. Attiah said to the *New York Times* his 'English wasn't great' and as he 'got settled in a little bit more, he found assistants or translators who helped him.'

Yet all this extra effort per piece had to come out of the $500 the *Post* paid him (a total of $11,000 for twenty-two pieces over a year, if one included the posthumous piece his translator sent to Attiah on 3 October). Doubtless it was one reason why he gratefully received the flexible writing help offered by his friend Maggie Mitchell Salem, who as director of Qatar Foundation International had the lobby budget and access to support staff.

The *Washington Post* would at its own expense translate the Arab-speaker's pieces in English back into Jamal's mother-tongue, potentially paying their translator more than Jamal himself as writer. It maintained control over the content published under the *Washington Post* banner in case the relevant editors couldn't read Arabic themselves. It is a moot point what would have happened if billionaire Jeff Bezos's newspaper had paid higher fees commensurate with the amount of work that a non-native speaker had to put into a piece written in idiomatic English.

On 28 December *Sabah*'s investigative team Abdurrahman Şimşek, Ferhat Ünlü, and Nazif Karaman published their book *Diplomatik Vahşet* (Diplomatic Savagery) in Turkey. It was published by Turkuvaz Books, which, like *Sabah*, is owned by Çalik Holding the conglomerate previously headed by Erdoğan's son-in-law, Berat Albayrak, subsequently finance minister.

The sources of the book were Turkish officials with first-hand knowledge of the top-secret recordings, the *Sabah* journalists wrote. The book revealed that the 7.5 minute clip given to foreign intelligence agencies was edited from recordings made before and after Jamal's arrival. The voices on the clip were predominantly 'negotiation-team' leader Maher Mutreb's and pathologist Salah Tubaigy's. It was the first time *Sabah*'s team returned to recording leaks since the Apple Watch debacle.

Their source leaked that the audio covered the hour before Jamal's arrival, and that a discussion had been taped between Mutreb, Tubaigy, and royal guard al-Harbi from MBS's personal security detail. Since the men spoke before his arrival, the book made clear why there was no doubt in the minds of Turkish investigators that Jamal's murder had been pre-meditated.

'We'll ask him to come back to Riyadh', said Mutreb. If he doesn't 'we will kill him here and get rid of the body.'

To this Tubaigy responds, 'I have never worked on a warm body until now, but I can handle that easily. Normally while working on a cadaver, I put on my headphones and listen to music. And I drink my coffee and smoke my cigarette.'

'Jamal is tall, around 1.80 meters,' he adds. 'The joints of a sacrificial animal are easily split, but dismembering still will take time.'

'After I dismember, you will wrap them in plastic bags and put them in the luggage and carry' the body parts out, Tubaigy instructed the others. Mutreb then orders his men to set out the tools and materials they brought. On the recording metal items can be heard, said the writers of the book.

In other words, Tubaigy had not, after all been salivating over Jamal's death. It was the way Turkey had initially edited the audio that had caused the revulsion around the world. Though hard-boiled, out of context they had made the pathologist sound like a blood-thirsty Hannibal Lecter salivating over Jamal's body and made the Saudi secret intelligence officer who listened to the clip speculate he was on 'heroin'. Turkey had intentionally manipulated the recording to turn it into Pulp Fiction.

As the objective had been achieved, the new point – unfolding in the December book – was to move away from Pulp Fiction and focus on buttressing the Turkish case that Riyadh's rendition plan was meant to end with pre-meditated murder – a 'truth' more suited to Erdoğan from December.

In 2019, the UN rapporteur would also be given new material underlining this latest narrative. Mutreb and Tubaigy had continued their conversation right until 1.02pm when Jamal was due to arrive any minute. 'Mutreb asked whether it will "be possible to put the trunk in a bag?" Dr. Tubaigy replied 'No. Too heavy.' He expressed hope that it would "be easy. Joints will be separated. It is not a problem. The body is heavy. First time I cut on the ground. If we take plastic bags and cut it into pieces, it will be finished. We will wrap each of them." "Leather bags". There was a reference to cutting skin' (UN detail 91).

In fact, Turkey's secret service even gave Tubaigy a human side in 2019. On the recording given to UN rapporteur Callamard the pathologist was heard worrying, 'My direct manager is not aware of what I am doing. There is nobody to protect me'.

When Jamal enters the consul-general's office around 1.20pm for tea and is grabbed by his arm, Mutreb says, 'Come, sit down. We came to take you to Riyadh.' Jamal immediately answers, 'I won't go to Riyadh.'

Mutreb says all will be 'forgiven' if he comes back and the men ask him to text his son Salah, 'My son, I am in Istanbul. Do not worry if you don't hear from me for a while'.

The recording that Callamard would hear underlined the story in book how the Saudis leveraged Salah – the only child for whom Saudi Arabia was still home – to get to Jamal.

At 1.22pm, Mutreb asked for the brand of Jamal's phones to get him to type the message.

'"Send a message to your son." "Which son? What should I say to my son?".' There was silence and it seemed as if Jamal briefly considered this option.

'"You will type a message – let's rehearse; show us." "What should I say? See you soon? I can't say kidnapping".'

'Cut it short', Mutreb pressured Jamal. '"Take off your jacket." "How could this happen in an embassy?" "I will not write anything." "Cut it short." "I will not write anything." "Type it, Mr Jamal. Hurry up. Help us so that we can help you because at the end we will take you back to Saudi Arabia and if you don't help us you know what will happen at the end; let this issue find a good end".'

After 10 minutes of this, at 1.33pm, Jamal said 'There is a towel here. Are you going to give me drugs?' Mutreb responded, 'We will anaesthetise you' (UN detail 94, reconstructed from memory as MİT prohibited note-taking).

Mutreb orders his officers to grab Jamal. MBS's royal guard al-Harbi tries to cover Jamal's mouth, but is repelled by him. Finally the five men, including al-Harbi, al-Zahrani another royal guard in MBS's personal security detail, al-Madani, and Saif al-Qahtani, pull a plastic bag over his head, securing it with a piece of nylon.

It takes 5 minutes before the last sound of his rasping breath is heard. Jamal Khashoggi dies at 1.24pm in this new version, some 10 minutes after entering the consulate. But on the recording that the UN delegation will hear, the last word they hear Jamal speak is at 1.33pm. They then hear sounds of a struggle, and Tiger Team operatives say: 'Did he sleep?' 'He raises his head.' 'Keep pushing.' 'Push here; don't remove your hand; push it.' The delegation then hears 'movement', 'heavy panting' and 'plastic sheets'.

Jamal's body-double al-Madani and travel companion Saif al-Qahtani (they entered the consulate together at 11.03am, possibly with Tubaigy) now take off his clothes for al-Madani to put on to leave through the consulate's back door an hour and a half later at 2.52pm.

In order to decrease spillage and creating a mess in the consulate, Tubaigy inserts a tube in Jamal's arm, which proved only effective in part. Turkish forensic experts later removed fresh paint from the walls of the consulate and found traces of Jamal's blood behind it. Officials leaked this to Qatar-based al-Jazeera in a documentary aired on 3 March 2019.

Earlier officials had leaked to *Haberturk* that their investigation had revealed marble floors and skirting boards were cleaned with two types of chemicals. They had nonetheless found tissue there – mainly on the skirting boards though they did ultimately admit that the DNA could not be matched with Jamal's. Turkish investigators also said the three rooms where they found evidence of the plot had been repainted after 2 October.

As Tubaigy furiously begins dismembering the body, it is a race against time. Over half an hour, orders rain down on the other men present who are struggling with what they are witnessing – 'quickly bring the bags', 'what are you waiting for', 'why are you standing there!'

Five bags are then transported to the consul-general's residence in the Mercedes Vito van that leaves after 3pm to drive the few hundred yards to his home address. They drive into his concealed garage port to unload and then park the van in front.

The Saudi's forensic cleaning of the consulate and residence, the book revealed, was executed in several stages. The assassins themselves did the first rough clean on the afternoon of 2 October, followed by a thorough one by Saudi consular staff. But the real detailing had been done by the 'wipers', the chemist al-Zahrani and toxicologist al-Janubi, who were part of the delegation of the governor of Mecca, Prince bin Faisal.

Diplomatik Vahşet now claimed, in yet another pivot back that there was really no evidence how or where the Tiger Team disposed of the body. Turkey's so-called investigation was like a wind vane on this point.

In Turkey, there were persistent rumours that Hatice Cengiz was a UAE spy and in on the plot to assassinate Jamal. The three journalists discounted this theory, as Cengiz did everything she could to expedite the involvement of the highest levels of government rather than merely alert the police.

On the vexed question where the recording came from, the *Sabah* journalists of *Diplomatik Vahşet* recorded yet another mixed bag of stories in the wake of their embarrassing Apple-Watch scoop.

On the one hand, Ferhat Ünlü, said in an interview, 'There are a number of intelligence scenarios, forecasts and speculations about how [the] records are obtained. In order not to speculate, we left that part unclear.' But *Sabah,* reporting on the book, also leaked what was said at a meeting between Turkey's and Saudi Arabia's security chiefs – Hakan Fidan and Abdulaziz al-Howairini. The latter said Saudi Arabia found ten bugs in their consulate. Fidan had retorted that 'anybody could be listening'. Perhaps that was the truth.

In yet another variation of having one's cake and eating it, English-language website dailysabah.com.tr (edited by *Sabah*) claimed that the recordings weren't 'unlawfully achieved' by Turkey in its attempt to paint a picture of Turkey as a punctilious defender of 'human conscience'.

Instead it said, cryptically, that 'the recordings were automatically saved, meaning that Turkey did not deliberately listen to the consulate and save the recording.' This tortuous phrase had in common with *Sabah*'s Apple Watch story that it suggested someone other than Turkey had made the recording – in case the truth, like a criminal, always returns to the scene of the crime.

As to the use MİT made of the recording of discussions inside the consulate, *Diplomatik Vahşet* said – as per above – that 'sound analysts... solved MİT's question within two hours' upon listening to the conversations in Arabic on 2 October. This made sense, because on 17 November *Yeni Şafak* had leaked to great effect that Jamal's body-double al-Madani had said 'a man whom we killed 20 minutes ago'. Even in Arabic those words left little to the imagination.

It meant that, according to the new book's time-line, listening some 30 minutes in from the moment of Jamal's arrival at 1.14pm would have made clear beyond any doubt that Jamal was assassinated and dead from 1.34pm. Why would analysts need another hour and a half to analyse those few words? Unless of course, al-Madani spoke those words quite a bit later into the recording.

Not only that, al-Madani was putting on Jamal's clothes while he spoke those words, complaining as he tried to squeeze into Jamal's smaller size shoes. It seemed from *Diplomatik Vahşet*'s time-line that, doing whatever he was still doing inside the consulate, al-Madani was dressed in Jamal's clothes from close to 1.34pm until 2.52pm, when he left the building through the back entrance and was caught on CC-TV. That meant almost an hour and a half of walking around in Jamal's clothes in the consulate. While possible, it didn't seem probable.

Whether the *Sabah* journalists acted, in fact, as a serving-hatch for

MİT and the Turkish government was addressed head on by Vice News/HBO. On 19 October, Andrew Potter of the news site visited *Sabah*'s Abdurrahman Şimşek and Ferhat Ünlü and challenged them on this point. Citing the fact that they had published most of the Khashoggi leaks, he questioned whether they weren't being 'used' by 'unnamed sources inside the Turkish government' to do their bidding. Although *Sabah* had so far shown pitch-perfect timing, the two men defended themselves to Vice News/HBO (reported on ahvalnews.com) that they had published their leaks if anything 'a little early' for the government's liking.

Presumably, another 'accelerator' to MİT's understanding on 2 October should have been brigadier-general al-Madani. Of all the operatives, he held the pointed, smoking gun in the blazing spotlight of all the evidence MİT claimed it had that evening. When the sound analysts heard for the first time the words 'it is creepy to wear the clothes' of a man who has just been killed, this linked his words without much doubt to the man who had already visually been 'quickly' (as leaked by MİT to the *Wall Street Journal* on 22 October) identified as Jamal's body-double by Turkish authorities through MoBeSe CC-TV footage and from his passport records arriving on the Gulfstream IV at 3.29am earlier that morning. And yet the brigadier-general went through Atatürk's passport control next day at 0.18am to board his plane to Riyadh at 1.20am at his leisure. This was over seven hours from the moment the Turkish investigations commenced under urgent presidential orders.

The Turkish investigators who spoke to the UN delegation in 2019, didn't pick the 'within two hours' version that the readers of *Diplomatik Vahşet* were being told. They picked the version that the *Wall Street Journal* had been given on 22 October.

On the 'same evening' of 2 October MİT had its 'raw recordings', Turkey told the UN team as the *Journal* had been told. The first operative, Maher Mutreb, arrived at the consulate at 9.55am and the last operatives, including Tubaigy, left the consulate at 7.40pm. One would expect the raw data to cover almost ten hours, but the UN report only mentions that there were 'seven hours' (detail 108: their report also mentioned 'at least seven hours of recordings' under detail 41a, but there it seems to refer to recordings during a 'two-day period' before 2 October).

But, as authorities had previously leaked to the *Journal* on 22 October, the recordings were 'complex and it took them several days to reach a firm conclusion'. None of it was easy, apparently. Just listening to these audio recordings didn't 'divulge' their stories, the UN delegates were told. 'Background noises have to be interpreted; conversations thought to be insignificant initially can become meaningful once more information comes to light. In this instance, some of the available recordings were less clear acoustically than others, making identification of those speaking difficult and making interpretation of what was happening at any given time difficult too' (detail 41d).

In 2019, there was no talk of sound analysts solving 'MİT's question within two hours'. In fact, they now seemed to admit that they got the recordings spectacularly wrong. Their first assessment was that Jamal 'had been injected with something, passed out, and taken alive from the consulate in some box or container', the told the UN. Having the recording seemed to have been no help at all for quite a long time. It took sound analysts 'several days' to rectify their mistake. In this version, Turkish authorities were no further than if they only had external evidence until Thursday 4 October or so.

Although the UN report passed no comment on the discrepancy between 'official' leaks to the Turkish press, nor on what brigadier-general al-Madani said on the recording the delegates listened to, it did observe, again, Turkey's lack. Turkish authorities undoubtedly have more information and intelligence about events in the Saudi Consulate than they were willing or able to share with the inquiry

Turkey now also claimed in the book that there was no audio where consul-general al-Otaibi pleaded 'Don't do it here, I'll get into trouble'. Erdoğan had claimed credit for the consul-general's sacking in his speech to the Turkish parliament on 22 September and in his November

Washington Post piece he had yet again made a point of singling out the consul-general – a minor figure in the plot – demanding al-Otaibi would be charged as he 'lied through his teeth to the media'. Erdoğan was implying he and his own officials were better than that.

Also, if al-Otaibi did say those words, they implied that the Riyadh's orders relayed to the consul-general had not mentioned the execution. It weakened Turkey's case that it had been a pre-meditated assassination. This might still have been the Tiger Team op's instructions taking Jamal first to Yalova and then for burial to Belgrad Forest. But Turkey's proof for that was at best circumstantial as it only had hours of audio inside the consulate.

Was there any chance that the key agents would be punished? The authors of the book said the consul-general's family was very well-connected, and al-Otaibi would likely receive immunity from prosecution in the kingdom. Professor lieutenant-colonel Tubaigy was in a luxury Jeddah villa with a pool. Nor was Mutreb under arrest, it was claimed separately in Middle East Eye, though the news site hadn't been able to verify this independently.

Although MBS's right hand man Saud al-Qahtani was relieved of his command of the Centre for Studies and Media Affairs, he, like Michael Flynn at the time in the US, continued to brief his team members sources reported. He was for a while still in charge of the Saudi Federation for Cyber Security and in control of the extensive secret files he had compiled over the years. The Centre itself was folded under the leadership of Dr Nasir Al-Biqami, a Saudi official with a Master's from Loughborough University and a 2001 PhD from Nottingham University – both in 'information management'. His brief was very wide indeed and he had on 17 April 2018, met a Vatican delegation to discuss the 'moderation of extremism'. The UN inquiry report of 19 June 2019 said 'Subsequent reports, including official statements from Western governments, have suggested however, that at least Mr al-Qahtani is still in place, performing his advisory functions.'

Sabah also reported the book's surprising claim that Mutreb never said to al-Qahtani 'tell yours [boss] the deed is done' which first appeared in the *New York Times*. It was the most direct piece of evidence linking Jamal's execution to MBS and now the journalists passed on MİT's statement had been misreported by the *Times*. It seemed that Erdoğan had decided to drop his attempts to implicate MBS directly. He had him exactly where he wanted. Another indication that Turkey was retreating from the high point of its narrative came months later. Authorities now disowned the proof that instruments of torture had been brought into the country. To the UN team, the Istanbul prosecutor denied having the airport X-rays of the luggage of the Saudis involved (those travelling on the getaway jet, the sitting-duck, nor even of the officers travelling on commercial flights). The UN report noted without further comment that this was contradicted in December in *Diplomatik Vahşet* (detail 87 footnote).

On 1 January Arab-Spring online publication Rassdnews, or RNN – claiming to be a populist, independent network after 'CNN' – in Egypt, voted Erdoğan 'the world's most prominent president' at 72 per cent. The news was gratefully reported by *Sabah* and others in Turkey. Deposed Egyptian Muslim-Brotherhood ex-president Mohamed Morsi was second at 52 per cent, the oddball trio of Donald Trump, Vladimir Putin and King Salman brought up the rear for 2018, according to RNN.

31

What Lies Ahead

On 30 January, UN special rapporteur Agnes Callamard was in Istanbul to investigate the murder. While Saudi Arabia had not agreed to give access to the consulate, Turkish authorities allowed Callamard to listen to the edited audio clip that MİT had distributed to intelligence agencies.

She presented a preliminary statement of her week-long fact finding mission on 6 February, saying that 'woefully inadequate time and access was granted to Turkish investigators to conduct a professional and effective crime-scene examination and search required by international standards for investigation.'

However, she also said that Turkey was guilty of the same charge with respect to her investigation, as investigators did not 'fulfil their pledge to provide access to forensic, scientific and police reports'. It was a damning conclusion for both countries.

Her charge of a lack of interest in the truth and cherry-picking through the evidence could also be levelled at Turkey's unofficial leaks to the media following 2 October. Apart from Erdoğan's personal press statements, spokespersons for Turkish government institutions rarely went on the record. Even these statements were contradictory. From the moment of access to the consulate even the investigations of the Istanbul chief prosecutor seemed to have more to do with optics and angling for headlines than a 'transparent' process under the rule of law.

As for the unofficial, anonymous leaks of evidence to the press, these often provided suggestive imagery that fit into Turkey's 'Pulp Fiction' storyboard that prevailed in October. Turkey then dropped 'torture' from the story board from November after Saudi Arabia admitted to pre-meditated murder. Taken together, the second-hand leaks to the press created conflicting time lines, lacked detail, made unsubstantiated claims, provided words that were supposedly said on a recording but then not said, and words that were presented to lead to a false impression as in the case of Tubaigy's being 'on heroin' or MİT's aggrandisement.

Instead of creating clarity, once it had released the information on Saturday 6 October that Jamal had been murdered, Turkey had used the leaks increasingly to show that Saudi Arabia acted in bad faith whereas Turkey supposedly acted in good faith.

But all it had done was chop and change the leaks to whatever point was needed at one time to embarrass Riyadh. While it had successfully forced the palace to admit high-ranking royal officials had assassinated Jamal during a rendition, after 15 November its behaviour had become as duplicitous as Riyadh's use of the media for power games. To Turkey's surprise it worked abroad because facts mattered in countries where the press was not on the government's leash. Regardless of the exact detail surrounding it, Jamal's assassination by Saudi officials inside state offices had become undeniable through Turkey's otherwise unreliable process.

Erdoğan claimed to 'have moved heaven and earth', but all that Turkey had done publicly was to issue arrest warrants while keeping evidence secret from everyone. Nor had it asked the UN to investigate or set up an independent inquiry in Turkey. In comparison, once Saudi authorities launched one investigation after another they almost seemed loquacious in their official statements and conclusions, ahead of the criminal case. Turkey's most public act was a secret one – giving a severely edited audio clip to the secret services of Saudi Arabia, the United States, Germany, France and Britain that established only a minimum of bare facts in much the same way the short CC-TV clips did. The access given to UN rapporteur Callamard – who particular thanks Istanbul chief prosecutor Irfan Fidan – for her report created the most official record of the 'crucial information' about the murder. But it was no more than partial access as the report carefully details.

Diplomatik Vahşet was the most comprehensive catalogue of Turkish leaks in one place on 24 December. Its 'facts' offered yet again small but important differences compared to previous leaks. It contained Apple-Watch style mysteries that were simply glossed over.

In the book the three *Sabah* journalists – Abdurrahman Şimşek, Ferhat Ünlü, Nazif Karaman (the first two with selfies with Erdoğan on their twitter masthead) – recreated a time line that matched what had been filtered to the media so far: Jamal dies in some 10 minutes after entering the consulate at around 1.24pm and Tubaigy dismembers the body in about half an hour till around 1.54pm while the other operatives simultaneously pack the parts in the suitcases.

While that may well have been accurate, it meant that the majority of time spent in the consulate by the Tiger Team members remained unaccounted for. The van with Jamal's remains left the consulate's backcourt at 3.08pm for the consul-general's residence. It meant that over 80 minutes remained unaddressed.

Çetiner Çetin, *Haberturk*'s contact to the Turkish Khashoggi investigators, did address this hiatus in his piece written in Turkish on 19 November. After the first minutes (11 according to his piece) of '*mêlée* and fight', followed 110 minutes of silence during which 'the Saudi team allegedly ran jammers'. These jammers explained the almost two hours of silence, as leaked by Turkish officials.

Then three men pierce the silence of the recording when they run downstairs. One of the three was an IT person. He reset the nineteen internal CC-TV cameras that had been turned off before Jamal's arrival, and he wiped all data. One of the other two wanted the front-door of the consulate locked.

This anonymously leaked story by security officials preceded the one described in *Diplomatik Vahşet*. Çetin was also given detailed information about the location of the recording microphones. They were placed in 'Unit A', the consulate's public section, and 'Unit B', the administrative offices behind it on the ground floor. In this narrative, Jamal was apprehended by 'four voices' the moment he entered the door to the public section and was taken straight to the 'Unit B' offices behind it where the 11-minute '*mêlée* and fight' ensued with the cursing and shouting of 'seven voices', in addition to Jamal's. The three new voices included Maher Mutreb's, the negotiation-team leader, and Mohammed al-Otaibi's, as well as an unidentified third one.

After the *mêlée*, nineteen calls were made from 'Unit C', the consulate's upper-floor comms, encryption, and sound-sealed rooms. The reason why, Çetin writes, the microphones picked up these nineteen calls despite the signal-jamming was because listening devices were placed at the bottom of the stairs of the consulate. They recorded talking voices and detected four calls to al-Qahtani by Mutreb. Their first call was 13 minutes after Jamal's arrival.

After some 2 hours, Çetin writes on 19 November, the crew left through Unit B and piled their luggage into the consular Mercedes Vito van caught on MoBeSe CC-TV angled at the consulate's back entrance at 3.08pm. The van parked two hundred yards away at the consul-general's residence, together with the consular Audi with another group of Tiger Team operatives. From '46 minutes' after the Tiger Team leaves the residence, Çetin writes, al-Otaibi did not leave his home until his departure back home days later, in a remarkably precise but seemingly irrelevant detail.

The article went on to explain that 'Turkish authorities have no recording of the killing because there were no recording bugs in 'Unit C'. He then said that the three rooms that were repainted according to the Turkish forensic team were in Unit C upstairs, which was also where the marble floors were cleaned with two chemicals. They also found Tubaigy's finger-prints on two electrical outlets in these rooms.

Yet in *Diplomatik Vahşet*, the authors wrote that the recording heard everything, from the Mutreb's decision to murder Jamal down to metal objects being put down in preparation Tubaigy's dismemberment of the body well before Jamal's arrival.

Was what Çetin said about 1 hour and 50 minute 'silence' because of signal jamming nonsense, or was the detail based on the at least three hours of recordings in *Diplomatik Vahşet* another Apple-Watch story?

If *Diplomatik Vahşet*'s new information was accurate then Jamal Khashoggi died about 30 minutes before Tubaigy got involved to dismember and have the body packed up in a frenzy. Al-Madani left the consulate's backdoor at 2.52pm on CC-TV. The Vito van with the suitcases would leave some 15 minutes later to head for the consul-general's residence. The five other cars dispersed at the same time. Bearing in mind that *Diplomatik Vahşet* claims Jamal died around 1.24pm, Jamal Khashoggi's time of death was at the latest between 2.15 and 2.30pm. Such a time would leave 60 to 75 minutes unaccounted during which Jamal was still able to talk.

On 13 October, Jamal's birthday, *Sabah* had reported leaks by Turkish officials what was on the audio ahead of the transcripts that would follow the days ahead. In fact the reporters who also wrote *Diplomatik Vahşet*, wrote then that Jamal 'was interrogated, tortured'. Leaking to the Middle East Eye news site, Turkish officials had leaked this as early as 7 October and had added that Jamal was 'beaten'. Yet at the end of December, during the publication of *Diplomatik Vahşet*, this aspect of the Khashoggi affair lay fallow.

Whether one believes that Jamal was interrogated or not, and whether he was tortured in the process of extracting answers, depends on one's view of the balance of probabilities. What was the likely point of a nineteen-men operation equipped with torture tools? When Mutreb decided – on the section of the consulate audio recording shared with foreign intelligence agencies, if Jamal doesn't agree to come back 'we will kill him here' – did he mean injecting Jamal as quickly as possible with a killing drug? Or did he want to try to extract at least some of the answers Riyadh was hoping to get by interrogation in Saudi Arabia (if Jamal agreed to fly back 'voluntarily') or Yalova (if not)?

The affirmative seems inescapable. The one thing Jamal as a former intelligence official was certain of if Saudi authorities detained him at the consulate was that they would interrogate him. He just didn't think they would be heavy-handed or, for example, knew about his secret talks with al-Baghdadi and the US Muslim Brotherhood. There were a minimum of ten operatives in the consulate (six cars left at 3.08pm and seven men and two cars are seen at the consul-general's residence minutes later). Did they really only spend that time mopping the floor after pathologist Tubaigy dismembered Jamal from MİT's putative time of death – 1.24pm? The conclusion he was tortured seems inescapable, as that an *omertà* had been brokered between Turkey and the palace.

The UN report noted the absence proof here, too, but without further analysis: 'The exact time of Mr. Khashoggi's death could not be confirmed with certainty. The ten minutes reference is based on the fact that after ten minutes, Mr. Khashoggi voice was not heard' (detail 92 footnote 39). At 1.39pm in the recording Turkish intelligence told the UN delegation they heard a bone saw, but they 'could not make out the sources of the sounds they heard' (UN detail 96).

Nor was the access Turkey gave the UN very transparent. In The UN rapporteur noted that they were 'prohibited from making notes' once the recording reached Jamal's voice (detail 94 footnote 40). The report gave no analysis of Turkey's reason for this obfuscation, but it also said that they were hampered in yet another way, in that they could not 'retain any transcript' (detail 41c). Though no journalist ever got to hear the recordings first-hand, the UN delegation was otherwise treated no different than members of the press.

The UN rapporteur did, however, address the issue of obfuscation in respect of the select number of recordings the UN delegation were allowed to listen to. They were 'not allowed to have clones of the recordings'. The point of this was preventing access to metadata of the recording such as 'when, how the data were created, the time and date of creation and the source and the process used to create it' (UN detail 41b). If the recordings had been sliced together, as the 7-minute Pulp Fiction edit of Tubaigy had been only the Turks would know. That clip had been given to foreign secret-services in October, but, from audio copy they had been handed, none had been able to conclude that Tubaigy's words were spoken before the execution – which would have weakened Turkey's leverage from the story it was putting out there.

MIT told the UN delegation it had at least 7 hours of recording over a two-day period, but only played seven phone calls totalling 45 minutes. The delegation also listened to 'a recording of the killing' and recordings dated from '28 September to 2 October'. There was 'much more recorded information than that made available', the UN report concluded (UN detail 41a).

The Turkish torture-interrogation meme was last leaked by both a Saudi and a Turkish source to *Independent*'s Borzou Daraghi on 30 October. The 'negotiation team' interrogated Jamal whether there was any record of his sensitive 9/11 work for Saudi intelligence under Prince Turki and the names of his associates after his self-exile. This interrogation took either 1 (the Turkish source close to Turkish authorities) or 2 hours (the Saudi source close to Saudi authorities). But these sources were not officials themselves. Turkish officials stopped using the two words after 19 October, the day on which Saudi Arabia admitted Jamal had died at the hands of palace officials.

There was no upside for Turkey to be transparent. Erdoğan's international leverage would be lost if Turkey made everything public, and that included the conclusions by the Istanbul prosecutors. Like MBS, Erdoğan had stipulated that the facts would be distributed and redistributed in a flexible manner. For the Turkish (and the Saudi) media this this was business as usual.

Leverage had the advantage of making MBS beholden to Turkey and turning Erdoğan's own pariah status around. The Khashoggi affair had deflected the attention away from Turkey and he aimed to maintain that advantage for as long as possible by keeping the pressure up on the US and Saudi Arabia. 'Relations went down and suffered a lot, over Syria, over the Muslim Brotherhood, over the US, over Yemen', according to Vehbi Baysun, a history and literature scholar at Ibn Haldun University in Istanbul, cited by Daraghi in his piece.

Apart from the seesaw beauty contest between MBS and Erdoğan over Jamal, easing Saudi pressure on Qatar, the brotherhood, and US, support for rebellious Kurds in Syria, etc would be a coup for Turkey. It would bring its own diplomatic and financial rewards for Turkey's listing economy. At his economic forum, for example, MBS made a conciliatory remark about Qatar and, on 25 April, the news broke that the US and Turkey were negotiating joint patrols in Kurdish safe zones in Manji, Northern Syria. The fruit of Erdoğan's Khashoggi campaign was plentiful.

Timed a few days after Agnes Callamard's press statement, Hatice Cengiz published her own book *Jamal Khashoggi* in Turkey. It was co-written with a Turkish war correspondent who did the last interview with Muammar Gaddafi and was now editor of the authoritative Turkish magazine *Foreign Policy* for which Hatice had written, as well as a Turkish freelance journalist who had contributed Turkish pieces to the BBC News Türkçe news site.

The book was published by Kopernik, a dual-language publisher with offices in Istanbul (kopernikkitap.com) and Gaithersburg, Maryland (kopernikpublishing.com). Among many rejections, it said on its website 'we reject double-standards', and promised the best of Turkish writing – including 'pulsating' thrillers and 'subliminal' poetry. On its publication board was Mehmet Erdoğan, a onetime civil servant in Turkey's Public Relations Directorate and a literary critic.

In a quick guide to the book on publication in Turkey on 7 February, *Sözcü* (Observer), one of the few non-AKP papers left in Turkey, described Hatice as a baker's daughter from Bursa. The *New York Times* added in an interview of 3 May 2019 that Hatice had gone to the religious school in Bursa.

From the Bursa *imam hatip* religious state school Hatice went for three years at the prestigious al-Azhar university in Cairo. The cost of tuition and living expenses would have been around $30,000 its website estimates. The *Times* also included the information that it was her father who paid for her three years in Cairo, as he was 'a wealthy kitchenware merchant in Istanbul'. The family it seems moved away from Bursa at around the time she herself went to Cairo for her studies. It also seems that her father changed from owning a bakery to owning a kitchenware emporium in Bursa, and then Istanbul, that was successful enough to cover the Cairo costs of six times Turkey's average wage.

Asked what advice Jamal would give her Hatice thought he would say to her, 'Continue where you left off. You're a different person now. You'll be the prophet of Oman', referring to the Shia-Sunni divide. She planned to travel the Middle East by backpack to do research and write to get over the emotional emptiness she felt following Jamal's assassination.

Before backpacking, however, Hatice Cengiz started on a tour of human rights conferences – giving talks and taking part in discussions as once Jamal had. She would also on 16 May 2019 give testimony before the US House Foreign Affairs Committee at a hearing on 'the danger of reporting on human rights'. When she spoke, she was at times close to tears and spoke emotionally about the life they were going to have in DC. Chris Smith, a US congressman on the committee, said that her 'written testimony was really a love letter' to Jamal.

She said that here had been 'no truth', no one knew where the body was nor why he was killed. Furthermore, 'seven, eight months later we see nothing has been done and that is why I'm here today'. She regretted that 'the world' was pulling its punches. She hoped that Congress could initiate an 'international investigation' and thought that 'President Trump could initiate this as well'.

Asked by the chair of the committee, Democratic congresswoman Karen Bass, what she thought the US government should do, she angled her answer at Saudi Arabia:

'The legal process in Saudi Arabia was not transparent. We don't know why he was killed. We don't know where the body is. If congress, if it undertakes an international investigation to put pressure on Saudi Arabia to share its information with the public and the United States that could be one thing, there could also be sanctions against Saudi Arabia.'

In the book Hatice also published her formal interviews with Jamal for the first time, whose recordings had brought them together from 6 May 2018.

Jamal addressed Saudi Arabia's structural problems, from 'skyrocketing numbers of guest workers to the diminishing oil income'. MBS 'needs to realise Vision 2030. Actually, it would be enough if he could realise one third of the things Erdoğan has achieved in Turkey', Jamal said from the grave. He praised his presidential friend for opening up Turkey to Syrian refugees and Egyptian exiles, though he also criticised the shrinking space for opinions in public in what was going to be his new host country.

Specifically Jamal's objection to MBS was that 'Mohammed bin Salman believes he is an extraordinary leader, like Atatürk.' 'He thinks he is the only one who can save us from radicalism and poverty.' MBS should be like his grandfather King ibn Saud the founder of the kingdom instead, Jamal argued. 'Even to him, people could go with different opinions', but instead 'the crown prince never listens to anyone'.

That rankled Jamal most. It wasn't that he was necessarily convinced MBS's economic policies were wrong as such. In all honesty, 'He didn't really know whether he would consider MBS a failure in ten years' time', said Hatice.

On 29 October, Kirsty Wark had asked Hatice whether the fact of the two of them getting married could be seen by the Saudis as a 'provocation'.

'If he had ever expected that marrying a young Turkish woman would be seen as a political provocation, I would have thought he would not have allowed this relationship to move forward', she had responded to Wark's question.

In her own book, Hatice gave the answer from her own point of view and said, 'I wouldn't have accepted the marriage proposal if I knew this would happen'.

She had never had the same intensity of feeling for anyone else, though she also candidly admitted to the *New York Times* in May 2019 about their marriage, 'Let's not think of it as a romantic proposal'.

'We were not children – we were two adults, and we immediately had a very rational conversation about how we could share it, how we could make it work.'

In her Turkish interview with *Sözcü* in February, Hatice revealed that her heroine was Gertrude Bell, whose travels through and writings on the Middle East she discovered during her three-year religious studies in Cairo. She later saw Queen of the Desert, the Werner Herzog biopic of Bell in 2015, with Nicole Kidman and James Franco in the role of the nine-year older Henry Cadogan, whom Bell had wanted to marry. While panned by the critics, Hatice loved the movie. She felt a great affinity with the pan-Arab motivation that drove Bell, and her courage. And maybe, yes, Gertrude Bell was a 'serious spy'.

In February Kroll analysed the WhatsApp messages between al-Qahtani and MBS, and, reviewing the report, the Saudi chief-prosecutor concluded non were connected with the Khashoggi rendition. In early March, the *Guardian* published news reports on MBS's weakening position thought to be 'baseless' by Riyadh officials. Before and after his father's visits to Egypt that month, MBS was increasingly absent in public and at officials meetings. The king had also received the damning conclusions of an investigation into political prisoners, which MBS had resisted. MBS was relieved of some investment and governmental authority, and on a trip to Egypt the king replaced his royal personal security detail with thirty staunch loyalists.

A month and a half after King Salman's 'human-rights' interventions, thirty seven Saudis were beheaded by sword around the kingdom 'for adopting terrorist and extremist thinking and for forming terrorist cells to corrupt and destabilise security'.

On 17 March, at the second trial hearing in Riyadh cultural attaché al-Muslih said he didn't know Jamal's body was in the van he drove to the consul-general's residence; al-Balawi said that Mutreb had ordered him to dissect Jamal's body. Earlier on 30 January, brigadier-general al-Madani argued that it was his duty to impersonate Jamal. Similarly, al-Balawi and the two al-Sehris said they were executing orders and covered Jamal's mouth when he started screaming. The UN report noted later that no screaming was heard on the recording their delegation heard (UN 213), and called for the suspension of the trial because of it 'is held behind closed doors; the identity of those charged has not been released nor is the identity of those facing death penalty' (UN 16), noting that some statements by Saudi chief prosecutor al-Mojeb 'and the identity of 11 perpetrators currently on trial do not match' (UN 6).

On 30 March, Amazon and *Washington Post* billionaire Jeff Bezos's security advisor of 22 years wrote in the Daily Beast that 'the Saudis had access to Bezos's phone, and gained private information' which they then leaked to the *National Enquirer*, a tabloid run by a friend of Donald Trump's, David Pecker, and led to Bezos's divorce. This was part of a campaign of harassments against Amazon and Bezos since October 2018.

President Erdoğan, MBS fiend and the world's greatest imprisoner of journalists, was given opeds in Bezos's *Washington Post* print edition on 2 November and on 19 March. It was as often as Jamal's pieces had appeared in the main paper, including his posthumous one. On 19 March Erdoğan wrote, 'Western leaders must learn... to embrace Muslims living in their respective countries'. A report published around the same time by UK foreign secretary Jeremy Hunt stated that the AKP portrayed Christians as a 'threat to the stability of the nation' and as 'not real Turks but as western collaborators'.

On 1 April, Erdoğan's party narrowly lost the mayoral elections against the opposition in both Ankara and Istanbul. The election board cancelled the outcome due to perceived irregularities on 7 May, ordering a rerun in both cities. 'Those who rely on the guns in their hands, those who rely on the power of the media cannot build democracy', Erdoğan had said after the coup in Egypt. 'Democracy can only be built at the ballot box'. Erdoğan's strong-man appeal was waning among Turkish metropolitan voters after the Khashoggi affair.

On 3 April, CNN revealed that Jamal's children received houses, a lump sum of 1 million riyals ($267,000) and $10,000 a-month stipends further to Riyadh's official admission that palace officials had killed their father. King Salman himself had approved these payments.

Depending on guilty verdicts against the eleven accused, the siblings could look forward to further compensation that would bring the total close to $70 million. Under Sharia law this would depend on the family accepting 'blood money', CNN reported, whereby the accused offered money to avoid the death penalty. In the past the palace had picked up the bill in similar circumstances and paid between 100-200 million riyals ($27 and $54 million).

Only Jamal's eldest son Salah still lived in Saudi Arabia, and had received a house worth $4 million, while his three siblings received more modest accommodations. As the three intended to remain in the US, where they had naturalised, they would not receive any of the benefits according to Saudi officials, CNN also reported.

On 10 April, Salah posted on his twitter account 'no settlement discussion had been or is discussed', but, he continued, 'Acts of generosity and humanity come from the high moral grounds they possess, not admission of guilt... We... thank acts of good not disavow.' The UN inquiry 'obtained information regarding a financial package offered to the children'.

To what extent had US intelligence closed its eyes prior to 2 October so as not tangle with Trump administration priorities? On 9 May 2019, *Time* magazine reported that the CIA issued public 'Duty-to-Warn' notices to Jamal's contacts Iyad el-Baghdadi, Omar Abdulaziz, and another who asked not to be part of the publicity. The first two lived in Norway and Canada, rather than the US, and were geographically beyond the scope of the duty-to-warn directive. The three men were told to 'avoid travel to a wide swath[e] of countries in Europe and Asia where Saudi Arabia has particular influence, and to move family members out of at least one particular country, Malaysia'.

There is one Middle Eastern country that has not been mentioned so far. It is the only one in the region that is suspected of already having nuclear weapons – Israel. It is also one of the four nations in the world that never signed the 1968 Non-Proliferation Treaty (India, Pakistan, and

South Sudan, a country minted in 2011, are the others).

Israel's policy has been to ensure that none of its neighbours join the select club of nations with atomic weapons. It has effectively sabotaged nuclear power plants in Iran and Iraq to destroy facts on the ground establishing themselves in those nations. Yet its response to the Trump administration's plan to sell nuclear technology to Saudi Arabia has been mute as was its response to tearing up the 2015 Iran Treaty. It seems not to consider the Saudi royal family a threat to its existence and tacitly supported special envoy Jared Kushner's mission in this area.

Did a benefit materialise for Israel during this period? On 23 March 2019, Donald Trump said that it is time to recognise Israel's sovereignty over the strategically important Golan Heights that Israel has occupied since the 6-day war in 1967. On June 16, Netanyahu's cabinet inaugurated Ramat Trump (Trump Heights), a rebranded thirty-year-old settlement of ten people in the Golan Heights.

On 3 April 2019, Bloomberg revealed footage of Saudi Arabia's first atomic facility.

'There's a very high probability these images show the country's first nuclear facility', Robert Kelley, a former IAEA director told the TV station. Argentina's state-owned INVAP SE sold the unit to Saudi Arabia, which planned to start later in the year.

Although this was merely a small training and research facility, Saudi Arabia had hoped to conclude its tender for two nuclear reactors, issued by MBS in September 2018, by selecting the vendor a few months later. It was talking to US, Russian, South Korean, Chinese and French firms. The tender is now expected in 2020, by which time the Khashoggi 'hubbub' will be in the past.

On 8 April, Erdoğan visited Putin in Russia to discuss the ongoing formalities to purchase the s-400 air-missile defence system and joint-efforts against the Kurds in Syria now that the US was withdrawing. It was his third visit in three months.

Time Line

2015 Michael Flynn visits Saudi Arabia several times sponsored (through his company Flynn Intel Inc.) as consultant of IP3 International, a consortium formed by retired US generals to execute the 'Iron Bridge' together with 6 nuclear power companies. Its sole focus is to build 40 nuclear power plants and uranium enrichment facilities in Saudi Arabia (although it is called 'a Marshall plan for the Middle East' that will bring stability through business).

18 November 2016 Michael Flynn is appointed as Donald Trump's National Security Advisor.

November 2016 Jared Kushner meets MBS's delegation in New York, including energy minister Khalid al-Falih

December 2016 Michael Flynn resigns as advisor to IP3. Michael Flynn omits to detail his IP3 sponsored trips to Saudi Arabia for the security clearance required for his appointment.

20 January 2017 (Inauguration Day) Michael Flynn texts that the 'project is good to go', instructing IP3 'to put things in place.'

Week following 20 January 2017 The Iron Bridge is adopted as the administration's energy policy. IP3 sends a draft Cabinet Memo to Michael Flynn to appoint Donald Trump's close personal friend billionaire Tom Barrack as special representative to implement Iron Bridge.

13 February 2017 Michael Flynn resigns as Donald Trump's National Security Advisor and (later) pleads guilty to lying.

2 March 2017 The Trump-administration official in charge of Iron Bridge says 'I speak with Michael Flynn every night.'

Mid-March 2017 Billionaire President Donald Trump tells billionaire Tom Barrack that he can lead the implementation of Iron Bridge. The administration official in charge is lobbying so 'that Jared Kushner can present it to the President for approval.'

14 March 2017 Billionaire Donald Trump meets billionaire MBS in the Oval Office with his son-in-law Jared Kushner and discusses Iron Bridge in the context of '$200 billion in direct and indirect investments within the next four years.'

17 March 2017 IP3 writes to MBS proposing a 'partnership to acquire Westinghouse between IP3 and Saudi Arabia.' The partnership would then build the 40 nuclear installations.

18 March 2018 MBS says on 60 Minutes 'if Iran developed a nuclear bomb, we will follow suit as soon as possible.'

21 March 2017 Billionaire Tom Barrack submits a White Paper on The Iron Bridge that calls for his appointment as representative 'with the rank of ambassador or Special Envoy'.

29 March 2017 Westinghouse Electric Company (owned by IP3 member Toshiba) files for bankruptcy.

November 2017 Saudi Arabia opens the formal process for bids for 'their first reactors'.

2017 The Trump administration issues 7 secret '810' authorisations to US nuclear energy companies to share to share sensitive technological information with Saudi Arabia despite the fact that Saudi Arabia has not given up its right to enrich uranium or reprocess spent fuel (under a '123 non-proliferation agreement.'

Winter 2018 Saudi Arabia is aggressively paying to lobby the Trump administration for a license for Westinghouse to build 16 nuclear reactors for $80 billion in Saudi Arabia.

8 May 2018 Donald Trump rips up the 2015 Iran Treaty to the dismay of many, re-igniting the threat of an Iranian nuclear bomb.

May 2018 Jamal Khashoggi meets Hatice Cengiz, PhD student at the University of Istanbul, at a conference. It is the beginning of a relationship that would lead him to propose to her in marriage a few months later.

Summer 2018 US Intelligence agencies intercept secret Saudi plans to move against Jamal Khashoggi, a US resident and Washington Post blogger. The information is disseminated to US intelligence stations in security briefings. The Trump administration takes the decision not to act on Government Order ICD19-'Duty to Warn' to let Khashoggi know.

1 August 2018 Hedgefund Brookfield completes its $4.6 billion acquisition of bankrupt Westinghouse from IP3 consortium founder Toshiba

3 August 2018 Hedgefund Brookfield completes its $1.1 billion upfront-payment for a 99 year lease on 666 Fifth Avenue owned by Kushner Companies, saving the Kushner-family company from impending bankruptcy by defaulting on a $1.4 billion mortgage repayment with accrued interest due in January 2019.

September 2018:

British intelligence intercept chatter about an impending plot against Khashoggi

Jamal Khashoggi is told by the Saudi Embassy in Washington DC, headed by Prince Khalid bin Salman, his friend and MBS' brother, that he needs to pick up divorce forms required for his new marriage in person at the consulate in Istanbul. He asks whether there is an arrest warrant for him in Saudi Arabia and is assured that this is not the case.

The Saudi consul-general orders the installation of a tandoori oven that can reach 1000 degrees – the temperature commonly used for incinerating human remains – in the garden of his residence.

Khashoggi visits the consulate on Friday 28 September at 11.50am in vain for the divorce papers and is told to come back on 2 October.

Saturday 29 September, Khashoggi speaks at the Middle East Monitor conference in London and is interviewed on BBC World Service's NewsHour.

Monday 1 October
4.30pm The first trio of elite Saudi soldiers arrive on a scheduled flight at Atatürk Airport and are captured on CC-TV: maj. Naif al-Arifi, 32, royal guard Muhammed al-Zahrani, 30, and brig. gen. Mansour Abahussein, 46. They checked in at the Wyndham Grand and make a reconnaissance tour in consular Mercedeses to Belgrad Forest (at 6.28pm) and Yalova near Istanbul

10.15pm Jamal Khashoggi flies from Heathrow to Istanbul on Turkish Airlines flight TK1984

Tuesday 2 October Atatürk Airport

1.45am	*Three Saudis arrive on scheduled flights – lt Meshal al-Bostani, 31, royal guard Khaled al-Otaibi, 30, and Abdulaziz al-Hawsawi, 31 – and check in at the Wyndham Grand*
3.29am	*A Saudi-government Gulfstream jet with tail marking HZ-SK2 lands at Atatürk Airport from Riyadh carrying nine Saudis: prof. lt-col. Salah Tubaigy, 47, Turki al-Sehri, 36, sgt Maj.*

	Waleed al-Sehri, 38, lt Thaar al-Harbi, 39, brig. gen. Maher Mutreb, 47, royal guard Fahad al-Balawi, 33, Col. Badr al-Otaibi, 45, Saif al-Qahtani, 45, and Mustafa al-Madani, 57
4am	*Jamal Khashoggi arrives on Turkish Airlines flight TK1984 and is captured on later leaked CC-TV entering his Istanbul apartment at 4:58am with his fiancée Hatice Cengiz. He is captured on CC-TV leaving his flat at 12:17pm*

Saudi consulate

9.55am	*Brig. gen. Mutreb enters the consulate alone in a suit; other death squad members follow*
11.05am	*Saif al-Qahtani and Al-Madani, dressed in a check shirt, sneakers and jeans, enter the consulate together*
11.50am	*Consul-general al-Otaibi calls Khashoggi to finalise the paper work. Khashoggi confirms he will be visiting the consulate after 1pm*
12.50pm	*Non-Saudi staff working at the consulate are told to leave the building without delay*
1.14pm	*Jamal Khashoggi is captured on later leaked CC-TV entering the consulate, handing his phone over to Hatice Cengiz at the security gate.*
1.14pm	*The second Saudi-government Gulfstream jet, with tail marking HZ-SK1, is airborne from Riyadh for Istanbul.*
1.30pm	*While former London-embassy colleague brig. gen. Maher Mutreb yells 'traitor' and Jamal Khashoggi pleads 'I can't breathe', he is strangled and dismembered in pieces, possibly still alive, by prof. lt-col. Tubaigy with a bone saw (his body parts are disposed of and his fingers, head and a video of the operation may be prepared for sending on to Riyadh on Saudi-government Gulfstream HZ-SK1 landing at 5:15pm*
2.52pm	*Impersonator al-Madani is captured leaving the consulate's back door with a false beard in Khashoggi's clothes but his own trainers on later leaked CC-TV footage; Hatice Cengiz doesn't see him as*

	she is waiting at the front
3.30pm	*The consulate closes with no sign of Khashoggi*
3.45pm	*Six vehicles, including two vans with blacked-out windows, leave the consulate*
4.29	*Al-Madani is captured on later leaked CC-TV footage in Istanbul wearing his own clothes, he is with Saif al-Qahtani*
5.30	*Khashoggi's fiancée Hatice Cengiz is seen on CC-TV outside the consulate*
5.50pm	*Hatice Cengiz alerts the Turkish authorities who open an investigation (says President Erdoğan)*

Atatürk Airport

5.15pm	*The second Saudi-government Gulfstream jet, with tail marking HZ-SK1, lands and waits*
6.20pm	*HZ-SK1 takes off with six of the Saudi squad: Mutreb, Waleed al-Sehri, Turki al-Sehri, al-Balawi, al-Harbi, Badr al-Otaibi (the Saudi prosecutor will demand the death penalty against the first four); its first destination is Cairo, Egypt, before returning to Riyadh*
10.54pm	*Before take-off the first Gulfstream jet with tail marking HZ-SK2, is searched by police for the presence of Khashoggi further to Hatice Cengiz's raising the alarm. It is allowed to take-off for Dubai, before flying on to Riyadh with seven of the Saudi hit team: Abahussein, Tubaigy, al-Zahrani, Khalid al-Otaibi, al-Arifi, al-Bostani, al-Hawsawi (the Saudi prosecutor will only charge the first two)*
00.10am	*Khashoggi impersonator al-Madani and Saif al-Qahtani leave Turkey on a scheduled flight*

Tuesday October 2 Southaven, Mississippi (GMT -6), Donald Trump speaking at a rally for Senator Cindy Hyde-Smith

'You have to pay.'

DONALD TRUMP: We protect Saudi Arabia. Would you say they're rich? And I love the king, King Salman. But I said 'King – we're protecting you – you might not be there for two weeks without us – you have to pay for your military. You have to pay'... They have got to reimburse us.

Wednesday October 3 Moscow (GMT +3), Russian Energy Week 2018
Vladimir Putin seated next to Saudi energy minister Khaled al-Falih

'A traitor.'

VLADIMIR PUTIN: Watching some media outlets, I see that some of your colleagues are pushing forward the theory that Mr Skripal is almost some kind of human rights defender. He is simply a spy, a traitor to his homeland. You get it? There is such a thing – a traitor to one's homeland. He is one of them. [Applause!] Imagine: You are a citizen of your own country, and all of a sudden you have a man who betrays his own country. How will you, or any representative of any country sitting here, look at him? He's simply a scumbag, that is all there is to it.

rferl.org/a/putin-slams-traitor-sergei-skripal-bastard/29523407.html

Wednesday evening October 3 Riyadh (GMT +3) MBS interviewed by 6 Bloomberg journalists

'I would know that.'

Bloomberg: So... U.S.-Saudi relations are just as good now as they were 24 hours ago before the President said 'You have to pay'?
MBS: Yes of course... I love working with him. I really like working with him and we have achieved a lot in the Middle East... We have good improvement in our trade – a lot of achievements, so this is really great.
[...]
Bloomberg: What's the Jamal Khashoggi story?
MBS: We hear the rumors about what happened. He's a Saudi citizen and we are very keen to know what happened to him. And we will

continue our dialogue with the Turkish government to see what happened to Jamal there.

Bloomberg: He went into the Saudi consulate.

MBS: My understanding is he entered and he got out after a few minutes or one hour. I'm not sure. We are investigating this through the foreign ministry to see exactly what happened at that time.

Bloomberg: So he's not inside the consulate?

MBS: Yes, he's not inside.

Bloomberg: Turkish officials have said he's still inside.

MBS: We are ready to welcome the Turkish government to go and search our premises. The premises are sovereign territory, but we will allow them to enter and search and do whatever they want to do. If they ask for that, of course, we will allow them. We have nothing to hide.

Bloomberg: Is he facing any charges in Saudi Arabia?

MBS: Actually, we need to know where Jamal is first.

Bloomberg: So he might be facing charges in Saudi Arabia?

MBS: If he's in Saudi Arabia I would know that.

Bloomberg: So he's not the person mentioned by Saudi Press Agency?

MBS: No, definitely not.

October 18 Vladimir Putin at the Valdai Discussion Club in the Russian Blacksea resort Sochi

'I hope America will not go as far as Saudi Arabia did.'

Ragida Dergham: Thank you, my name is Ragida Dergham. I am Founder and Executive Chairman of Beirut Institute. It's a think tank for the Arab region with a global reach… On Saudi Arabia, of course, the world is preoccupied with the developments, and I'm wondering what consequences or… Do you see that there may be consequences, on your particular relationships, Russian-Saudi relations, given that you have been eager to have good relations and beyond.

VLADIMIR PUTIN: Now concerning Saudi Arabia. What is it that is bothering you? I can't understand. We have built really good relations with Saudi Arabia in recent years. Please, specify your question about Saudi Arabia. What is it that is perplexing you in this regard? Why should our relations with Saudi Arabia break down?

Ragida Dergham: As you know, because of the developments in Istanbul, at the Saudi Consulate, there is a big interest worldwide in the investigation regarding the assassination or the killing of Jamal Khashoggi, the journalist who was our colleague and has been a participant in the Valdai Group. So this is what I am talking about. Right now, of course, there is pressure on President Trump that may reflect on the mid-term elections, and there are countries pulling out and countries being concerned, I mean, media and others are concerned about continuing to be present in Saudi Arabia given the alleged feeling that maybe someone in the government may be involved in this atrocity, of killing of Jamal Khashoggi. That is what I meant. Do you think it will impact your relations with Saudi Arabia at all?

VLADIMIR PUTIN: As far as I know, the journalist, who has disappeared and whom you have just mentioned, lived in the United States of America. He lived in the US, not in Russia. In this sense, the US, of course, bears certain responsibility for what has happened to him. This goes without saying.

He was the one to go to the United States for asylum. In this connection, I would like to say the following. First, we should wait for the results of the investigation to become available. How can we, Russia, start spoiling relations with Saudi Arabia while being unaware of what has really happened over there?

As far as I can judge, this man was to a certain extent a member of the Saudi elite. In some way or other, he was connected with certain ruling circles. It is hard to say, what is going on there.

But we can see that complicated processes are also taking place within the US elites. I hope America will not go as far as Saudi Arabia did. But we don't know what, in fact, has happened over there. So why should we take any steps directed at downgrading our relations, if we do not understand what is really happening?

If someone understands it and believes that a murder has been committed, then I hope that some evidence will be presented and we will adopt relevant decisions based on this evidence. This gives me a pretext to say something else.

From time to time, there are steps taken against Russia and even sanctions are imposed, as I have repeatedly said, on the basis of flimsy excuses and pretexts. They groundlessly claim that we have allegedly used chemical weapons, even though, incidentally, we have destroyed our chemical weapons, while the United States has failed to do so despite the obligation to that effect it assumed.

So, there is no proof against Russia but steps are being taken. According to claims, the murder was committed in Istanbul, but no steps are being taken.

Uniform approaches to problems of this kind should be sorted. To reiterate: Our policy towards Saudi Arabia has evolved over a long period of time, over many years. Of course, it is a misfortune that a man has disappeared, but we must understand what has really happened.

valdaiclub.com/events/posts/articles/vladimir-putin-meets-with-valdai-discussion-club/

12 February 2019 billionaire Tom Barrack, representative and beneficiary of The Iron Bridge said in Abu Dabhi of the Khashoggi assassination: 'For us to dictate what we think is the moral code there … I think is a mistake.' Echoing Vladimir Putin's words of 18 October, the Lebanese American also said, 'the atrocities in America are equal or worse than the atrocities in Saudi Arabia.'